AF323779

INDIVIDUALISATION AT WORK

To Maria Markus and Michael Pusey

Individualisation at Work
The Self between Freedom and Social Pathologies

NORBERT EBERT
Macquarie University, Australia

ASHGATE

Cover design by Anna Lena Kuhn.

Published by
Ashgate Publishing Limited
Wey Court East
Union Road
Farnham
Surrey, GU9 7PT
England

Ashgate Publishing Company
Suite 420
101 Cherry Street
Burlington
VT 05401-4405
USA

www.ashgate.com

British Library Cataloguing in Publication Data
Ebert, Norbert.
  Individualisation at work : the self between freedom and social pathologies.
  1. Individualism. 2. Socialization. 3. Industrial sociology.
  I. Title
  302.5'4–dc23

Library of Congress Cataloging-in-Publication Data
Ebert, Norbert.
  Individualisation at work : the self between freedom and social
pathologies / by Norbert Ebert.
     p. cm.
  Includes bibliographical references and index.
  ISBN 978-1-4094-4266-0 (hbk) -- ISBN 978-1-4094-4267-7 (ebook)
1. Individualism. 2. Individuation (Psychology) 3.
Organizational sociology. I. Title.
  HM1276.E24 2012
  302.5'4--dc23

ISBN 9781409442660 (hbk)
ISBN 9781409442677 (ebk)

Printed and bound in Great Britain by the
MPG Books Group, UK.

Contents

Preface

The changing relationship between individual and society lies at the very core of Sociology as a discipline. The most recent changes in the nature of this relationship have been described as individualisation. Although individualisation has been and still is hotly debated in Sociology a fundamental issue persists: the concept remains vague. As a consequence, individualisation is in theoretical as well as empirical studies often reduced to mean atomisation, self-realisation or social isolation. Sociological debates of individualisation all too often take individual claims for self-realisation as their starting point. Individualisation is, however, a social phenomenon, not an individual one. In this book I seek conceptual and theoretical clarity and depth by distinguishing three social aspects of individualisation: structural individualisation, normative individualisation and organised individualisation. It provides empirical evidence on the basis of qualitative interviews. I refer to those aspects of individualisation as 'social' as they do not originate in the individual but in individuals' interactions; they are neither just individual nor just social. It is in the social sphere where individualisation is at work enabling social freedoms, while equally being at risk of developing social pathologies.

Given the pace of social change in late modern societies, sociological analyses are always at risk of lagging behind. Investigations like this one, therefore, are intrinsically at risk of being nothing but a sociological snapshot of social conditions in a fast changing world. Yet, this study is premised on something that – I believe – runs deeper than a look at those fleeting fashions to which sociology – and even this book – is by no means immune. This fundamental premise is the belief that human beings are able to build and sustain a social order that allows them to spread the wings of their emancipatory capacities in a way that does justice to their own human nature. Given the plurality and diversity of human beings, I have no doubt that this is an inherently difficult and open-ended task, a task that is never going to be completed, yet one that is worth pursuing. As a matter of fact, it is the social dynamics of organising this pursuit that allow individuals to be at their best as creative and reasoning beings. Therefore, the reflections presented in this book, theoretical as they may be, have their starting point in individuals' practical experiences of everyday social interactions. This is important, since the normative critique of contemporary individualisation that I present is not intended to identify pathologies in individuals' abilities to be ever more individualistic rational actors. The potential pathologies that I want to bring to the fore are social pathologies that have their origins in deficient modes of normative integration. Without hesitation, I admit that my investigation is to a large degree driven by the hope that "a moral culture could be so constituted as to give those affected, disrespected and ostracised, the individual strength to articulate their experiences in the democratic sphere" (Honneth 1994: 269).

Writing a book can in itself be a very individualising challenge. Trying to find words to thank those who have been on my side during an exciting and challenging task, I realise that I cannot but fail in finding the right ones. Above all, I deeply thank Maria Markus and Michael Pusey for their extraordinary wisdom and guidance. I cannot possibly do justice to the seeds of respect, trust and knowledge you have patiently, carefully and generously nurtured in me when I was bare of understanding. Over the years this project has taken me much further than Down Under. I am humbled by the generous friendships and collegiality that surround me. This goes for the whole Department of Sociology at Macquarie University in Sydney. My debt is particularly great to my friends and colleagues Harry Blatterer for reading through large parts of the manuscript, to Selvaraj Velayutham who persistently and patiently reminded me to get started in the first place and to Shaun Wilson for listening and encouraging me on many train trips home. Above all, however, I am grateful to and hold great respect for my colleague and friend Pauline Johnson. This book would not have come true without the determination with which she builds and guides the department. Lucian Daniel Kafka and Benjamin Mudaliar are probably both completely unaware of the enormous contributions they have made to this book which is all the more reason to thank them both for cordial friendships. Last but not least, I am grateful to my dear brothers, the "Fab Five" of Lörrach, you are fabulous indeed. That is where I belong.

Sydney, January 2012

Introduction

In the article *Freedom and the Individual*, originally published in 1913, Georg Simmel wrote:

> The general European consensus is that the era of the Italian Renaissance created what we call individuality. By this is meant a state of inner and external liberation of the individual from the communal forms of the Middle Ages, forms which had constricted the pattern of his life, his activities, and his fundamental impulses through homogenising groups. These had, as it were, allowed the boundaries of the individual to become blurred, suppressing the development of personal freedom, of intrinsic uniqueness, and of the sense of responsibility for one's self. (1971: 217)

Almost a hundred years later, individualisation is perhaps more topical than ever and is still associated with a sense of liberation. Moreover, most people have no qualms in identifying personal freedom, intrinsic uniqueness and responsibility for one's self as elementary features of contemporary individualisation or self-realisation. Yet Zygmunt Bauman claims that:

> '[i]ndividualisation' now means something very different from what it meant 100 years ago and what it conveyed in the early times of the modern era – the times of extolled human 'emancipation' from the tightly knit web of communal dependency, surveillance and enforcement. (2002: xiv)

And so it is worthwhile to briefly overview the transformation of the very meaning of the concept of individualisation. The classical sociological theorists associated individualisation mainly with the transition from pre-modern to modern societies and thus with the liberation of the individual from rigid normative structures. Later, Talcott Parsons' term 'institutionalised individualism' became influential in describing individualisation in industrial societies as 'an individualistic system of goal achievement' (1964: 183). This concept comprises a more general definition of norms and values, permitting individuals to have a greater level of choice.

Today, it is most prominently Ulrich Beck who defines contemporary individualisation as the individual's release 'from industrial society into the turbulence of the global risk society' (1994: 7). Beck and Beck-Gernsheim specify what, in their opinion, characterises contemporary individualisation. 'For the first time in history,' they write, 'the individual is becoming the basic unit of social reproduction' (2002: xxii). Part of those reproduction processes is, as

Beck and Beck-Gernsheim point out, that they 'not only permit, but demand, an active contribution by individuals' (1996: 27). As a consequence, individualisation as a process of liberation has become ambiguous in late modernity. It can no longer be described merely in terms of individuals having the capacity to free themselves from restrictive structures. The compulsion for individuals to use their capacities and abilities to handle freedom becomes an equally important, if not more important, aspect of how individualisation works in late modern societies. This, however, also affects underlying questions of differentiation and integration without which contemporary forms of individualisation cannot be reconstructed.

Individual liberation, however, must not be equated with independence from social structures. From its beginning, sociology has linked individualisation and structural differentiation, be it on the basis of a Durkheimian social division of labour, Weberian rationalisation processes, Parsons' or Luhmann's systemic differentiation or the Habermasian uncoupling of systems and lifeworlds. In fact, it is Habermas who grasps well the core of modern liberation processes. He stresses the interdependence of structure and individualisation when he writes that 'an autonomous ego and an emancipated society reciprocally require one another' (1976: 71). More recently, Axel Honneth points out that 'the claim of an increase in the autonomy of the individual subject ultimately remains tied back to the viewpoint of the participant in social interaction' (2004: 464). And so the sense of liberation associated with individualisation not only depends on the social structures that individuals live in, but is grounded in the very nature of social interaction by which individuals construct their social world.

Quite often people refer to self-realisation rather than individualisation. I will predominantly use the term individualisation as a more encompassing concept, since it enables me to distinguish various important aspects of my argument. These have their origin in two key concepts of sociology, namely 'socialisation' and 'individuation' (Habermas 1976). Individuals are what Giddens identifies as 'knowledgeable actors' (1979: 144), but they can only be so with the aid of the structures through which individuals have acquired and learned a particular kind of cultural knowledge. While we can say that individualisation is structurally enabled, individuals do not just act passively according to given rules and norms; they are not just reflexive, but reflective, impulsive, creative and spontaneous actors. They have 'the ability to give one's own needs their due in … communicative structures' (Habermas 1976: 78). Individuals not only act on the basis of learned norms and values, but equally we have the abilities to make normative claims. We continuously seek approval for these claims from the wider community in terms of a 'struggle for recognition' (Honneth 1996: 83). Individualisation thus can also be described as normative individualisation, where individuals use their autonomy to make a difference to an existing normative infrastructure.

At first sight, a heightened sense of individual autonomy on the basis of a more differentiated social order seems to weaken the relationship between individual and society. In fact the converse is true, because the integration of individuals into society becomes more complex and ambiguous – or even paradoxical. As Beck states:

> The place of traditional ties and social forms (social class, nuclear family) is taken by secondary agencies and institutions, which stamp the biography of the individual and make that person dependent upon fashions, social policy, economic cycles and markets, contrary to the image of individual control which establishes itself in consciousness. (1992: 131)

While most people in everyday life associate individualisation predominantly with a sense of liberation and self-realisation, the increasing organisational dependencies seem to go rather unnoticed. Investigating these organisational dependencies and their consequences on individualisation is one of the major motivations underpinning this book. It is not that the ties between individual and society evaporate, but they seem inconspicuously to transform. The more rigid nexuses based on traditional forms of ascription or institutionally defined unitary goals are increasingly fragmented and pluralised. An ambiguity emerges at this point. On the one hand, individualisation is strongly affiliated with a sense of liberation and differentiation. On the other hand, it is characterised by individual dependencies on agencies, institutions and networks of organisations that become the reference points for an individualised form of integration. The striving for individual autonomy and the reproduction of society fundamentally draw on each other. As a consequence, 'the borders between culture and the economy, lifeworld and system, [can] no longer be unambiguously determined' (Honneth and Hartmann 2006: 11). The negotiation of those blurred boundaries between lifeworld and system, the individual and organisations are the defining feature of individualisation in late modernity and are the subject-matter of this book.

The social context within which processes of individualisation, differentiation and integration are currently taking place can be described as network capitalism. In *The Coming of Post-Industrial Society*, Daniel Bell writes:

> The major intellectual and sociological problems of the post-industrial society are ... those of 'organised complexity' – the management of large-scale systems, with large numbers of interacting variables, which have to be coordinated to achieve specific goals. (1973: 29)

My argument is that 'organised individualisation' assigns the key role to the individual in the coordination and reproduction of those ambiguous complexities. One of the main reasons for this lies in the transformation of capitalism, which has not only undergone changes, but is still in the midst of them. Profound processes of economic restructuring centred on the notions of flexibility, deregulation and privatisation have established networks as the primary, yet quite 'fluid' pattern of social interaction for both organisations and individuals. As Jeremy Rifkin writes: 'The most important feature of the modern market system ... [is] access between servers and clients operating in a network relationship' (2000: 4–5). The underlying change, however, is the shift towards a knowledge economy where 'productivity and competitiveness are … a function of knowledge generation and information processing; firms and territories are organised in networks of production, management and distribution' (Castells 2001: 52). In the same vein, Peter Drucker states that 'the absolutely decisive "factor of production" is now neither capital, nor land, nor labour. It is knowledge' (1995: 5). While these are crucial topics, it is my conviction that the processing, handling, generation and use of knowledge cannot do without the abilities, capacities and qualities that no one else but individuals can provide. My interest, therefore, lies in the effect of these developments on individualisation.

Most importantly, however, the administration of those markets lies in the hands of modern corporations, as the primary form of organisation in late modernity. As Craig Calhoun points out, modern corporations have 'received very little attention in sociological theory even though it is central to modern institutional arrangements' (1992: 215). He points out that 'corporations, large-scale markets, and other organisations of indirect relationships have grown in size and importance throughout the modern era. … Computers and new telecommunications technologies continue this pattern' (1992: 218). With those transformations of Western capitalism occurring over the last decades, individualisation has slowly become an ideological organising principle on the institutional and organisational levels of late modern political and economic systems. Individualisation as individuals' striving for self-realisation has become the 'engine room' for the self-motivated realisation of systemic imperatives. Boltanski and Chiapello in their study *The New Spirit of Capitalism* refer to this as 'people's commitment to capitalism' (2005: 162). The deep-seated sense of liberation that individuals hold is 'inverted into compulsions and expectations' (Honneth 2004: 474) through an increasing marketisation and corporatisation of late modern societies.

My aim is not to provide an all-encompassing sociological theory of the modern corporation; this must be left to future investigations. However, modern corporations hold a key position in my argument. They represent the 'organised' part of the phrase 'organised individualisation' because they guide and influence individual behaviour on the basis of norms and values that are in principle not negotiable. Although my empirical study concentrates on the contemporary workplace, this influence reaches far beyond the immediate corporate sphere into the various spheres of contemporary society, and defines to a large degree late modern work societies and their varied forms of integration.

These developments are underpinned by an often unarticulated shift in the power relationship between civil society, the state and the market on an institutional level; and the transition, on an organisational level, from publicly controlled organisations to profit-driven corporations. While the market has become the primary institution of our time, the corporation can be said to be the primary form of organisation. This shift in power, however, stems from the distinction between legitimation and justification. While civil society, on the basis of normative individualisation, has the power to legitimate a political order, the state can legislate in order to both protect the norms and values emerging from civil society discourses and to (re)regulate market rules, so as to ensure economic prosperity and its own existence. The impact of marketisation and corporatisation on the possible negotiation of norms and values amounts to 'organised individualisation', on an organisational level, and on an institutional level, a potential 'legitimation crises' in the Habermasian sense (see e.g. 1979) as we can see in the aftermath of the global financial crisis in 2008 and the debt crisis in European nation states in 2011.

Sociology has ignored corporations as major organisational players in modern societies. This is largely the result of the assumption that they are merely systemic associations. They cannot be based on anything other than concrete social relationships, however, mediated by power, money and scientifically generated knowledge. For corporations to be put into the sociological limelight, one needs to fundamentally acknowledge that 'the member of an organisation is simultaneously and ineradicably a speaking subject, a labouring subject, and an embodied subject' (Clegg 1989: 194) of a larger social order. Thus, on an organisational level, corporatisations shift power relationships by controlling individuals' discursive and reflective capacities. Individualisation becomes a structural demand, while its normative aspects are rationalised and instrumentalised for organisational purposes.

This book investigates contemporary individualisation as it emerges from late modern processes of structural differentiation and its implications for various forms of integration. The aim is to explore the evolving structural underpinnings and normative aspects of individualisation under conditions of contemporary network capitalism. Particularly in the contemporary workplace, where the individual and the organisation meet directly, but also in the wider community, individualisation becomes an ideological and ambiguous process of liberation. Individualisation starts to serve as a means for systemic coordination and reproduction, rather than a liberating negotiation of society's normative infrastructure. This seems to be – according to my investigation – the main specificity of present-day developments.

The sociological approaches to the relationship between individual and society have predominantly been characterised by an opposition between the individual striving for autonomy on the one hand, and restrictive, mainly economic or governmental structures on the other. Investigating the characteristics of contemporary individualisation offers us clues that this theoretical model of oppositions may no longer hold. The relationship between individual and society has become more fluid and permeable and, as a result, ambiguous. Contemporary individualisation is characterised by a convergence of individuals' emancipatory capacities as thinking and acting human beings and the systemic coordination and reproduction of society. This results not so much in an opposition or contradiction between individual and society, but in intensified frictions along the demarcation between systems and lifeworlds that lead to a general proliferation of ambiguities. Moreover, these tensions and ambiguities assign the responsibility to negotiate between systemic and normative processes on to individuals. As the collective reference points like class and status break away, communicative processes no longer stand in clear opposition to instrumental or strategic economic actions. For individuals, these modes of action have become rather immediate and are increasingly difficult to distinguish. Equally, forms of systemic and social integration are easily mistaken for one another. Hence, contemporary individualisation is characterised by the individualised negotiation of the meshed boundaries between systems and lifeworlds, social and systemic integration, normative self-organisation and organisational (systemic) dependencies. We are, therefore, not necessarily speaking about a Habermasian colonisation of the lifeworld through systems – although it is certainly an obvious risk. The focus is, rather, more on a proliferation of ambiguities concerning the boundaries between systems and lifeworlds. As I argue in this book, the negotiation of these complexities and ambiguities is the crucial and defining moment of contemporary individualisation.

Part of my approach to individualisation is to challenge the possibilities and limitations of the Habermasian systems – lifeworld distinction. While these concepts are used at times metaphorically or counterfactually, they lead to a complex of practically important, contemporary sociological problems. My investigation, therefore, tests to a degree their empirical applicability, to see whether these ideas can help to explain and conceptualise social action in late modern everyday life.

One of the reasons for the emergence of an individualised border between systems and lifeworlds, has its origin in the last thirty years of economic development. This period has been variously described as the end of Fordist organisation of production, post-Taylorism (see e.g. Bradley et al. 2000) or the neo-liberal reform project. Whatever the label, I will mainly refer to these processes on an institutional level as intensified marketisation and on an organisational level as progressive corporatisation. While these developments essentially frame contemporary individualisation and have to be dealt with to some extent, they are not the main focus of this book. Rather, the crucial point is how they have transposed the individual striving for autonomy and individualisation into an essentially self-propelled productive force in contemporary network capitalism, so that the individual has become an 'entrepreneur of the self' (Gordon 1987: 300).

On an organisational level, various management tools embrace autonomy, so as to encourage individuals to make their own decisions. Although significant for my investigation, the focal point is not on managerial techniques as such. What is of interest here are the instrumentalising pressures which make individuals' desires and motivations match those of the corporation. As a consequence, individuals are trusted because their own thinking and feelings automatically trigger the right decision for the organisation. The individual is expected to be involved with his/her whole personality to benefit the business. It is a distortion of individuals' capacities to make a difference to an existing normative infrastructure. These capacities, driven by a sense of liberation, become a means for the realisation of organisationally given goals, forming the cornerstone of 'organised individualisation'. Moreover, the result of individuals mistaking that reversal for their own choice and free decision becomes the self-fulfilling justification for more of the same, namely, more deregulation and greater marketisation. The result is that individuals have to be flexible, show initiative and motivation, to an as yet unknown degree.

It would be wrong, however, to construe these rather complex developments as deliberate or totally instrumentalising. Neither the market nor corporations should be regarded as the culprits nor perpetrators of a single defining feature of late modernity. The world we live in is the result of separate and yet interdependent social processes: individualisation, as individuals' striving for liberation and autonomy; structural differentiation, as contradictory, ambiguous or even paradoxical forms of rationalisation in society's various spheres of action; and integration, as a range of ways and opportunities for individuals to participate in and contribute to the reproduction of society. As a result, under the institutional transformations of Western capitalism over the last twenty years, individualisation has developed into an ideology and productive force of a largely deregulated economic system at both the institutional and the organisational level.

Some Methodological Comments

Individualisation is in theoretical as well as empirical studies often reduced to mean atomisation, self-realisation or social isolation of the individual. This book seeks to gain conceptual and theoretical clarity and depth by distinguishing three aspects of individualisation: structural individualisation, normative individualisation and organised individualisation. As part of that work, it provides empirical evidence gathered from twenty qualitative interviews with managers from internationally operating corporations. This constitutes the empirical core and basis of this study (Chapters 5 and 6). It is their experience and organisation of individualisation at work that makes them – at least for this study – my primary object of observation, from which I take many cues to develop a closer understanding of contemporary individualisation. However, further studies could be conducted that separate those two aspects, that is, generating and moulding the conditions of 'organised individualisation' for others, and being an employee/worker at the receiving end of those processes. It is because these two aspects collide in the role of the manager that I have chosen her or him as my object of study. Another advantage of this approach is that it also allows me to gain important insights into emerging management practices 'on the ground', and how they relate to the broader managerial perceptions of economy and society. These interviews, however, are a heuristic tool and not an empirical, quantitative warrant. I have used the interviews as cues for the theoretical development of my own argument. While my study is to a large degree a theoretical and analytical investigation, the interviews provide firstly, a pre-theoretical grounding in individuals' real life experiences, and secondly, stimulate a theoretical alertness to issues that otherwise might easily go unnoticed. Generally, this study follows a Critical Theory approach. By this I mean that it is grounded in the emancipatory interests of ordinary individuals in contemporary workplaces, that is, in social reality itself (Honneth 1994: 256).

The overall aim is a conceptual and thought-provoking normative critique; that is to say, an analysis of those norms and values on the basis of which institutions, organisations and individuals produce and reproduce society in everyday life (see Honneth 2011: 23). I do not claim my findings are true for everybody, since their respective socio-economic background, status, class, religion, ethnicity and gender might generate vastly different experiences in today's diverse societies. Nevertheless, my goal is to capture some of the characteristic features of contemporary individualisation, and to raise questions about its possible social pathologies that might need further investigation. The premise of this book therefore can be formulated as follows:

> Individualisation has become an ambiguous, but defining feature of late modern societies. In principle, it is characterised by an increase in individual autonomy, as well as a convergence of normative and systemic processes, that is at some risk of instrumentalisation (structural individualisation). While it still carries a sense of liberation, individuals are equally required to negotiate a fragmented, pluralised and ambiguous social order on their own terms. I argue that under conditions of marketisation and corporatisation the emancipatory qualities and motivations defining individualisation are sidestepped and transformed from a normative negotiation (normative individualisation) process into a means for the coordination and reproduction of systemic imperatives fuelled by individuals' qualities and capacities for self-realisation. I therefore conceptualise the ambiguous features of contemporary individualisation as 'organised individualisation'.

Weighing up the various aspects of individualisation against the social conditions of late modernity I argue in this book that the specific characteristics of late modern individualisation are best conceptualised and normatively critiqued on the basis of three distinct forms of individualisation, that is, structural individualisation, normative individualisation and organised individualisation. With the aid of those distinctions we might gain a better understanding of how and where individualisation is at work in late modern societies.

Chapter 1
Structural Individualisation

This chapter establishes the broad context for my argument by examining the structural underpinnings of the relationship between the individual and society in late modernity. I argue that what underpins the relationship between the individual and society is a proliferation of functional and normative ambiguities. In order to demonstrate this, I will concentrate on three main points:

First, structural differentiation did not come to a halt with the rise of modernity. Indeed, I contend that with ongoing processes of structural differentiation late modern societies can no longer be described as simply functionally differentiated; increasingly these societies are hyper-differentiated. Secondly, the origins of both functional and normative forms of differentiation are concrete social relationships. These relationships rest on communicative action that in late modernity goes beyond the uncoupling of systems and lifeworld, thus leading not only to systemic hyper-differentiation but also to hypertrophied lifeworlds[1], that is, a normative overload that does not or has not yet translated into stable communicative structures. In this a fundamental ambiguity emerges as individuals gain more autonomy, while also becoming subject to a greater risk of instrumentalisation. Thirdly, under these circumstances, the ties between individuals and society increasingly come to manifest themselves as a web of systemic imperatives that can no longer be described as 'institutionalised individualism' or as individual responses to systemic dependencies. Individualisation becomes an ambiguous process. While it is structurally enabled, it is also more and more systemically organised. This puts individuals increasingly at risk of becoming active hubs not only for systemic coordination, but also for the reproduction of their own systemic dependence.

1. From Structural Differentiation to Hyper-differentiation?

As modern society began to take shape, sociologists became ever more able to distinguish, in both theoretical and empirical ways, amongst the various components that constituted this modern society. In this, the theory of structural

---

1   I borrow the expression 'hypertrophied' from Habermas (see quote below). He does not explain the term in detail. There are two sides to hyper-differentiation. I refer to the structural aspect as hyper-differentiated, whereas the normative side of it I describe as hypertrophied. What I mean by it is a normative overload, pluralisation and fragmentation of the lifeworld.

differentiation, although not all-encompassing, has become one of the most useful sociological 'tools' for the analysis of various aspects of social change, be it in pre-modern, modern or late modern societies. In general terms, Alexander and Colomy get to the heart of structural differentiation when they write: 'The process of differentiation refers to tendencies that societies have, when certain background conditions are present, to respond to social conflicts or abrupt disruptions by developing more specialised structures' (1985: 15).

My argument here is concerned in particular with the consequences of social change in late modernity underpinning individualisation, the economy and integration (Schimank 1996: 14). These consequences manifest in a strikingly distinctive fashion in the general shifts towards marketisation, towards the increased relevance of corporations and towards work-organisational changes (these ideas will be discussed in greater detail in Chapters 3, 4, 5 and 6). This is the terrain in which I will locate my investigation to exemplify how the negotiation of functional and normative processes becomes a task which characterises individualisation today. Given the relevance of the economy and work in contemporary society, these developments hardly remain confined to the economic sphere; indeed, they spill over into a variety of other areas of everyday life, such as the family, friendships or in leisure activities.

Georg Simmel's (1890) discussion of the inseparability of 'Vergesellschaftung' (socialisation as continuous formation of society) and 'Individualisierung' (individualisation), Ferdinand Toennies' differentiation between 'Gemeinschaft' and 'Gesellschaft' (1955) and Émile Durkheim's analysis of changing social divisions of labour (1964) were among the first sociological works to point to the complex interplay of structural differentiation, individualisation and social integration. These, of course, have not been the only ones to highlight this interplay. Indeed, it was Max Weber in particular who was most concerned with an increasingly fragmented and pluralised modern society. His approach offers much for the present investigation of the characteristics of late modernity, as well as the ambiguities characterising the relationship between systems and lifeworlds.

Max Weber conceptualised the differentiation running through modern society on the basis of incompatible and largely autonomous value spheres (1978[1946]: 147), with each autonomous sphere driven by its 'own specific mode of rationality' (Brubaker 1984: 30). Thus, the sphere of law strives for justice, the sphere of science searches for truth, the sphere of economy maximises profits, the sphere of politics seeks power, while art works towards ultimate beauty. Accordingly, multiple, parallel, contradictory and conflicting logics of rationalisation operate in contemporary society (Brubaker 1984: 9). Importantly, these conflicting value spheres, based on various types of purposive rationality, challenge individuals' sense of coherence and continuity. They trigger what could be called an 'inner differentiation' that puts processes of individualisation at risk of being 'organised' by external and systemic forces (Brubaker 1984: 68). For Weber, it was the process of parallel rationalisation that sat at the heart of fragmentation and pluralisation. Following and building on Weber, I am arguing in this section that late modern society is not only functionally and normatively differentiated, but functionally as well as normatively hyper-differentiated, generating ambiguities between the various spheres of action.

My concern here is not with the emergence of incommensurable value spheres with the rise of modernity, but with the ongoing structural differentiation between and within those value spheres, and their effect on individuals. Weber provides us with a theoretical starting point for the understanding of hyper-differentiation as a major source of ambiguities, and as a central characteristic of late modern society. While the consequences of hyper-differentiation are widely celebrated as an increase in individual choice, I contend instead that while individuals enjoy hitherto unheard-of standards of living, the risk of instrumentalisation, of being trapped in all-consuming processes of rationalisation and bureaucratic organisation (something Weber referred to as an 'iron cage' (1974[1930]: 181), has equally increased.

Talcott Parsons has built upon and reconceptualised Weber's ideas in a variety of interesting ways. Although not opposed to the concept of structural differentiation, he took a more 'harmonising' approach. While differentiation – according to him – leads to the emergence of various systems in society, 'functional prerequisites' (Parsons 1963: 348) are supposed to realise 'harmonising' 'normative orientations'. The problem is, however, that a 'harmonising' normative approach no longer holds for late modern society as ongoing processes of structural differentiation cannot but lead to a normative pluralisation and fragmentation. Thus, hyper-differentiation also means that ambivalent or contradictory norms and values might be realised.

Some aspects of Parsons' systemic approach can be found – alongside considerable contributions from Durkheim and Weber – in the work of Niklas Luhmann. For Luhmann, modern societies are characterised by subsystems which are of equal importance for the reproduction of society. One of Luhmann's main concerns was to analyse how we engage with complexity that is the proliferation of ambiguities in contemporary network capitalism and work-organisation (Chapter 4). 'The world does not pose a problem in terms of its ontology, but regarding its complexity' (1974: 115, my translation), writes Luhmann, and therefore considers the formation of systems as a consequence of the human condition. Social systems compensate for the lack of instincts by reducing complexity, while they also provide orientation through the formation of institutions and organisations. As Luhmann suggested,

> The function of social systems is to capture and reduce complexity. They help to mediate between the external complexity of the world and the anthropologically very restricted ability of human beings to consciously process experiences. (1974: 116, my translation)

This suggestion leads us to a paradoxical situation that has been pointed out by Habermas: the reduction of complexity through one system increases the complexity of the world for other systems. Hence, reducing complexity also increases complexity (Schimank 1996: 138). This is precisely what characterises the structure of late modern societies: differentiation leads to further differentiation resulting in hyper-differentiation. As I will argue later in this chapter, late modern lifeworlds are not far behind when it comes to an increase in complexity and ambiguity.

A more detailed look at some of Luhmann's ideas can bring my argument regarding hyper-differentiation and the resulting ambiguities more to the fore; Luhmann's ideas will also be relevant at various points later in the discussion, particularly in the assessment of work-organisational changes in Chapters 5 and 6. In particular, Luhmann's ideas of self-referential 'autopoietic systems' (1996: 57) and 'selections' (1996: 195, 588) are most important. Echoing Weber, Luhmann described structural differentiation along the lines of incommensurable 'binary codes', such as truth vs. lies, justice vs. injustice, solvency vs. insolvency, power vs. powerlessness. These constitute the general sources for the formation of systems on the basis of 'selections' (1996: 195, 588) which on an organisational level equates to decisions (see Chapter 4). As the orienting guidelines for reducing complexity, these binaries specify the autopoietic reproduction of a particular subsystem. That is, systems reproduce and differentiate themselves only in reference to themselves and – in contrast to Durkheim and Parsons – not necessarily as part of a bigger whole fulfilling one particular function in the realisation of a coherent normative infrastructure. Self-referentiality can thus be considered the cornerstone of systemic continuity, a point particularly interesting when we consider corporations (as discussed in Chapter 4), but also important in relation to the role of the state and the economy (as discussed in Chapter 3).

Importantly, binary codes alone are not a sufficient force to drive structural differentiation. Accordingly, Luhmann completes them with programs (1996: 432), formal organisations, and, similar to Parsons and Habermas, with symbolically generalised media like money, power or truth (1996: 222). Formal organisations create their own systemic continuity by enforcing a program independent of persons. In Luhmann's conceptualisation, systemic differentiation and the omnipresence of organisations go hand in hand.

All this is relevant for the present discussion because 'self-referentiality' and 'selections' can be looked upon as fundamental sources of ambiguity in conditions of late modernity. On the one hand, systems try to secure their own existence and continuation by differentiating themselves from other systems, whilst on the other, this also means de-differentiation, within systems, subsystems and organisations, by way of aligning components and elements of the environment to one particular systemic or organisational logic. Thus hyper-differentiation intensifies the friction between systemic differentiation (increasing complexity) and de-differentiation (reducing complexity). The resolution of one problem through further differentiation might cause counterproductive differentiations somewhere else and vice versa. Hence a paradox: what structurally underpins individualisation is the concurrence of hyper-differentiation and de-differentiation, which, moreover, increasingly collide on an organisational and individual level, leaving individuals to deal with the resulting ambiguities.

It is along similar lines that Ulrich Beck coined the term 'second' or 'reflexive modernity' (see e.g. 2003; 2001); this he defines as a further 'modernisation of modern societies' (1995: 187) and a 'radicalisation of modernity that dissolves the premises and contours of the industrial society and opens up avenues into another modernity – or counter modernity' (1994b: 23, my translation). The commonality linking first and second modernity is that of structural differentiation as the 'engine room' of social change. Beck and others have argued that structural differentiation does not disappear with second or late modernity, but that it becomes subject to the very processes it itself is based on, that is, modernisation, rationalisation and differentiation. The structural differentiation that led to the rise of first modernity also came with certain unwanted side-effects or irrationalities that can no longer be resolved with further differentiation or rationalisation (1994b: 34, 38). Hence, differentiation itself becomes an ambiguous issue that can no longer be resolved by more of the same (Beck 1996: 46). If resolution was to succeed, modernity might run the risk of destroying its own basis (Schroer 2000: 387). Again, and most importantly, the negotiation of and engagement with these ambiguities is shifted onto individuals.

As we have seen, hyper-differentiation is paradoxical. Firstly, structural differentiation continues to be the driving force of social change, which is why Beck sees 'second modernity' as a continuation of – not a break with – modernity. Differentiation does not stop with the emergence of incommensurable value spheres, but these spheres themselves are subject to further differentiation. Secondly, the continuation of structural differentiation leads to both a functional and normative fragmentation and pluralisation of industrial society (Beck 1994b: 28). The paradox of hyper-differentiation comes fully to the fore with increasingly complex and functionally independent systems and their organisations, while at the same time lacking, or even demanding, coordination by individuals.

So far, my argument is that late modern society is characterised by a shift from structural differentiation aiming to reduce complexity to a hyper-differentiation, resulting in an increase in complexity and ambiguity. The functional pluralisation and fragmentation of society intensifies frictions along the systemic intersections of late modern society. Although not clear-cut, these boundaries increasingly emerge between individuals and organisations.

2. Beyond the Uncoupling of Systems and Lifeworld?

Hyper-differentiation and its effects, however, can only be fully grasped if their origins and normative underpinnings are not only anchored in, but emerge from, concrete social relationships. I will address this with the help of Jürgen Habermas's differentiation between systems and lifeworld. Habermas did not dismiss the ideas of the classical theorists, or of Parsons or Beck; rather, he raised fundamental questions regarding a theory of modernity, useful for the present. In Habermas's opinion such a theory must be able to explain what leads to the emergence of systems and to hyper-differentiation. He identified communicative action as the fundamental process of structural differentiation, or for him, the 'uncoupling of systems and lifeworld' (1987: 153). In contrast to the classical theorists and Parsons, this enabled him to both pinpoint the causes for possible distortions, malfunctions and social pathologies, and also raise hope for emancipation on the basis of social interaction.

According to Habermas, structural differentiation can be readily described as both a growing social division of labour and an increasing release of purposive rationality. Importantly, structural differentiation cannot, according to this schema, be separated from the question of its origins, which he sees as lying in communicative action. By establishing a dialectical relationship between the individual and society – built on a basis of communication – as the primary paradigm of social evolution, Habermas has been able to account not only for structural differentiation, but also for the formation of the normative infrastructure of society. This is in stark contrast to Parsons. That is, Habermas matches the systemic processes of structural differentiation with ongoing communicative processes, which he describes as the 'rationalisation of the lifeworld'. For him, communicative action fundamentally underpins the dialectical relation between individual and society from which both systems and lifeworld emerge.

> Under the functional aspect of *mutual understanding*, communicative action serves to transmit and renew cultural knowledge; under the aspect of *coordinating action*, it serves social interaction and the establishment of solidarity; finally, under the aspect of *socialisation*, communicative action serves the formation of personal identities. The symbolic structures of the lifeworld are reproduced by way of the continuation of valid knowledge, stabilisation of group solidarity, and socialisation of responsible actors ... Corresponding to these processes of *cultural reproduction, social integration, and socialisation* are the structural components of the lifeworld: culture, society, person. (Habermas 1987: 137–38)

The lifeworld represents the communicatively established normative infrastructure of society, operating as a stock or reservoir of taken-for granted knowledge which always exists unproblematically, but which can always be communicatively problematised and potentially re-negotiated (Habermas 1987: 124). As such, it encompasses both values and norms. This conception allows a first glimpse on what the term 'organised' means, namely the eclipse or instrumentalisation of the possibility to negotiate norms and values.

Most importantly for my discussion, communicative action is also the starting point for the emergence of systems. Like individual and society, systems and lifeworld are distinct but not separate. As a result of ongoing processes of rationalisation, the lifeworld gains levels of complexity that finally result in a communicative overload, where language is partly replaced by 'steering media' such as money and power.

> The rationalisation of the lifeworld makes possible a heightening of systemic complexity, which becomes so hypertrophied that it unleashes system imperatives that burst the capacity of the lifeworld they instrumentalised. (Habermas 1987: 155)

This is exactly the case when concrete social relationships become not only mediated (see Calhoun 1992), but have to be mediated in order to be socially manageable. Yet they are still social relationships. The reduction of complexity in the lifeworld is the starting point for the uncoupling of systems and lifeworld. On this point Habermas agrees with Luhmann. However, for Habermas systems emerge from the dialectical relation between individuals and society, while for Luhmann, 'systems theory ... has no need for a concept of the subject. It replaces it with the concept of self-referential systems' (1995: 29).

Following Habermas, contemporary hyper-differentiation is the result of a hyper-rationalised, hypertrophied (normatively overloaded) lifeworld that is caught up in the process of finding and forming appropriate steering media and systemic structures in order to reduce the 'new' complexity. Thus late modern society is not only structurally hyper-differentiated, but is also normatively overloaded and thus characterised by a hypertrophied lifeworld. This suggests that we are living in a period of structural and normative transition that goes beyond the uncoupling of systems and lifeworld on a meta-level. That is, the uncoupling of systems and lifeworlds also operates on organisational and individual levels, where the conflictual and paradoxical uncoupling of the individual and organisation defines the junction between systems and lifeworlds. Communicative action not only drives the uncoupling of systems and lifeworlds, but equally contributes to the formation of hyper-differentiated systems and normatively overloaded and pluralised lifeworlds as the main source of contemporary ambiguities structurally underpinning contemporary individualisation.

While systems emerge from communicative action, they also reach back into the communicative structures of society. That is, when social relations are subject to steering media – when they are monetarised and bureaucratised in a Weberian sense – Habermas suggests that a 'colonisation of the lifeworld' occurs, and that this constitutes a potential origin of social pathologies. In such an arrangement, the dialectic between individual and society becomes a one-way-street, where systemic imperatives increasingly distort opportunities and channels for communicative action. Habermas's point is that

> a progressively rationalised lifeworld is both uncoupled from and made dependent upon increasingly complex, formally organised domains of action, like the economy and the state administration. This dependency, resulting from the mediatisation of the lifeworld by system imperatives, assumes the

> sociopathological form of an internal colonisation when critical disequilibria in
> material reproduction – that is, systemic crises amenable to systems-theoretical
> analysis – can be avoided only at the cost of disturbances in the symbolic
> reproduction of the lifeworld – that is, of 'subjectively' experienced, identity-
> threatening crises or pathologies. (1987: 305)

What this suggests is that the maintenance of systemic continuity takes priority over communicative action, but individuals' lifeworlds become dependent on those systemic processes.

What does this mean for my characterisation of late modernity as hyper-differentiated? Firstly, systemic hyper-differentiation may be the result of hypertrophied lifeworlds. Secondly, the fragmentation and pluralisation of systems may point to the fact that such systems are no longer tied back into communicative processes in lifeworlds. Finally, systemic hyper-differentiation again has an effect on already hypertrophied lifeworlds. This indicates that hyper-differentiation is the result of the hypertrophied lifeworld that does not develop into systemic processes reducing complexity, but instead leads to a pluralisation and fragmentation of systemic imperatives which impose themselves back onto an equally pluralised lifeworld trying to ensure systemic continuity. The transitional deficiencies in integration leave individuals in a position where they themselves have to negotiate the various intersections between systems and lifeworlds in their more immediate organisational environment.

It is not inevitable that problems arise in the coexistence of functional and normative processes of differentiation. Indeed, neither process can do without the other. Whereas the lifeworld is responsible for social reproduction, systems are supposed to take care of material reproduction under the normative guidance of the lifeworld. Accordingly, an understanding of society only as systems seems to be one-sided, as Archer has argued:

> Because the social world is made up, inter alia, of 'structures' and of 'agents'
> and because these belong to different strata of social reality, there is no question
> of reducing one to the other or of eliding the two and there is every reason for
> exploring the interplay between them. (1996: 691)

Both functional and normative processes of differentiation are essential. Yet the defining features are not functional interdependencies, but the embeddedness of both systems and lifeworld, in a normative infrastructure that emerges from and is subject to communicative action. While this should also be the case for hyper-differentiated late modern societies, the means of achieving this might be lacking.

In late modern societies both systems and lifeworlds are characterised by complexity, by functional and normative pluralisation and fragmentation. From a lifeworld perspective, this should (theoretically) translate into new steering media and systems growing out of hypertrophied communicative action. From a systemic point of view, systems have become independent from lifeworlds, and their systemic imperatives can no longer relate reflexively to communicative action. This results in the subtle instrumentalisation of individuals' abilities to negotiate and re-negotiate a society's normative order. Therefore, what further characterises hyper-differentiation is the concurrence of both processes. While the opportunities, abilities and capacities for communicative action have improved, the risk of an instrumentalisation of exactly those communicative processes has escalated. I argue that today an individualised negotiation and re-negotiation of the boundaries between systems and lifeworlds revolves around these ambiguities between hyper-differentiated systems and hypertrophied communicative processes. What do this mean for individualisation in contemporary society?

3. Individualisation: Structurally Enabled or Systemically Compelled?

For Habermas, the dialectical relationship between the individual and society leads to an uncoupling of systems and lifeworld; I argue that in late modernity there occurs a process of uncoupling between the individual and the organisation. Anthony Giddens has attempted to address similar processes in his theory of structuration. 'Structure,' he argued, 'is both the medium and outcome of the practices which constitute social systems' (1981: 27). More importantly, structures are the 'rules and resources, recursively implicated in the reproduction of social systems' (1984: 377). Consequently, he holds, 'structure must not be understood as simply placing constraints upon human agency, but as enabling' (1993: 169). Most importantly, he places 'the production and reproduction of society as the accomplished outcome of human agency' (1993: 170). It is the enabling character of structures on the one hand, and the potential mutability of normative structures through individual action on the other, that Giddens describes as the 'duality of structure' (see e.g. 1993: 109). What I am centrally concerned with in this section is the enabling character of structures and their impact on individualisation. I will deal with the abilities of individuals to shape structures in Chapter 2.

At this point my interest begins with the assumption that processes of structural differentiation seem to go hand in hand with processes of individualisation. Simmel, Adorno, Horkheimer, Beck and others have identified the origins of individualisation in the Italian Renaissance, as a state of internal and external liberation of the individual from the communal forms of the Middle Ages (Beck 1992: 127; Schroer 2000: 59; Simmel 1971: 217). From these accounts follows that the more differentiated a society, the more individualised its members appear to be. On the basis of my earlier elaborations on hyper-differentiation I argue that in conditions of late modernity individualisation is not only structurally enabled, but an increasingly systemically driven compulsion. It is this ambiguity – between the sense of liberation and the concomitant compulsion that together define contemporary individualisation – that sits at the heart of the negotiation of the demarcation between systems and lifeworld.

With the rise of modernity, individualisation became structurally enabled, as functional differentiation also means role-differentiation. As the social division of labour increased, roles became pluralised and subject to individual choice. Simmel, for example, has described individuality as the result of individuals' memberships in various social circles; individuality is, in this picture, a mix or 'web' of group affiliations:

> The groups to which the individual belongs form so to speak clues of the kind that every additional one defines him more precisely and unambiguously … The more there are, the more unlikely it is that other people hold the same combination of circles, that these many circles intersect in the same way at one point. (1968: 312, my translation)

The same goes for individuals that are part of different spheres of action as members of different organisations and institutions. More importantly however, for Weber individualisation also emerges as a normatively triggered 'inner rationalisation' (see also Adorno 1993: 75; Brubaker 1984: 24), or, the rationalisation of the individual 'based on constant self-scrutiny and methodical self-control' (Brubaker 1984: 9). This connects with Weber's conception of the Protestant Ethic, which persists in a secularised or corporatised conduct of life (see my discussions of a universalised work ethic in Chapter 3 and corporatisation in Chapter 4). Parsons' term 'institutionalised individualism', which I will discuss in greater detail below, seems also to refer to the same phenomenon. First however, let us clarify the notion of individualisation.

As I have already noted in the introduction, in the present stage of modernity the meaning of individualisation has changed considerably. While some of the classical theorists' concepts and ideas are still important, Ulrich Beck has developed a useful understanding of individualisation in contrast to them:

> The difference, to Georg Simmel, Emile Durkheim and Max Weber, who theoretically shaped this process [individualisation] and illuminated it in various stages early in the twentieth century, lies in the fact that today people are not being 'released' from feudal or religious-transcendental certainties into the world of industrial society, but rather from industrial society into the turbulence of the global risk society. They are being expected to live with a broad variety of different, mutually contradictory, global and personal risks. (1994a: 7)

Yet what classical and contemporary (or modern and late modern) processes of individualisation have in common is the form which liberation takes. The question is whether we can really speak of a 'release' in contemporary society or whether there are simply new ties and webs within which the liberating process functions.

Beck has distilled three general dimensions of individualisation:

Modernisation... leads, and here we have arrived at the general model, to a triple 'individualisation': disembedding, removal from historically prescribed social forms and commitments in the sense of traditional contexts of dominance and support (the 'liberating dimension'); the loss of traditional security with respect to practical knowledge, faith and guiding norms (the 'disenchantment dimension'); and – here the meaning of the word is virtually turned into its opposite – re-embedding, a new type of social commitment (the 'control' or 'reintegration dimension'). (1992: 127–28)

Beyond these three general dimensions, Beck and Beck-Gernsheim have posed and answered the following question: 'But what then is specific about individualisation and second modernity? ... the individual is becoming the basic unit of social reproduction for the first time in history' (2002: xxii). This seems true; yet this reproduction process has very specific characteristics connected to the predominance of corporations as the main form of contemporary organisation. The underlying theme and my focus here are the changing forms of social integration. For classical thinkers, individualisation released the individual from traditional, more rigid sources of integration into the emerging industrial society; contemporary forms of individualisation supposedly set the individual free from industrial society's forms of integration, such as status and class. This is the core argument of Beck's article *Beyond status and class*, in which he wrote:

Against the backdrop of a comparatively high standard of living and social security, a break in historical continuity released people from traditional class ties and family supports and increasingly threw them onto their own resources and their individual fate in the labour market, with all its attendant risks, opportunities and contradictions. (Beck 2002: 30)

Beck identified various forces that drive contemporary processes of individualisation. In this he singled out the ongoing processes of differentiation that I have tried to capture more precisely as hyper-differentiation:

The compulsion to lead your own life, and the possibility of doing it, emerge when a society is highly differentiated ... Constantly changing between different, partly incompatible logics of action, they [individuals] are forced to take into their hands that which is in danger of breaking into pieces: their own lives. (Beck 2000: 165)

Although his analysis of differentiation is in some ways not nuanced enough, Beck hinted at the role of differentiated labour markets and workplaces as driving contemporary processes of individualisation (2002: 32–33). Education and job qualifications seem to be other key factors defining individualisation as they provide individuals with the credentials to individualise career opportunities. Yet education also creates competition and a need for the individual to stand out, as everyone has a similar degree of education, experience and knowledge (Beck 2002: 33).[2]

Beck and Beck-Gernsheim isolated the core of contemporary individualisation with this:

> [I]ndividualisation is a social condition which is not arrived at by free decision of individuals ... Individualisation is a compulsion, albeit a paradoxical one, to create, to stage-manage, not only one's own biography but the bonds and networks surrounding it, and to do this amid changing preferences and at successive stages of life, while constantly adapting to the conditions of the labour market, the education system, the welfare state, etc. One of the decisive features of the individualisation processes, then, is that they not only permit, but demand, an active contribution by individuals. As the range of options widens and the necessity of deciding between them grows, so too does the need for individually performed actions, for adjustment, co-ordination, integration ... Opportunities, dangers, biographical uncertainties that were earlier predefined within the family association, the village community, or by recourse to the rules of social estates or classes, must now be perceived, interpreted, decided and processed by individuals themselves. The consequences – opportunities and burdens alike – are shifted on to individuals who, naturally, in face of the complexity of social interconnections, are often unable to take the necessary decisions in a properly founded way, by considering interests, morality and consequences. (1996: 27)

The essence of individualisation in late modernity amounts therefore to individuals being structurally forced to coordinate and integrate themselves when the more collective means to do so have begun to break apart or become deficient. As Baumann argued,

> To put it in a nutshell, 'individualisation' consists in transforming human 'identity' from a 'given' into a 'task' – and charging the actors with the responsibility for performing that task and for the consequences (also the side-effects) of their performance: in other words, it consists in establishing a de jure autonomy (although not necessarily a de facto one). No more are human beings 'born into' their identities ... Needing to become what one is is the hallmark of

---

2   Individualisation as a struggle to balance uniqueness and sameness appears to work hand in glove with a struggle for social recognition (Honneth 1996); I will introduce this position as a theoretical concept in greater detail in Chapter 2. Also beyond the scale of this study, Gabriele Wagner investigates the link between recognition, individualisation and gender (2004).

> modern living – and of this living alone … Modernity replaces determination of
> social standing with compulsive and obligatory self-determination. (2002: xv)

Yet it is not entirely adequate, in my opinion, to simply state that individuals have become the basic unit of social reproduction. Indeed, this is a flawed stance because the process of individualisation involves much more than this. The significant development for individuals in contemporary society is not that institutional or more collective reference points might break away, but rather they are replaced with organisational reference points to which individuals have to respond. In addition, by responding they are forced to reproduce various organisational dependencies. At this point it is worth examining Becks' approach with the aid of Luhmann and Parsons as his perspective resonates with both.

Briefly again, Luhmann portrayed individualisation as a largely systemic process: the individual as a psychic system is just an another autopoietic, self-referential system in a generally systemic environment (Luhmann 1996: 346). Yet psychic systems have a special position. They have consciousness which can trigger, disturb or influence communication (Luhmann 1996: 355). Individualisation emerges as a technocratic and quantitative selection process of system formation;[3] a process by which psychic systems position themselves in regard to their systemic environment (Schroer 2000: 273–74). For Beck and Beck-Gernsheim, the essence of contemporary individualisation then comes down to the following definition: 'The Western type of individualised society tells us to seek biographical solutions to systemic contradictions' (2002: xxii). Building on Beck – yet sharpening the argument with the aid of Luhmann – I contend that individualisation becomes the organising principle for the systemic coordination of hyper-differentiated late modern societies. Individuals do not passively adapt, but are compelled to become active hubs for systemic coordination and social integration alike. Meanwhile, the power to achieve both depends largely on systems and their organisations. Thus, the decisive point is not that individuals are the basic unit of social reproduction, but the terms on which individuals negotiate or re-negotiate the conditions of social reproduction. Is individualisation an organising principle turning individuals into mere hubs for systemic coordination, or do they gain opportunities for social integration? Above all, individuals have become active hubs for the reproduction of the very systemic processes that they are dependent upon. Individualisation has become a process of coordinating and coping with hyper-differentiated social structures and facing an infinite number of paradoxical institutional and organisational imperatives:

> [I]n order to survive the rat-race, one has to become active, inventive and
> resourceful, to develop ideas of one's own, to be faster, nimbler and more
> creative … Individuals become actors, builders, jugglers, stage-managers of

---

3   In reference to Simmel this kind of individualisation could also be called 'quantitative individualisation' (see Honneth 2004).

their own biographies and identities, but also of their social links and networks. (2000: 166)

More to the point, what individuals juggle and reproduce is not merely their own biography. Indeed, whilst juggling and reproducing their own biography they simultaneously reproduce and establish systemic imperatives that are beyond the means of individual normative negotiation. Thus, individualisation is not only structurally enabled but also systemically imposed.

Apart from the strong systemic features in Luhmann's conception, Beck and Beck-Gernsheim also resurrected Parsons' term 'institutionalised individualism'. This is problematic, because Parsons' conception does not match the hyper-differentiated context of late modernity. In particular, it does not take the dependence on organisations into account. As Beck and Beck-Gernsheim write:

> To put it in a nutshell – individualisation is becoming *the social structure of second modern society itself*. Institutionalised individualism is no longer Talcott Parsons' idea of linear self-reproducing systems; it means the paradox of an 'individualising structure' as a non-linear, open-ended, highly ambivalent, ongoing process ... Thus the theoretical collectivism of sociology ends. (2002: xxii)

But it is not individualisation itself that has become the structure of late modernity but hyper-differentiation. And while the end of the theoretical collectivism of sociology is worth noting, this conception largely ignores the need and increasing lack of a collective organisation of consent in everyday life. Here Beck's notion of individualisation needs to be more differentiated. Moreover, Beck and Beck-Gernsheim identify institutional dependencies as crucial characteristics of contemporary individualisation. Again in reference to Parsons they argue:

> [I]ndividualisation does not by any means imply that the increased freedom of choice is the same thing as a breakdown of order. Rather, what we see here, as elsewhere, is what Talcott Parsons has called 'institutionalised individualism'... You may and you must lead your own independent life, outside the old bonds of family, tribe, religion, origin and class; and you must do this within the new guidelines and rules which the state, the job market, the bureaucracy, etc. lay down. (1996: 36)

To be sure, Parsons might have regarded individualisation as structurally enabled, but more importantly, he saw it as an individual responsibility to contribute to the reproduction of society according to the normative infrastructure. The responsibility that lies with the individual is to realise the institutionalised values of a 'good society' (Parsons and White 1964: 195) through 'an individualistic system of goal achievement' (Parsons 1964: 183). For Parsons, the term 'institutionalised individualism' referred to the fact that all members of society work more or less for the realisation of the 'good society'. The dilemma is that 'institutionalised individualism', or 'instrumental activism' (Parsons and White 1964: 196) as he has also labelled it, delineates a subtle social determinism: what has to be realised is more or less pre-given. Space opens up in regard to how values can be realised individually, and ultimately structural differentiation can serve that purpose. Thanks to this, all members of society share a normative infrastructure.

In late modern societies, however, this is no longer the case; institutionalised individualism as the Becks use it becomes problematic. What people share is not a common normative infrastructure, but the fact that they live in a hyper-differentiated context. Although the context is the same for everyone, it is faced and addressed individually. It is not just that individuals may and must lead their own independent lives, they must do so within modernity first and foremost. What has changed is that possible ways of living are so infinite in conditions of late modernity that life is experienced as a kind of bombardment with choices. Both their systemic imperatives and their normative underpinnings are fragmented and pluralised, leaving individuals with 'no choice, but to choose' (Giddens 1991: 81). Moreover, whichever choices individuals make they reproduce their own systemic dependence by doing so. What Beck and Beck-Gernsheim fail to address is that individualisation is not just about the release of the individual from industrial society into risk societies. While individualisation is in that sense structurally enabled and has the potential to be about shaping the social context in which we live, it can also be instrumentalised and become an organising principle for systemic processes. To talk about structural individualisation then means firstly, that individuals are increasingly released from social structures to shape their own live; secondly, however, it also means that individualisation is systemically compelled by structures that are beyond individuals' control.

The Parsonian term 'institutionalised individualism' is now – thanks to the newly emerged hyper-differentiated context and the proliferation of organisational and individual ambiguities – inadequate to describe the features of contemporary individualisation. In a hyper-differentiated society it is precisely the Parsonian idea of a 'good society' that becomes pluralised, fragmented, contradictory and contentious. The very idea of 'institutionalised individualism' is pluralised and, as I will argue in Parts II and III of this book, it is increasingly dependent on a plurality of organisations, many of which are corporations or are at least run like corporations. Thus rather than describing contemporary individualisation as another form of 'institutionalised individualism', I argue that the contemporary fragmentation and pluralisation of collective forms of identification is better described as 'organised individualisation'. This allows me to specify what the fact that individuals have become the basic unit for the reproduction of society means while the negotiation of systemic and normative boundaries has shifted on to an organisational and individual level.

In contrast to Parsons and Luhmann, but building on Beck and Beck-Gernsheim, I suggest that contemporary individualisation is neither merely about an individualistic realisation of a normative infrastructure, nor is it about a forced individualised response to systemic dependencies. What structural individualisation is about is the negotiation of systemic and normative boundaries on an individual and organisational level in a hyper-differentiated context. The will to actively form an identity and to realise a more or less autonomous individual life is potentially instrumentalised and becomes an organising principle for the reproduction of these systemic dependencies. The following chapter will investigate the characteristics of these boundaries and the ambiguities that arise from them.

Chapter 2
Normative Individualisation

So far I have presented individualisation not only as something that is structurally enabled and increasingly systemically compelled, but also as a key factor in the reproduction of systemic dependencies. In this Chapter I deepen my argument by suggesting that what characterises contemporary individualisation is the need and ability to individually negotiate the normative boundaries between systems and lifeworlds. I describe the ability to negotiate as normative individualisation and I elaborate the concept in in three steps. Firstly, by looking at the formation of the 'social self', I portray socialisation as an individual's learning of their society's normative infrastructure. With the aid of a brief differentiation between social character and identity, I argue that hyper-differentiation prolongs and transmutes socialisation into a continuous state of becoming, in which individuals constantly have to re-learn, adapt and cope with fast changing and contradictory norms in late modern societies. Yet importantly, individualisation also comprises the abilities held by individuals to make a difference to the normative infrastructure in which they live. That is, it is through the process of individuation (a process not the same as individualisation; more will be discussed on this below) that individuals develop the capacity to respond to their normative infrastructure. Accordingly, and secondly, I contend that normative individualisation means that individuals have to increasingly use their qualities and abilities to negotiate the divide between systems and lifeworlds. However, it is this ability to negotiate on an organisational level which underpins the risk of normative individualisation being instrumentalised into 'organised individualisation'. Thirdly, as the demarcation between systems and lifeworlds is turned into an individual task, integration also becomes an individual responsibility as processes of hyper-differentiation appear to challenge existing forms of integration. I claim that an individualised form of integration can only be successful – if it can be successful at all – on the basis of a balanced combination of structural and normative aspects of individualisation, while it is important to see that normative individualisation is not possible without a social sphere that structurally enables individuals to negotiate norms and values in the first place.

1. Socialisation: A Continuous State of Becoming?

Research on the capacities of individuals has traditionally been conducted within the realms of psychology, whilst the role of the individual in society fits more readily into the discussions of sociology or social psychology. In order to elaborate my argument regarding individuals in late modern society having to continuously learn their society's paradoxical normative underpinnings, I will draw on the more socio-psychological notion of 'the self'.

The abundance of definitions of the self or of its various aspects does not necessarily indicate the existence of any conceptual clarity.[1] In these definitions, some prioritise the inner self as 'relatively stable and invariant, resistant to external influences, and self-preserving' (Gaertner and Sedikides 2001: 19). Others, like Baumeister and Tice (2001: 76), have placed their emphasis on social factors. Turner for example has claimed that there is an impulsive side to the self that is constrained or channelled through the social or institutional settings of society (2001: 245). Regardless of their different emphasis, most approaches are explicitly partial, designed to point out one particular quality of the self in particular (Forgas and Kipling 2002: 11). In one way or another, most approaches deal with various elements of 'self-realisation' which, similar to individualisation, carries a sense of liberation that originates in Romanticism (Hattie 1992: 12) and Enlightenment ideals (Hall 1992: 275). The modern concept of self-actualisation also mirrors this thinking by focussing on the self reaching its full potential (see e.g. Maslow 1968: 33). In any case, self-realisation has become one of the highest (though also probably most overrated) values of late-modern societies (Ashmore and Jussim 1997: 228). In this, external as well as internal expectations are high: the self is expected to possess many contradictory qualities like autonomy and independence, but also the ability to conform and cooperate. Some therefore appropriately describe the overemphasis on self-realisation as a kind of 'treasure hunt' (Baumeister 1997: 31) or '*Ich-Jagd*' – a constant chase for the *real* ego (Gross 1999: 11).

While it is not my task to provide a comprehensive review of the various understandings of the self or of self-realisation, I want to emphasise that what is supposed to be realised, the self, is neither simply given at birth, nor can it be understood as some 'tabula rasa'. The self is neither a mere passive receiver of society's norms and values, nor a totally repressed, fixed or hidden entity that strives to break free. If we regard the individual as a competent actor that is shaped by social structures as well as shaping those structures, the question remains: how does the individual become a competent actor in society? The following statement by Berger and Luckmann constitutes a basic – yet central – starting point to explore this in greater detail: 'Man's self-production is always, and of necessity

---

1   In one of the earliest multipartite models of the self, William James (1907) proposed that the self can be divided into the material, the social and the spiritual self. Freud developed the most influential of the multipartite models by differentiating between the Id, the Ego and the Superego (see e.g. 1974). More recent formulations continue these approaches when they discuss, for example, public and private selves (Scheier and Carver 1981), reflexive consciousness, interpersonal relation and executive function of the self (Baumeister 1998), or individual, relational and collective self (Sedikides and Brewer et al. 2001).

a social enterprise' (1971: 69). George Herbert Mead depicts this in greater detail when he argued:

> When a self does appear it always involves an experience of another; there could not be an experience of a self simply by itself … When the response of the other becomes an essential part in the experience or conduct of the individual; when taking the attitude of the other becomes an essential part in his behavior – then the individual appears in his own experience as a self; and until this happens he does not appear as a self. (1972: 195)

But it is not sufficient to portray the self as a social self; there is more to its constitution. In particular, the Chicago School of Symbolic Interactionism, originating mainly in George Herbert Mead's concepts, gave high priority to the process of negotiation. 'Meaning is viewed as an emergent of this fluid and reciprocal process of interaction' (Gecas 1982: 10). Individuals are seen as active and creative actors who are able to construct their social environment and themselves. Accordingly, the social self is seen as a dynamic, changing actor, never 'becoming anything', but always 'in the state of becoming'. This suggests that the self not only negotiates the social order, but the very process of negotiating defines its very nature and existence. The individual is not socialised once, but is always in the process of socialisation; it is not set or fixed, but constantly undergoing change in the process of social interaction (Charon 1979: 30). Thus it is social interaction that fundamentally characterises the permeable boundaries between the individual and society, and the normative flexibility of human beings. As explicated by Joas,

> The prototypical case is of social relations in which action does not take the form of mere translation of fixed prescriptions into deeds, but in which definitions of the relations are, rather, jointly and reciprocally proposed and established. Social relations are seen, then, not as stabilised once and for all but as open and tied to ongoing common acknowledgments. (1987: 84)

This open-ended malleability forms, we can suggest, the basis for the currently popular demand for an openness to 'life-long learning'; it also seems a necessity and essential quality of individuals in hyper-differentiated work societies. To further clarify this I will base my following discussion on the differentiation of 'socialisation' and 'individuation'.

Starting with a discussion of socialisation (I will address individuation separately in section 2 of this chapter), Mead's concept of the 'generalised other' is most relevant here. 'The attitude of the generalised other is the attitude of the whole community' (1972: 154). These attitudes become normative guidelines for the self's own behaviour and thus shape the individual. This fundamentally constitutes the first meaning of normative individualisation. Beyond this, Mead went on to differentiate between 'I' and 'Me' as constituents of the self.[2] In this, the internalisation of norms and values refers to the formation of the 'Me'; the reaction to that socially constructed 'Me' is what Mead termed the 'I'. Building on Mead, Habermas described socialisation as the learning of culture through which a child is integrated into a specific social system. This process results in the formation of what Habermas called role identity (1976: 74).

Mead's 'Me' bears some similarity to what is commonly referred to as 'social character'. This term is useful for the consideration of some of the challenges involved in learning a normative infrastructure in late modernity. Erich Fromm has explained 'social character' in the following way:

> In studying the psychological reactions of a social group we deal with the character structure of the members of the group, that is, of individual persons; we are interested, however, not in the peculiarities by which these persons differ from each other, but in that part of their character structure that is common to most members of the group. We can call this character the social character. The social character necessarily is less specific than the individual character ... The social character comprises only a selection of traits, the essential nucleus of the character structure of most members of a group which has developed as the result of the basic experiences and mode of life common to that group. (1942: 239, original emphasis)

The underlying assumption here is that there exists a rather stable normative infrastructure that to some extent shapes a person's self (Gleason 1983: 925). Once internalised, the 'moral order of society' (a concept Hunter uses in order to describes social character (2000: 16)), develops into an inner authority and a means of social control. It is, however, not an overt form of control, but one that resides inside the individual. Almost automatically, Freud comes into mind here: 'From the point of view of instinctual control, of morality, it may be said of the id that it is totally non-moral, of the ego that it strives to be moral, and of the super-ego that it can be super-moral' (1974). Along the same lines, Fromm has written that the individual 'by adapting himself to social conditions ... develops those traits that make him desire to act as he has to act' (1942: 243). This was also the focal point of character studies conducted in the 1950s and 60s (e.g. Gerth and Mills 1954; Riesman et al. 1961), before identity became the predominantly used term. One of Riesman's central questions, for example, was: 'How is it that every society seems to get, more or less, the social character it "needs"' (1961: 5)? Readopting this question to the context of the present discussion one could ask: How is it that individualisation in contemporary society becomes an organising principle, and

---

2   Kant (1997 [1781]) introduced a distinction between 'the self as an object' and 'the self as a subject'. This was further pursued by Schopenhauer (1995 [1819]) in his distinction between 'the known' and the 'knower', which James pursued further by differentiating between 'I' and 'me'.

is it an internalised form of control or a loss of control by individuals to external forces? The following statement by Hunter gives a clue:

> When … principles, maxims, and habits are internalised deep in our consciousness, they act as moral compasses, providing the bearings by which we navigate the challenges of life. Far from a philosophical abstraction, moral culture guides our behavior, thinking, and expectations of others. Consciously or not, we refer to these compasses constantly, not only when we are confronted by moral dilemmas but in the rhythms of everyday life. (2000: 25)

'Character' as a concept has re-emerged in some more recent works, such as those of Sennett (1998) or Hunter (2000), that claim that the normative stability in contemporary societies is corroding. My point is that the term 'social character' tells us something about the socialisation process in contemporary society: that it has become a continuous lifelong state of becoming, something part of the definition of contemporary individualisation. The fact that a society's normative infrastructures under conditions of hyper-differentiation are characterised by fluidity rather than normative stability explains the decline of the term character and the rise of the term identity, to which I now turn briefly.

It is conceivable that 'identity' became a more prominent concept than 'character' as it seemed more able to capture the process underscoring the ongoing formation of who we are[3]. The expression 'identity' was hardly used before the 1940s, but we can barely do without it today.[4] The development of the term commenced, we can suggest, in the work of Erik H. Erikson, who put a particular emphasis on continuity.[5]

What my argument gains from a brief elaboration on identity is a deeper understanding of the term, which becomes clear when one considers the Latin root *idem*, meaning the same. One of the main differences between terms like personality, self, character and identity seems to lie in the growing difficulty to define what – if anything – actually remains the same. What was considered rather stable in regard to social character, nowadays appears to be more fragile, fragmented, pluralised or even paradoxical (Weigert et al. 1986: 19). We find

---

3   For a more philosophical understanding of the term 'identity' see (Ebert 2003).

4   A. Wheelis' *The Quest for Identity* (1958) exemplifies the emerging use of the term. For a more detailed overview of the development of the term and its use in various disciplines see, for example, (Weigert et al. 1986).

5   Anselm L. Strauss and other members of the school of symbolic interactionism made identity a technical term for sociological psychology. For Strauss, identity is mostly about how we see others and how they see us (1969: 9). Erving Goffman in his work *Stigma* used the term and differentiated between three kinds of identity: social, personal and ego identity (1986). Others, such as Talcott Parsons, have referred to the concept as a rather 'fashionable term' because of the increasing structural differentiation of society which leads to a pluralisation and weakening of clear-cut social roles and increased choices (1968: 11).

ourselves in the same and yet individually very different situations. Our sameness lies in the fact that we live in the same society and that we can learn and adapt to different norms and values. What we share is a hyper-differentiated context in which the normative commonalities shared by all members of society have considerably diminished. The commonality is not what we learn, but that we have to continuously and individually learn and adapt. Putting the emphasis on the paradoxical character of this situation, we could say that we have in common what divides us. Thus what underpins socialisation is the constant learning of and adapting to a fragmented, pluralised and fast changing normative infrastructure. The flexibility of human socialisation has meant that in contemporary societies a continuous exercise of normative adaptation has become the fundamental characteristic of individualisation. Most importantly, what guides individuals is not an internalised form of control, but external systemic imperatives beyond the control of those individuals. It is not that people in earlier societies did not have to keep adapting to social change; rather, my point is that the pace of change has stepped up, thus intensifying individualisation as continuous processes of learning and adaptation. This can also be taken as the first characteristic of normative individualisation.

2. Shifting the Boundaries: Towards Organised Individualisation

Although both concepts – social character and identity – seem to imply a sense of stability and guidance for individual behaviour, Mead stressed that society cannot only expect its members to internalise given norms, but also has to provide opportunities for individuals to shape these norms:

> The value of an ordered society is essential to our existence, but there also has to be room for an expression of the individual himself if there is to be a satisfactorily developed society. A means for such expression must be provided. (1972: 220)

Erich Fromm took a similar stance, concluding that society needs to allow individuals

> to grow, to develop and realise potentialities which man has developed in the course of history – as, for instance, the faculty of creative and critical thinking and of having differentiated emotional and sensuous experiences … it also seems that this general tendency to grow … results in such specific tendencies as the desire for freedom and the hatred against oppression, since freedom is the fundamental condition for any growth. (Fromm 1942: 246)

These statements suggest that individualisation is not only about society shaping individuals structurally or normatively (socialisation), but also about individuals shaping society and its structures. On the basis of what Giddens calls 'knowledgeable actors' (1979: 144; 1981: 28) structures can be conceptualised not as impervious but as the result of social processes. What makes them processual are the debates and controversies that surround them and, indeed, make them. While Giddens' definition and idea of structures as rules and resources might be disputable in its details (see e.g. Sewell 1992), my interest at present lies in what characterises individuals as 'knowledgeable actors'. More specifically: what are the characteristics that allow us to define individualisation as the ability to negotiate and re-negotiate the demarcations between various incommensurable value spheres?

This question takes us back to Habermas, who extends Mead's approach precisely on this point. For Habermas, identity, or more precisely ego-identity (his preferred term instead of self or character), is more than a purely descriptive concept (1976: 70). For him, ego-identity develops. It is a symbolic term for the organisation of the self, responding to recurring challenges, problems and situations. He describes this development as individuation – which is not the same as individualisation – but constitutes an essential aspect of the latter.

Habermas basically concurrs with Mead's idea of the social construction of the self. Socialisation for him refers to the learning of culture through which a child is integrated into society. This process results initially in the formation of what Habermas calls role identity (1976: 74). His crucial refinement was that individuals are not only socialised on the basis of normative expectations of 'generalised others', but the self also matures and learns to make a qualitative difference to the generalised other, the normative infrastructure of society. This process of maturation, during which the self acquires various abilities and capacities to engage with the learned culture, is what pervades Habermas's conceptualisation of individuation. It refers to an individual's growing independence in relation to social systems (Habermas 1976: ibid) and thus the ability to debate and contest a society's normative infrastructure. Whereas role identity can be understood as the learned ability to appropriately use symbolically grounded communicative structures, ego-identity refers to an individual's 'ability to give one's own needs their due in these communicative structures' (Habermas 1976: 78). To be clear, what I call normative individualisation cannot do without social structures that enable it. This is of utmost sociological importance as most debates about individualisation misconstrue this process by reversing it. Often the individual is taken as the starting point, while my point here is that it is the social that constitutes the individual.

The capacity to discursively make normative claims (Habermas 1976: 90) is a core aspect of my understanding of individualisation. Thus, individualisation is not only structurally enabled or compelled, but can also be described as normative individualisation, which refers to the abilities of individuals to make a difference to the social order in which they live. They do so by expressing needs, wishes, desires, criticisms, comments and opinions, but also by confirming, contesting or challenging society's existing normative underpinnings. Individualisation is not only about the structural choices of roles or the one-sided internalisation of norms and values, and it is also not simply about individuation. Individualisation is about the individual as a fully integrated member of society that is trusted to make not only functional, but also normative contributions to the reproduction of society.

Here we face another fundamental ambiguity. As I have argued in Chapter 1, individualisation becomes a reproduction mechanism for systemic dependencies. While this is certainly the case, I am now arguing that individualisation is also about individuals making a normative difference to society. The intention is not to question Habermas's concept of individuation. Rather, I want to go beyond the concept of individuation and specify more precisely those qualities that develop out of individuation and enable individuals to negotiate the normative infrastructure of society. Under conditions of hyper-differentiation and structurally compelled individualisation, individuals have to increasingly use these qualities to individually negotiate the divide between systems and lifeworlds, because the collective forms to do so are fragmented, pluralised and thus weakened. While individuals might develop the competences to freely articulate their needs, will and opinions, these abilities need to be matched by a society that provides space to freely do so, in accordance with, but also – when appropriate – in opposition to a society's normative infrastructure. As Habermas wrote: '[A]n autonomous ego and an emancipated society reciprocally require one another' (1976: 71). Individualisation, therefore, needs both an autonomous individual that is able to critically assess the existing normative infrastructure and an emancipated society that renders norms and values discursively accessible. It is this interdependence that describes the permeable space of autonomy. To be sure, autonomy does not mean total independence. Indeed, both autonomy and independence only come into view as relational. This suggests that there is no totally independent, autonomous, true or hidden self, yet equally there are no independent, autonomous and impervious structures 'out there' dominating the individual. Hence, it makes only sense to talk about individual autonomy as relational or as the space within which social interaction can unfold between individuals in a commonly agreed upon manner, that is, not in an externally imposed way. It is exactly this interdependent dynamic which I try to capture with structurally enabled individualisation on the one hand, and normative individualisation on the other.

All kinds of contradictions, paradoxes and ambiguities arise in this endeavour. The increase in individual autonomy itself inevitably leads to a normative pluralisation and fragmentation of the lifeworld, which then again underpins socialisation as a continuous state of becoming. While the autonomy to make normative claims has increased in late modernity, so too have the contradictions and number of claims. At the same time, the collective means to coordinate and negotiate lag behind. Thus, as a consequence of hyper-differentiation, an increase in individual autonomy at least complicates the collective normative negotiations. When individuals make use of their abilities to voice normative claims, they cannot but trigger social change. This challenges the idea of continuity and certainty on institutional, organisational and personal levels. In this, the self's sense of continuity is strongly related to the concept of identity. Erikson's theory of ego identity development is useful in understanding this, because he is most fundamentally concerned with the development of a sense of continuity and coherence (Côté and Levine 2002: 177). Accordingly, the question of personal continuity comes down to two fundamental perspectives: subjectively individuals experience themselves as continuous entities in varying contexts and over the passage of time; objectively persons are being experienced from the perspective of others as continuous entities in changing situations and over time (Côté and Levine 2002: 94). In regard to individualisation, personal continuity refers to the capacity of an individual to master and maintain a stable self-image both subjectively and objectively across situations and through time (Côté and Levine 2002: 92–93). As Erikson argued, 'the term identity expresses such a mutual relation in that it connotes both a persistent sameness within oneself (self-sameness) and a persistent sharing of some kind of essential character with others' (1960: 37). This suggests that a sense of temporal-spatial continuity depends on individuals' capacities to handle the discontinuities that have flourished in late modernity. In systems theoretical terms, this capacity could be understood as a means for reducing complexity not only on a personal, but also on an organisational level. The failure to do so is essentially what Erikson's concept of identity crisis encapsulates. It refers to a breakdown or an overload of an individual's ability to 'stitch together' a coherent self-image as discontinuities get out of hand. On this, Ewen, in reference to Erikson, defined identity-crisis as follows: 'The inability to achieve a sense of identity … [i]nvolves painful feelings of inner fragmentation, little or no sense of where one's life is headed, and an inability to gain the support provided by satisfactory social roles' (1993: 247).

The attempt to balance individual autonomy, change and continuity is equally present on an institutional level. In this, individual's efforts to change or challenge various norms and values can turn into what is a rather Sisyphean endeavour if they cannot be tied back to overall society; that is, if they are not manifest in the normative infrastructure represented by institutions or organisations. It is in this respect that institutions play a crucial role as intermediaries in the dialectical relationship between individual and society, as it is naïve to imagine millions of people negotiating norms directly with each other.[6] It is the fundamental characteristic of intermediary institutions[7] to mediate and coordinate the voices and actions of individuals where systems and lifeworlds intersect. As Hartmut

---

6   Quite often institutions are referred to as 'second nature' as their rules and norms make up for what Scheler (1961) and Gehlen (1988: 352) call 'Instinktarmut' (lack of instincts). But 'Instinktarmut' also means 'Weltoffenheit' (world-openness). Without going into further detail here, this anthropological condition can be considered the starting point for the elaboration of a dialectical relationship between individual and society.

7   The term was broadly introduced into sociology by Durkheim. See Berger and Luckmann (1996: 59).

Esser[8] has summarised: 'Institutions are certain socially defined sets of rules that are valid for overall society and that are anchored in actors' expectations. From these rules an unconditionally binding social behavior is derived' (2000: 6).[9]

It is important for the architecture of my argument to note that institutions are not the same as organisations. Organisations represent institutions that put their rules into practice. For example, government organisations implement policies; corporations as a form of organisation represent the market as an institution (see Chapter 4). In the final equation it is individuals, on behalf of organisations, that realise the institutionalised norms and values. Under conditions of hyper-differentiation, the role of intermediary institutions might shift onto organisations, where the boundaries between systems and lifeworlds have to be negotiated individually.

Because of the normative claims of individuals, a society's normative infrastructure is in constant flux and intermediary institutions are also subject to change:

> 'Institutions' are never something concrete to which we can point but are essentially processual; ever in a fluid process of becoming and never in a fixed state of being, because all structural properties and all actions are always potentially transformational. (Archer 1996: 689)

Yet institutions also seem to set the pace for social change. They transform social conflicts into social change, thereby creating a sense of stability in terms of continuous but not revolutionary change. The following quote from Berger and Luckmann describes exactly the 'joint-like' role of institutions in the relationship between individuals and society:

> On the one hand, we find institutions that enable individuals to carry their personal values from the private sphere into various areas of society and to put them forward in a way where they become a formative influence for overall society. On the other hand, there are institutions that treat individuals more or less as passive objects of their symbolic services. Only the former are intermediary institutions … They are intermediary as they mediate between the individual and the established patterns of experience and behaviour in society. With the support of those institutions the individual contributes to the establishing and revising of the social stock of knowledge. Therefore, the existing stock of knowledge is

---

8   Esser refers in particular to Bronislaw Malinowski, Arnold Gehlen and Helmut Schelsky (amongst others), who introduced the term widely to sociology, mainly describing it as a pattern of general expectations everyone has to conform to on the basis of either tradition or law.

9   'Institutionen sind … bestimmte, in den Erwartungen der Akteure verankerte, sozial definierte Regeln mit gesellschaftlicher Geltung und daraus abgeleiteter 'unbedingter' Verbindlichkeit fuer das Handeln'.

not experienced as something that is authoritatively given or prescribed but as an
offer that has been shaped by all members of society and that is open for further
modifications. (1996: 59)

Hyper-differentiation, however, makes these mediating processes enormously
complex. The attempt to achieve a balance between personal, institutional and
organisational continuity and stability is conflictual in the Weberian sense as
elaborated above. It generates various ambivalences, while the responsibility to
negotiate and handle those contradictions and to maintain continuity on all three
levels is individualised. As hyper-differentiation breaks up the collective means
to organise consent, systemic forces turn the intermediary role of institutions into
a one way street of systemic imperatives. On an organisational level individuals
not only have to respond, but have to reproduce these imperatives (Chapter 4).
Such ambiguities seem to intensify with the growing flexibility, fragmentation and
pluralisation of all layers of the social order.

The ability to negotiate between systems and lifeworlds also means that
individuals develop the mental capacity to reflectively engage in, contribute to
and participate in the systemic and normative reproduction of society. Mead,
for example, described reflexivity as 'the turning-back of the experience of the
individual upon himself' (1956: 211). It is this concept of the self, as an internal
reference point, that lies at the heart of the 'reflexive project of the self' (Giddens
1991: 145). Or as Baumeister writes, '[s]elf-knowledge begins when attention
turns around toward its source, a phenomenon commonly called reflexive
consciousness' (1998: 699). Hence, reflexivity refers to the self's capacity to
reflectively step back and process information not only about oneself, but also
about the social environment. While this might result in normative claims in one
form or the other, it might also result in the systemic processing of information
as reflexivity seems to be particularly susceptible to instrumentalisation. That
reflexivity is a major individual resource for negotiating systemic and social
structures. This comes under duress in hyper-differentiated circumstances where
individuals are supposed to handle an abundance of ambivalent information which
might lead them to react reflexively rather than reflectively.

And yet society is not realised through thinking, but through the actions of
individuals. This is commonly referred to as 'agency', a somewhat unfortunate
or perhaps even misleading term. It either awkwardly suggests that individuals
are agents of a hidden or true self, which contradicts the deeply social processes
from which the self emerges, or that the individual is understood in structuralist
terms as a mere agent of external forces. Therefore, I will avoid the terms 'agent'
or 'agency' unless they refer to being an agent for something or someone. Instead,
I will refer to action and actors. While various theoretical approaches oscillate
between an emphasis on either 'totally free', 'totally institutionalised' or 'rational'
agents, I want to put the emphasis on individuals' abilities to negotiate the
institutional and organisational landscape through their actions as a major aspect
of individualisation.

The ability to feel as a competent actor is very much based on experiencing oneself as a causal actor in one's environment (Gecas and Burke 1995: 51), which is theoretically widely accounted for in a variety of concepts.[10] Without the ability to act 'the self would be … of minimal use or importance' (Baumeister 1998: 680) and a 'helpless, passive spectator of events' (Baumeister 1997: 192–93). In the context of my argument, I understand individuals as competent actors. As actors, individuals draw on already established norms or everyday knowledge, relate their actions to other individuals, places and meanings or use their imagination to direct action towards a future outcome. Hence, action is embedded in what Emirbayer has described as a temporal relational flow of social interaction (1998: 963), to which the nexus between time and money adds the dimension of efficiency to almost everything human beings do (see Chapter 3).

Yet, individuals cannot simply act as they please. Their actions are, before they are individual action, socially enabled. Actions are approved, disapproved and scrutinised by (the generalised) others around them. It is mainly from this Meadian understanding that Honneth developed his theory of social recognition and of a negotiable normative infrastructure.[11] As children gain full membership in a society they are trusted and recognised by others as individuals who can now normatively expect certain behaviour from others. As Honneth argued: 'Subjects encounter each other within the parameters of the reciprocal expectation that they receive recognition as moral persons and for their social achievements' (1994: 262). Accordingly, the very idea of mutual recognition is based on shared rights and expectations. All members of a society know what they can expect from others and what others expect from them (Honneth 1996: 79). This, of course, also becomes problematic under hyper-differentiated circumstances.

Honneth differentiated between three modern forms of recognition in liberal democratic societies: love, law and solidarity. Recognition based on love equips us with basic self-confidence. Legal recognition is based on the mainly Western idea of law that recognises everyone as equal and allows individuals to develop self-respect. Solidarity, the third type of recognition, is the most important one for my argument. This recognition is granted on the basis of a normative infrastructure that serves as a guideline for the evaluation of individuals' unique contributions, traits and qualities as useful or useless for the reproduction of society. As Honneth himself wrote:

> The cultural self-understanding of a society provides the criteria that orient the social esteem of persons, because their abilities and achievements are judged intersubjectively according to the degree to which they can help to realise culturally defined values. (1996: 122)

---

10   See for example Adler's idea of 'mastery' (1927), Bandura's 'self-efficacy' (Bandura 1977), or the concept of 'habitus' (see e.g. Bourdieu 1977).

11   He also builds his theory on Hegel's understanding of social recognition which is, however, irrelevant for my discussion.

Individuals' abilities and achievements, in particular in work (Honneth 1994: 267), are judged intersubjectively according to the degree to which they contribute to the realisation of the overarching normative infrastructure (Honneth 1996: 122). This enables individuals to develop self-esteem because they know others recognise them for the unique abilities they may not share with others, but which are recognised as providing useful contributions to society. The struggle for recognition conceptualises a possible dialogue between the individual and society without getting trapped in supposedly impervious and overbearing structures. As Honneth explained:

> In defending their spontaneously experienced demands, subjects have no option but to secure acceptance, again and again, from a counterfactually posited community that grants them greater freedom, as compared to the established relations of recognition. (1996: 83)

This leads to a never ending chain of challenges pushing the boundaries for more individual autonomy, institutionally paced social change on the basis of reflexivity and competent action in relation to existing normative understandings. However, if recognition is denied, it results in feelings of social disrespect and social exclusion (Honneth 1994: 262). Equally, the striving for social recognition becomes a source of guidance as it encourages individuals to 'do the right thing' in order to maintain and secure social recognition.

In late modern societies the emphasis appears to lie on the struggle rather than the successful granting of social recognition. Pluralisation, fragmentation and flexibilisation reduce the collective sources of social recognition as society seems to lose the sense of a shared and largely unitary normative infrastructure. The struggle for recognition therefore becomes an increasingly individual struggle on an organisational basis, at the end of which the desired outcome of social recognition can by no means be guaranteed or secured over any period of time. Whether an individualised struggle for recognition can be successful at all without collective consent is questionable. The granting of social recognition today is individualised insofar as it increasingly depends on organisations rather than an overarching normative infrastructure. Whether this individualised, organisational struggle can be successful depends on the negotiability of the norms and values underpinning organisations. This might well result in the granting of social recognition, but it might equally increase the risk of organisational disrespect and exclusion, as my discussion of corporate culture in Chapter 6 will demonstrate.

With this discussion I have introduced various aspects of individualisation that allow me to further specify the meaning of normative individualisation as the individualised negotiation between systems and lifeworlds. From this discussion communication, socialisation, autonomy, reflexivity, continuity, action and the struggle for social recognition emerge as processes that define the dialogue between the individual and society from various angles. What characterises normative individualisation is the negotiation of the increasingly permeable boundaries between systems and lifeworlds. The shift from structurally enabled, normative individualisation to 'organised individualisation', as well as the ambiguities that arise from it, can now be described as

- the ability to communicate as a means of negotiating norms and values versus simply giving / receiving information;
- the capacity to be socialised by and actively socialise others versus the internalisation and coordination of systemic and increasingly organisational imperatives;
- individual autonomy and independence as a relationally defined space to reflectively and actively organise consent versus organisationally dependent adaptation and instrumentalisation as systemically inflicted compulsory choice and reproduction;
- reflexivity as the ability to process information, make judgments and to be self-responsible versus being active hubs for systemic coordination of pregiven goals where individuals act reflexively rather than reflectively;
- the capacity to create and sustain personal, organisational and institutional continuity versus sustaining individual continuity in dependence of systemic continuity;
- competent individual action versus organisational agency (not only responding to, but reproducing systemic dependencies);
- granting and being granted social recognition on the basis of publicly accessible normative infrastructures versus granting and being granted social recognition on behalf of a systemically inaccessible organisationally prescribed normative infrastructure.

To be sure, while there might be a potential shift towards 'organised individualisation', it entails just as many risks of instrumentalisation as it opens up opportunities of individual autonomy. The instabilities and uncertainties that are said to beset late modern societies are in fact the consequences of an increase in individual autonomy.

3. Individualised Integration: An (Im)Possible Balancing Act?

In *The Division of Labour in Society* Durkheim asks the following question: 'How does it come about that the individual personality, whilst becoming more autonomous, depends ever more closely upon society? How can he become at the same time more of an individual and yet more linked to society?' (1984[1893]: xxx) This is in essence the question about the relationship between differentiation on the one hand, and individualisation on the other; it is the question about integration which under conditions of hyper-differentiation becomes ever more pressing. Integration in late modern societies has become a balancing act for individuals between systemic coordination on the one hand and social integration on the other. With the aid of three dimensions of integration – organisational, social and functional – I suggest that contemporary forms of integration are characterised by individuals having to balance both, systemic coordination and social integration. Individuals' ability to perform this balancing act is another defining feature of normative individualisation. However, these abilities can be used to realise given norms and values which equates to systemic coordination and integration, while the use of those abilities to negotiate norms and values would amount to social integration. What characterises late modern societies then are various coexisting, conflictual and above all individualised aspects of organisational, social and systemic integration. Each one of these forms of integration comprises aspects of both systemic coordination and social integration.

As this discussion has shown, Durkheim's understanding of integration rests largely on interdependencies of various functions of society (systemic integration). While this kind of integration has not become obsolete, under conditions of hyper-differentiation it is accompanied by an increase of complexities and interdependencies and so cannot but be partial, contradictory and in constant flux. Because of that these complexities are shifted not only from a social meta-level to a Weberian pluralised, fragmented and competitive organisational level (organisational integration), but to an individual level. Accordingly, individuals have to achieve integration themselves and they do so often with the aid of organisational memberships. To be sure, neither systemic coordination nor social integration can do without organisations. The crucial point here is whether individuals achieve integration on the basis of a normative infrastructure they themselves negotiate (social integration) or whether integration is conditional and aims at the individual implementation of non-negotiable systemic rules (organisation and systemic integration). In the latter case the role of individuals is one of becoming active hubs for coordinating systemic imperatives. But whether or not normative individualisation leads to organisational integration, social integration or systemic coordination depends on the ability of individuals to negotiate the norms that underpin and define the purpose of an organisation. This is what defines the difference between social integration and systemic coordination, at least on the analytic level.

Another important aspect of this issue comes into view when Parsons' systemic approach to integration is considered. Parsons portrayed society as a context of functionally differentiated but highly interdependent subsystems (1963b: 350). Integration occurs when the four functional prerequisites (adaptation, goal attainment, integration and latency) work together in a well-balanced manner (Parsons 1960: 196–97). These interdependencies are supported by 'generalised media of exchange' like 'money, power and influence' (Parsons 1963a: 355, 361) and the 'cybernetic hierarchy of control' (Schimank 1996: 112), referring to a hierarchy of subsystems. Parsons insisted that no matter how differentiated societies are, they are always based on normative orientations (Parsons 1964: 11). He is of course right in so far as institutions, organisations and individuals (or, in Habermasian terms, systems and lifeworlds), are guided by norms and values that are the result of concrete social relationships no matter how mediated they are. The decisive question, however, is whether these norms and values are based on a working dialogue between individual and society or whether they are beyond public control.[12] The abundance of contradictory and competing norms and values does not mean the end of normative integration in general; at the same time, integration on the basis of norms is highly fragmented, pluralistic and paradoxical and again, the responsibility to achieve integration or, in Parsonian terms, to harmonise the various systemic imperatives, seems to lie with individuals.

As I have pointed out above, Niklas Luhmann does not favour normative aspects of integration (1996: 318). Rather, he holds that each system adapts its own internal structures and programs to the externalities produced by other systems in order to maintain its own reproduction. Luhmann referred to this as 'interpenetration' (1996: 318). As this happens, the development of one system is linked to the development of others and vice versa. Luhmann calls this process 'strukturelle Kopplung' (structural linkage) (Schimank 1996: 191). He and others have identified three key mechanisms which drive systemic adaptation: material constraints (e.g. financial scarcity), reflexivity (e.g. considering environmental damage that puts future systemic reproduction at risk) and 'Kontextsteuerung' (politics or social movements) (see Schimank 1996: 192). In particular, the latter two seem to relativise a total functional fragmentation of modern society. I will put aside the question whether 'binary codes' or 'programs' might in the final equation mean the same thing as values or norms. What is important to note is that systemic 'self-referentiality' reduces social integration based on discursively established norms to processes of systemic coordination on various levels (institutional, organisational, individual). This amounts neither to a Durkheimian sense of integration on the basis of interdependencies, nor to Parsonian normative underpinnings. However, echoing the Weberian concept of value spheres, it describes functional aspects of integration under conditions of hyper-differentiation. Based on systemically defined membership roles individuals succumb to norms and values that force them to individually reproduce rather than negotiate rules and norms in order to ensure systemic continuity and their own integration. Individuals as psychic systems carry out the self-referentiality of other systems.

All aspects of integration (social and systemic) are present at an organisational level. Individuals are not only social entities that want or need to be integrated, but are also responsible for the occurrence of that integration. Individualised integration means that individuals have to achieve and sustain various organisational memberships either by negotiating, consenting to or complying with certain membership roles and rules. It also means that individuals can integrate themselves by contesting or accepting an existing normative infrastructure and they must individually bear the consequences of, for example, social recognition

---

12   As I have pointed out in Chapter 1 Parsons' inability to account for the emergence of norms is the weak spot of his theory identified by Habermas.

or the lack thereof. Finally, normative individualisation means that individuals integrate themselves by participating in and contributing to the ongoing social as well as systemic reproduction of society. Successful individualised integration is thus a balanced combination of systemic coordination and social integration on organisational levels that takes structural and normative aspects of individualisation equally into account.

How does this help us to understand the integration or disintegration of contemporary society? 'Is it', as Beck and Beck-Gernsheim asked, 'still at all possible to integrate highly individualised societies' (1996: 43)? That question can now be reformulated: Is it still at all possible to integrate hyper-differentiated and highly individualised societies? Without making concrete suggestions, Beck and Beck-Gernsheim alluded to potential forms of integration and the risks of disintegration in contemporary society when they wrote:

> Highly individualised societies can only be bound together – if at all – firstly, through a clear understanding of precisely this situation; and secondly, if people can be successfully mobilised and motivated for the challenges present at the centre of their lives (unemployment, destruction of nature, etc.). Where the old sociality is 'evaporating', society must be re-invented. Integration therefore becomes possible if no attempt is made to arrest and push back the break-out of individuals. It can happen if we make conscious use of this situation, and try to forge new, politically open, creative forms of bond and alliances. The question of whether we still have the strength, the imagination – and the time – for this 'invention of the political' … is, to be sure, a matter of life and death … Post-traditional societies threatening the cohesion of this civilisation can only become integrable – if at all – through the experiment of the self-interpretation, self-observation, self-opening, self-discovery, indeed, their self-invention. Their ⌊post-traditional societies'] future, their ability to have and shape a future, is the measure of their integration. (1996: 44–45)

I suggest that it is less about the 'break-out' of individuals but that integration ends up being an individualised balancing act between social and systemic processes on an organisational level. The fact that individuals can successfully handle this balancing act attests to their ability to achieve social as well as systemic integration.

The discussion thus far has shown that both the structural underpinnings of late modernity and normative individualisation are currently characterised by a fundamental ambiguity, namely a heightened sense of liberation and an increased risk of instrumentalisation. It has also demonstrated that a clear understanding of individualisation has to include the interdependence of differentiation, individualisation and integration. I have described processes of differentiation as a pluralisation and fragmentation of society on an institutional, organisational and individual level. What characterises this late modern context is both hyper-differentiated systems and hypertrophied lifeworlds. While broad overarching institutional reference points are weakened, organisational identifications that are subject to individual choice come to the fore. As a consequence, individualisation can no longer be sufficiently described as 'institutionalised individualism' or as mere responses to systemic imperatives. Rather, contemporary individualisation has to be understood along three interconnected lines: firstly, structures enable individualisation in terms of roles and choices; secondly, structures not only enable, demand and compel individuals to actively respond to systemic imperatives, but by responding individuals actively reproduce these imperatives; thirdly, individuals are able to be shaped by, and in turn shape, these structures.

Normative individualisation refers to individuals' ability to constantly re-learn, adapt and cope with fast changing and contradictory situations. But it also presupposes individuals' capacities to make a difference to the normative infrastructure in which they live, and they develop these capacities in the process of individuation. They use their qualities and abilities to negotiate the divide between systems and lifeworlds; it is this ability to negotiate on an organisational level which underpins the risk of normative individualisation being instrumentalised into 'organised individualisation'. But individuals are also engaged in the achievement of integration. As the demarcation between systems and lifeworlds is turned into an individual task, social as well as systemic integration become an individual responsibility. I claim that an individualised form of integration can only be successful – if it can be successful at all – on the basis of a balanced combination of structural and normative aspects of individualisation, while it is important to see that normative individualisation is not possible without a social sphere that structurally enables individuals to negotiate norms and values in the first place.

The shift towards what I call 'organised individualisation' gives rise to considerable ambiguities. Perceived uncertainties and instabilities not only demand a more active response by individuals, but also represent increased opportunities for individual autonomy. With this in mind, I now turn to developments in contemporary capitalism and ask how these impact on individualisation as the possibility to re-negotiate and negotiate society's normative infrastructure.

Chapter 3
The Individualisation of Society

The aim of this chapter is to scrutinise the link between what I have described as structural individualisation and normative individualisation in the public sphere and markets. Here the ambiguity between liberation and the risk of instrumentalisation finds a continuation in the conflict between politicisation and marketisation. By addressing those aspects, we will be able to develop an understanding of the individualisation of society as a social phenomenon as opposed to atomisation or even disintegration for which individualisation is often mistaken. The ambiguities that emerge from this provide strong breeding grounds for organised individualisation.

The individualised negotiation of the demarcations between systems and lifeworlds can facilitate public discourses about norms and values in civil society, generating not only social integration, but also guidelines for the state to regulate and intervene in the market. For such a discourse to successfully occur, however, a public sphere is required that enables individuals to participate. We can refer to this discourse as politicisation or what Habermas describes as the 'detour through norms' (1971: 118). Yet, there is a risk that the structures of the state as well as the market turn normative individualisation into an organising principle for systemic coordination and reproduction. Thus, they can not only enable normative individualisation but also sideline debates in the public sphere.

In particular, current tendencies towards marketisation marginalise public debates as a legitimating and socially integrating process. Both state-regulation and marketisation cannot provide institutional shortcuts to social integration. They themselves can only provide systemic integration, unless they can be tied back to genuine normative negotiation processes. It is in precisely this sense that marketisation can lead to legitimation deficits by reducing individualisation to an individual responsibility for the reproduction of systemic dependencies.

The conflict between politicisation and marketisation comes particularly to the fore with an individualised negotiation between systemic and normative aspects of work. The instrumentalising pressures resulting from a systemically threatening 'end of work' and a normatively defined 'universalised work ethic' deepen the tensions between democracy and capitalism for individuals in contemporary work society. Taken together, these tensions provide major breeding grounds for 'organised individualisation'.

1. Politicisation: A Detour through Norms or Systemic Organising Principle?

The economy is a decisive part of creating and sustaining any society and as such it is an integral part of individuals' lives. However, to argue that state-regulation as well as the material satisfaction of needs should be embedded in normative discussions, we need to start with Marx and the satisfaction of needs. According to him,

> we must begin by stating the first premise of all human existence and, therefore, of all history, the premise, namely, that men must be in a position to live in order to be able to 'make history'. But life involves before everything else eating and drinking, a habitation, clothing and many other things. The first historical act is thus the production of the means to satisfy these needs, the production of material life itself. And indeed this is an historical act, a fundamental condition of all history, which today, as thousands of years ago, must daily and hourly be fulfilled merely in order to sustain human life. (1970: 48)

As a consequence, who the individuals are depends on 'what they produce and … how they produce' (Marx 1970: 42). For Marx, the economy has a clear-cut function, namely the satisfaction and reproduction of existing as well as new needs. Apart from that, the relations of production also influence how individuals relate to each other. Here it is the economy that structurally enables individualisation. The mode of production might demand a particular coordination of the producing individuals. Even language and consciousness for Marx emerge from the need to coordinate linguistically not only the material reproduction of society, but also the social interactions of its members (Marx 1970: 51). From that point of view, it seems only logical to regard production processes as the nucleus of social life.

However, it is not only the material reproduction that necessitates coordination and cooperation. This is also true for the legitimation, definition and interpretation of needs in respect to the priority they are given and what mode of production is chosen for their satisfaction. Thus, the material reproduction of society not only satisfies material needs, but makes the contingency of needs in relation to the various spheres of society obvious (Polanyi 1957: 243–44). The coordination of the material reproduction through the state equally calls for a legitimation of the emerging political order as well as the definition and interpretation of a normative infrastructure into which the economy is supposed to be embedded.[1] This is where politicisation enters the picture.

Two fundamental steps have to be taken into consideration in order to gain a deeper understanding of politicisation and the risk of individualisation turning into an organising principle in late modern work societies: firstly, the theoretical shift

---

1   Boltanski and Chiapello in their study *The New Spirit of Capitalism* raise a similar question when they write: '[T]he process of capitalism is remarkably lacking in justification' (2005: 162).

from work to communication as the paradigm of social evolution; secondly, the differentiation between work and interaction and subsequently purposive-rational and communicative action. Both play an essential role in an individualised clash of systems and lifeworlds. It is only with the aid of those theoretical differentiations that it becomes clear what kind of individualisation is structurally enabled and what the risk involved in an individualisation of society are.

While Marx identifies the necessity of social coordination, he cannot account for the emergence of norms and values guiding the satisfaction of needs. Habermas therefore states:

> Whereas Marx localised the learning processes important for evolution in the dimension of objectivating thought – of technical and organisational knowledge, of instrumental and strategic action, in short, of productive forces – there are good reasons meanwhile for assuming that learning processes also take place in the dimension of moral insight, practical knowledge, communicative action, and the consensual regulation of action conflicts – learning processes that are deposited in more mature forms of social integration, in new productive relations, and that in turn first make possible the introduction of new productive forces. (1979a: 97–98)

The decisive point is that Marx regards society and intersubjectivity as materially produced, while Habermas considers both as 'linguistically established' (1979a: 99). The latter regards market activity not only as insufficient to account for the evolution of society, but equally as secondary to communicative action. With this shift, Habermas leaves the materially based view on social evolution behind and advances

> the thesis that the development of these normative structures is the pacemaker of social evolution, for new principles of social organisation mean new forms of social integration; and the latter, in turn, first make it possible to implement available productive forces or to generate new ones, as well as making possible a heightening of social complexity. (1979a: 120)

To be clear, work remains a central aspect of modern life, but Habermas makes a fundamental differentiation between instrumental and communicative action that 'permits us to separate the aspects under which action can be rationalised' (1979a: 120). I contend that this is not just a theoretical assumption, but it is the everyday situation in which individuals find themselves in late modernity. They have to rationalise their actions along the lines of communicative or instrumental action; however, they have to do so under systemic and normative pressures. The crucial point is whether the rationalisation of normative individualisation feeds either into a public discourse about norms, values and needs (politicisation) or results in an instrumentalisation of individualisation as an organising principle of state and market activity.

We can deepen this argument with the aid of Weber's concept of rationalisation. Habermas reformulates Weber's idea of rationalisation with the central distinction between work and communication. In more detail, he not only differentiates between work and interaction, but also between instrumental/purposive-rational/strategic action on the one hand, and communicative action/symbolic interaction on the other hand.

> By 'work' or purposive-rational action I understand either instrumental action of rational choice or their conjunction. Instrumental action is governed by technical rules based on empirical knowledge … The conduct of rational choice is governed by strategies based on analytic knowledge … Purposive-rational action realises defined goals under given conditions. But while instrumental action organises means that are appropriate or inappropriate according to criteria of an effective control of reality, strategic action depends only on the correct evaluation of possible alternative choices, which results from calculation supplemented by values and maxims. (Habermas 1971: 90–92)

In contrast to that, he defines interaction as

> communicative action, symbolic interaction. It is governed by binding consensual norms, which define reciprocal expectations about behavior and which must be understood and recognised by at least two acting subjects … While the validity of technical rules and strategies depends on that of empirically true or analytically correct propositions, the validity of social norms is grounded only in the intersubjectivity of the mutual understanding of intentions and secured by the general recognition of obligations … Learned rules of purposive-rational action supply us with skills, internalised norms with personality structures. Skills put us in a position to solve problems; motivations allow us to follow norms. (Habermas 1971: 92)

The distinction between various types of action allows Habermas to differentiate between an 'institutional framework' and 'subsystems', depending on which type of action predominates. The institutional framework of a society consists of norms that guide symbolic interaction, while the economy and the state operate primarily along the lines of purposive-rational action.

> Insofar as actions are determined by the institutional framework they are both guided and enforced by norms. Insofar as they are determined by subsystems of purposive-rational action, they conform to patterns of instrumental or strategic action. (Habermas 1971: 93–94)

The relevance of these distinctions for our topic lies in the following questions: If instrumental action and systemic imperatives are non-democratic, apolitical and non-negotiable (Habermas 1979b: 189), how can they become part of any kind of collective or individualised processes of contestation? The answer lies in a politicisation of the norms and values underpinning the purpose we assign to the state, the market, work and subsequently organisations in each of those spheres. This is what Habermas calls the 'detour through norms' (1971: 118) and what I refer to as politicisation. Economic processes and work can only be indirectly subject to politicisation on the basis of communicatively established norms (1979b: 195–96).

The politicisation of the normative infrastructure first of all presupposes that needs and norms are contingent and thus negotiable and re-negotiable (Markus 1995: 168). On the basis of that, both the material as well as the social reproduction of society can be subject to public discourses over the norms and values of society, opening up opportunities for individuals to debate and contest norms and values. Politicisation is the result of individual contestations that can translate into public discourses in civil society from which a normative infrastructure emerges, which then can become a guideline for the economy and work enforced and protected by the state. Politicisation, thus, refers to publicly conducted discourses that are based on individual abilities to make a difference concerning the definition and interpretation of a society's normative underpinnings. Structural and normative individualisation have to work hand in hand at this point for a genuine politicisation to occur. It requires social structures to be in place that allow normative individualisation.

Moreover, politicisation must not be equated with politics or the state. It is rather about the institutionalisation of communicative action as a source of legitimation outside, yet not independent of, purposive-rational systems like the economy and state-administration. The state could be seen as an empty structure that enables normative individualisation but equally puts individualisation at risk of becoming an organising principle for systemic purposes. Hence, the source of legitimation lies neither in the economy, nor in the state-apparatus or the political system. The politicisation of the normative infrastructure in hyper-differentiated societies is about an institutionalisation of plurality, in contrast to a one-sided domination of either state-administration or economic reason (Offe 1985b). The question is whether this plurality can be translated into a meaningful public debate that is neither systemically prescribed nor organisationally arranged.

Consequently, in the context of our discussion, politicisation does not refer to systemic self-regulation, but to normative self-organisation originating in individualisation as the ability to make a normative difference. And this is the benchmark against which we must measure individualisation as a socially integrating, legitimating and liberating negotiation process rather than in terms of atomisation or disintegration. As much as we might complain about increasing uncertainties, they equally provide us with the social freedom to negotiate; they give us more individual autonomy. Most importantly, I am not speaking about systemically provided choices that usually are portrayed to us as some kind of individual freedom. The space for these 'horizontal structures of negotiation and compromise' is not the political or economic system, but 'a democratic civil society' (Markus 1995: 162). It is here where, besides the political and the economic sphere, the broader public sphere enters the picture, not as another institution for systemic coordination, but as a locus for an individually driven rationalisation of the lifeworld potentially able to bring about social integration.

Maria Markus describes civil society as 'a public sphere, or multiplicity of public spaces, a structure of self-organisation of society, outside the institutional framework of the state but not independent of it' (1995: 167). As such, it can be regarded as an intermediary institution where the ongoing confrontation between the hyper-differentiated and individualised social order, the market and the state becomes the nucleus of a socially integrating relationship between the individual and society. In that context politicisation in civil society is not about homogenisation. One can imagine politicisation as a multilayered discourse for the social self-organisation of consent regarding all value-spheres rather than a particular kind of logic of organisation and structural arrangement. Most importantly, these processes emerge from difference rather than similarity. This also means that grand transcendental, pseudo-religious value horizons can no longer open up. Hyper-differentiation alone makes this a sheer impossibility, and as Luckmann writes: 'In modern societies homogeneous, unitary moral orders of this kind are no longer embedded in the social structure' (2002: 25).

The most important point to take from this complex discussion is that normative individualisation can only generate a sense of liberation if it feeds into politicisation, public discourses and the legitimation of the political order. Only if normative individualisation flows into public debates which subsequently manifest themselves in state-policies can we speak of a true politicisation of needs.

> The genuine politicisation of needs has occurred only when … the question of needs has been brought into a public discourse (or perhaps rather discourses) and became a subject of contestation. Such contestation has to be understood not purely in terms of negotiations concerning the satisfaction of needs (its modes and levels), but extends to questioning of their interpretation as well as of the competence of different public institutions and bodies to take over such interpretation. Politicisation of needs, in this sense, means the recognition of the contingent nature of needs and the awareness of their interconnection with the process of individual and collective *identity formation* and with different ways of life. (Markus 1995: 168)

Consequently, what lies at the heart of individualisation translating into politicisation, not only of needs, but of the normative infrastructure in general, is individuals' access to the participatory means for public discourses. They are the source of social integration and social coordination, legitimating a particular social and political order defined by various modes, hierarchies and priorities of living and working together as a society.

So far, our discussion has mainly been focused on politicisation. A brief look at questions of legitimation, state-regulation and marketisation will not only further clarify issues around politicisation and subsequently social and systemic integration, but is also essential for an identification of breeding grounds of 'organised individualisation'.

I will again turn here to Habermas who writes:

> We first speak of legitimacy in relation to political orders ... The state does not ... carry out social integration through values and norms, which are not at its disposition. But inasmuch as the state assumes the guarantee to prevent social disintegration by way of binding decisions, the exercise of state power is tied to the claim of maintaining society in its normatively determined identity. The legitimacy of state power is then measured against this; and it must be recognised as legitimate if it is to last. (1979b: 179–80)

Values and norms are at the disposition of individuals as members of civil society. Thus, 'only the rules and communicative presuppositions that make it possible to distinguish an accord or agreement among free and equals from a contingent or forced consensus have legitimating force today' (Habermas 1979b: 188). Accordingly, it is the democratic will-formation in civil society that legitimates state power. And yet,

> the modern state can be understood as the result of the differentiation of an economic system which regulates the production process through the market – that is, in a decentralised and unpolitical manner ... the state develops and guarantees bourgeois civil law, the monetary mechanism, and certain infrastructures overall the prerequisites for the continued existence of a depoliticised economic process set free from moral norms and orientations to use value ... the modern state directs its ordering achievements to delimiting a subsystem from its domain of sovereignty, a subsystem that replaces (at least in part) the social integration accomplished through values and norms with a system integration operating through exchange relations. (Habermas 1979b: 188–90)

Only from politicisation can a genuine legitimation of a social and political order emerge which takes individualisation into account as the ability to negotiate the normative infrastructure in civil society. The point made by Habermas that 'only political orders can have and lose legitimacy; only they need legitimation [and that] multinational corporations or the world market are not capable of legitimation' (1979b: 179) is crucial. Accordingly, only if individualisation translates into politicisation can it carry a sense of liberation that results from participation in the formation of norms and values. Individualisation through corporations and the market can be described as 'organised individualisation' as the underlying norms and principles are not the result of negotiations, but are organisationally prescribed or arranged resulting in a 'pseudo-negotiation' of norms and values.

The all-decisive point is thus individuals' access to the means and channels of communication in order to define the normative infrastructure according to which the economy, work and the state directly or indirectly function. To be sure, these are social channels that enable structural individualisation as a social phenomenon. Once this is the case, the social sphere can become the space where normative individualisation can occur and translate into politicisation. This is where the emancipatory potential of an individualised negotiation of systemic and normative processes lies in late modern societies. If this is not the case, 'deficits in democratic legitimation arise whenever the set of those involved in making democratic decisions fails to coincide with the set of those affected by them' (Habermas 1999: 49). Normative individualisation as the negotiation of the boundaries between systems and lifeworlds then does not flow into public debates and discourses about the normative infrastructure of society, but becomes an organising principle for systemic imperatives.

2. Marketisation: A Shortcut through Markets to Social Integration?

The discussion in section one of this chapter provides an idea of how the state and markets can become subject to communicatively-formed norms and values through politicisation. It also establishes an important triangular constellation of civil society (generating social integration and legitimation through politicisation), the state (providing systemic integration through regulation on the one hand, and social integration by protecting the space for politicisation on the other), and the market (producing systemic integration through marketisation). The state as well as the market can potentially turn individual processes of contestation and debate into pseudo-negotiations as organising principles for systemic imperatives. The follow-on question to address here is whether the current emphasis on marketisation can provide a shortcut to social integration, or whether it simply sidesteps and distorts the 'detour through norms'.

As the discussion has demonstrated, the legitimation of the normative infrastructure and the political order can only lie with civil society and not with the state or the economy. If the latter become, so to say, quasi-legitimating forces, we can speak of instrumentalisation. This obviously involves questions of power. Currently, marketisation is regarded as the panacea for the coordination of any aspect of society, while the politicisation of the normative infrastructure and the legitimation of the political order tend to be shrunk to a democratically elected state-apparatus. Thus, rather than searching for forms of legitimation and subsequent social integration that take the various aspects of individualisation equally into account, I hold that we are currently side-stepping legitimation favouring marketisation, thus increasing the risk of individualisation being instrumentalised by systemic imperatives. If the state and the market become hegemonic as systemically integrating forces, this becomes yet another breeding ground for 'organised individualisation'. That this might be the case becomes clear from a brief overview of the debate between the representatives of the various approaches to the coordination of the economy and society. The discussion usually focuses on either varying degrees of state-intervention/regulation or self-regulating markets. Looking at those debates will advance my argument by showing not only what marketisation means, but also how it affects the institutional interplay between civil society, the state and the market, thus providing the conditions for 'organised individualisation' by making the maintenance of systemic continuity an individual responsibility.

We can start our theoretical investigation with a look at Winkler's discussion of corporatism (1976). The concept does not automatically privilege a particular sphere of power and control. As a matter of fact, various forms of corporatism represent different spheres of power. Thus, corporatism neither dismisses the role of the state, nor that of the economy or civil society as power brokers. While the former two are clearly addressed, the latter appears rather implicitly in earlier discussions around corporatism. It seems, however, to gain relevance in more recent debates (see e.g. Molina and Rhodes 2002), including the debate on specifically work-related issues (see e.g. Dettling 2000: 207). What is of particular interest here is that the concept revolves around questions of ownership and control (Winkler 1976: 114), which become even more interesting in reference to networks and the emergence a so-called access economy (Chapter 4).

Although various economists suggest otherwise by referring to concepts like 'laissez-faire' and the 'invisible hand', the modern market cannot do without the state. The state always performs some economic functions. The question is to what degree, with what kind of goal-orientation and on the basis of what kind of legitimation and toward what kind of integration? Winkler differentiates between three roles the state can play (1976: 104). Firstly, a facilitative role is envisaged in classical economics where the state provides the platform for economic activity. Secondly, a supportive state offers protection, incentives and subsidies to encourage economic activity. It also provides welfare services for those who suffer under the inequalities generated by a competitive market system. The economic initiative lies with private business. Thirdly, the state takes on a directive role and tells private businesses what they must and must not do. The economic initiative here lies with the state.

Yet Winkler fails to explicitly point out the role of civil society in authorising and legitimating the state to play any role. In societies based on democratic principles, all three approaches of the state to the economy have to be grounded in the normative infrastructure emerging from politicisation. Once legitimated the state not only ensures a prosperous economy, but also facilitates and supports a thriving civil society. If it does not do so, not only civil society, but also normative individualisation are at risk of being instrumentalised by either the state or the market to ensure their systemic, that is, self-referential and autopoietic continuation in Luhmann's terms.

Historically and theoretically, the state's role has developed in various ways and directions. While the common denominator of the various approaches seems to be economic prosperity as the 'engine room' of a well-integrated society, they differ drastically in how they deal with questions of social integration.

Economic liberalism, Keynesianism, neo-liberalism, basic income models and ordo-liberalism wrongly equate economic prosperity, work and employment as systemically coordinating forces with social integration, while they largely sideline politicisation and legitimation, thus providing the institutional basis for individualisation as a systemic organising principle potentially resulting in deficits of social integration.

Karl Polanyi describes economic liberalism[2] as 'the organising principle of society engaged in creating a market system. Born as a mere penchant for non-bureaucratic methods, it evolved into a veritable faith in man's secular salvation through a self-regulating market' (2001[1944]: 141). Classical economics looks upon the market as 'perfect-in-principle', that is, as creating an equilibrium of supply and demand, prices and full employment. The central steering mechanism for self-regulating markets is the price mechanism.

> Market economy implies a self-regulating system of markets; in slightly more technical terms, it is an economy directed by market prices and nothing but market prices. Such a system capable of organising the whole economic life without outside help or interference would certainly deserve to be called self-regulating. (2001[1944]: 45)

On the basis of the price mechanism, the market and money become decentralised means of systemic coordination of instrumental action and as such they can potentially not just replace, but instrumentalise communicative coordination. As prices coordinate exchange and consequently also organise succeeding or proceeding production and consumption processes, it all appears as if the market arranged the division of labour according to a plan. Seemingly chaotic and independent actions of competing participants operate in the market as if they were guided by an 'invisible hand'. The important point is that the 'detour through norms' is replaced by a shortcut through markets. At this point market fundamentalists ask: why sustain a centralised intervening state apparatus if the decentralised market is more efficient in coordinating complex modern societies? Problems are then attributed to the 'detour through norms' or the state's intervention hampering the unfolding of market forces (Polanyi 2001[1944]: 150). Furthermore, if the market mechanism is considered to be flawless, the responsibility for unemployment or economic crises can easily be attributed to the

---

2   The leading ideas of *economic liberalism* came among others from Adam Smith's *The Wealth of the Nations* (1974 [1776]), David Ricardo's *On the Principles of Political Economy and Taxation* (1821) and John Stuart Mill's *Principles of Political Economy* (1970 [1817]). Fundamentally, they saw the striving for self-interest as the driving force for a progressive society that equally generates public welfare due to the so called *invisible hand* and *laissez-faire*.

state or individuals. The individual becomes not only the soft spot in a 'perfect-in-principle' market mechanism, but also in work-organisational contexts. The responsibility for systemic integration is passed on to individuals. This leads to integration without politicisation and thus a problem in legitimation, as we will see below. With self-regulating markets, systemic coordination takes priority over social integration, and so civil society, politicisation or normative individualisation are regarded as hampering the development of a prosperous society.

The world economic crisis in 1929 meant the downfall of classical economic theory, and Keynesianism became the prevailing economic policy after the Second World War. John Maynard Keynes realised that the economic liberal approaches of 'laissez-faire' and 'invisible hand' were of no use to end the depression and mass unemployment (Willke 2002: 18). His suggestions seemed simple and plausible: if the invisible hand is not sufficient to solve problems, a more visible hand is needed, namely state intervention. If the state was able to keep demand on a high level through public spending, this would result in higher employment. Hence, in times of depression and mass unemployment, the state is neither supposed to act according to laissez-faire, that is, let the market solve the problem itself, nor to worsen things by cutting back public spending. Instead, the state is supposed to support the economy with additional spending, even if that means running up debts (deficit spending). The obvious risk of inflation was secondary. Instead of focusing only on the market, Keynes envisaged a mixed economy where the state played an active role. As Offe writes: 'The argument in favour of the state regulation of economic activity arises out of the theory of market failure' (Offe 1985a: 73; Offe 1996: 73). Too much state intervention and regulation, however, is the main point of criticism put forward by neo-liberals. Subsequently, Keynesianism has become the epitome of regulation as a consequence of market deficiencies. It is the state's administrative power that is made responsible for hampering the unfolding of market forces. I will address the neo-liberal response in more detail later in this section. Most importantly for my debate at this point, however, is the fact that politicisation, the 'detour through norms', is replaced once again by another shortcut. In the final equation, the Keynesian welfare-state not only aimed to facilitate economic activity, but it also cushioned the harsh social inequalities resulting from market failures. This, however, only shifts the emphasis from systemic coordination through the market to systemic coordination through the state, while an active involvement of the citizenry other than economic activity is left out of the equation. Although Keynesianism addresses the issue of social inequality by taking care of market deficiencies, it does not draw on civil society. Thus, the deficiencies in social integration persist.

The belief in the market as a problem-solving order re-emerged with the rise of monetarism which was theoretically most prominently advanced by Friedrich August von Hayek and Milton Friedman. They can be regarded as the theoretical founding fathers of the neo-liberal doctrine, although they never called themselves neo-liberals. Both established a liberal reform project which in principle opposes state intervention and favours competition and free market forces. We do not need to go into the economic details of either Hayek's or Friedman's theory here. What is important, however, is that they both portray the market as a natural order.

One of Friedman's basic assumptions is that economic freedom foregoes political freedom. His argument is based on the understanding that markets create a voluntary and productive cooperation between its participants (Vanberg 2001b: 27). Both sides participate voluntarily as they both hope to gain something. The market is considered to be a natural order from which the normative coordination of society would automatically follow. Similarly, Hayek is convinced that a 'good society' cannot and must not be constructed or planned from above through state intervention. Consequently, he was opposed to any kind of social constructivism that assumed that the formation of 'better' human beings would automatically result in a better society. State interventionism and constructivism are in Hayek's words *The road to serfdom* (1946). Instead, he regards the economy and society as a spontaneous order that emerges from the interplay of complex and incalculable forces, the core of which is the market (Sally 2001: 7). If market forces are restricted and the task of running the economy is left to the state, the freedom of individuals would be severely restricted. Modern societies were far too complex to be systematically or even centrally organised. The market, however, would be able to organise society more efficiently.

There is a fundamental flaw in this argument. While I would not challenge the fundamental premise that neither a 'good society' nor 'better' individuals can be organised or arranged from above, or that the market and society emerge from the interplay of complex and incalculable forces, these forces are to be found in individuals' creative actions, their spontaneity and their very humanness. Even though Friedman and Hayek speak about connection between political and economic freedom, that is where their approach becomes problematic: it ignores that this interplay and its complexities are based on social interaction and concrete social relationships between individuals. They are the incalculable and spontaneous components of any social order, including the market. The fundamental flaw in Hayek's, but also Friedman's premise, therefore, is that they construct and prioritise the market as a natural order, while ignoring social interaction as its essential underpinning. This, however, is yet another road to serfdom, as it does not leave any room for the processuality of individuals' spontaneous debates and contestations from which a social order could emerge without being systemically imposed from above. Both approaches sideline individualisation, politicisation and thus social integration, while wrongly equating systemic coordination with social integration and marketisation with politicisation, which cannot but lead to deficits in legitimation and a systemic distortion of the negotiation process between systems and lifeworlds.

Notwithstanding the obvious social dysfunctions (Stiglitz 2002: 26) that seem to come with self-regulating markets, neo-liberal reform currently still rank high on political agendas to ensure economic prosperity, not only as an integrating force, but also to sustain the contemporary welfare state (Habermas 1989: 64). For the last three decades, marketisation has been presented as a panacea for all the problems related to work societies (see e.g. Ulrich 2002). Some exuberantly claimed that it was the beginning of a new era. The new economic structures were expected to create a golden age of economic prosperity characterised by permanent economic growth, a relentless increase in productivity, lasting low unemployment and immunity to the ups and downs of macroeconomic cycles. Just as the liberal movement of the 18th century strived for freedom, neo-liberalism claims to reduce extreme government regulations that are said to paralyse economic and consequently individual freedom. Hence, individual freedom of action has to be re-established through economic reforms and the market has to be freed from bureaucratic obstacles. The 'neo-liberal project' aims to shape economy and society in such a way that individuals can pursue their interests with a minimum of state intervention and regulation, but with a maximum of self-determination. However, self-determination in this context refers mainly to free economic choice rather than normative debates or discourses in the public sphere. Now, the responsibility to get the 'perfect in principle' market to work lies mainly with individuals (Bourdieu 1998: 98). From that point of view, market failure becomes individual failure. While this portrays individualisation as 'making oneself fit into the market', true self-organisation in terms of politicisation and not purely as the freedom of economic choice, is distorted and marginalised.

The realisation of a neo-liberal agenda finds expression mainly in the concepts of deregulation, privatisation and flexibilisation. Deregulation does not aim to abolish the state, but to reduce state regulation and bureaucracy to a minimum.

> In the name of increased economic efficiency, and in the interests of an expanded freedom of economic action, the political-theoretical demand for, and practice of, deregulation is directed at an alleged excess of state norms, rules, and prescriptions. Deregulation seeks its political justification in an argument which attempts to discredit postwar state regulation by showing it to be ineffective, mistaken, and unsustainable in the light of experience. (Offe 1985b: 72)

The major goal of deregulation is to reduce state control in order to increase the economic freedom of action equally for corporations and individuals. This goes specifically for those areas of society that used to be under some sort of government control like telecommunication, traffic, energy and water supply, provision of medical care, money markets, labour markets, superannuation, education and many more. These areas are taken over by privately-run corporations, hence the term privatisation (see e.g. Stiglitz 2002: 17). As private businesses, they are no longer run with the main goal of ensuring a certain quality of life for all members of society regardless of status or class, but largely with the aim of efficiency and profit-maximisation. While the market might be more cost efficient, it comes at the cost of equal treatment and access to health, education or even communication. In the context of individualisation, the neo-liberal agenda sidesteps politicisation through marketisation. In the final equation this means that deregulation and privatisation shift the priority from a cushioning state intervention to a more direct marketisation of social relations. The fatal assumption is that social integration is considered to follow from systemic integration. The process of legitimation and politicisation is turned upside down; normative individualisation is turned into individual responsibility for systemic integration.

Deregulation manifests itself through what is commonly referred to as flexibilisation resulting in more shift work, work on weekends and public holidays, overtime and other forms of strategically rationalising time, space and tasks (Geissler 2002: 58). While individuals can partly benefit from those changes, it is equally clear that it they who have to be flexible and not the markets or organisations. While Marx claimed that individuals become the appendage of the machine, flexibilisation turns the individual into an appendage of the organisation. The term flexibility seems to be omnipresent and has become established as a way of referring to a set of heterogenous practices framing any form of organisation. Hence, what is specifically characteristic about flexibility is the absence of a common denominator between the various practices, apart from moving away from the typical models of employment and work traditionally associated with them (Vielle and Walthery 2003: 6). Life-long employment, for example, is a thing of the past (e.g. Kocka and Offe 2000: 11).

Deregulation, privatisation and flexibilisation can create enormous uncertainties and time pressures for individuals (Bagnall 1999: 15). Individuals themselves become ultimately subject to market forces and are made individually responsible for their success or failure in the market-place (Stiglitz 2002: 22). Being unemployed gives many people the feeling of being a failure, inflexible, worthless or unqualified (Uske 2000: 169). Instead of the market being embedded in a normative infrastructure, individuals become entrenched in market forces. Habermas summarises the shift from a more socially oriented capitalism to intensified self-regulation along the lines of market-mechanisms:

> The new social policy … is not intended to protect people from the typical risks of working life, but, first and foremost, to supply them with the entrepreneurial skills of 'achievers', capable of looking after themselves. The well-known adage about 'helping people to help themselves' is thus given an economistic slant: it now conjures up a kind of fitness training that should enable everyone to assume personal responsibility and take initiative which will allow her to hold her own in the marketplace – not to end up as the kind of 'failure' who has to turn to the state for help. (1999: 53)

Yet, when it comes to coordinating the economy, the market is currently without alternative (Habermas 1999: 46). That does not mean it is an alternative for politicisation, legitimation and social integration. It also does not mean that neo-liberalism is without alternatives.

Some of Hayek's and Friedman's successors are aware of the fact that self-regulating markets are not the panacea for the ills of late modern societies. This goes in particular for the so called *Freiburg School* that formulates the market – in reference to Hayek – as a game (Vanberg 2001b: 19) that needs rules of 'economic constitution'. Founded in the 1930s at the University of Freiburg in Germany by economist Walter Eucken and jurist Franz Böhm, it adopted the Latin word *ordo* as a description of its approach, meaning an order that is desirable for human beings (Vanberg 2001a: 40). The ordo-liberals differ from economic liberalism and neo-liberalism mainly by emphasising the need for a political constitution in which the market is embedded. Similarly to Polanyi (2001[1944]: 142–45), they doubt that self-regulating markets, laissez-faire and the invisible hand are manifestations of a natural order. They see a need to attach the invisible hand of the market to the normative body of society that has to agree upon the rules of the game (economic constitution) in order to avoid the irrationalities of an all too rational self-regulating market, a view the Freiburg School actually shares with the Frankfurt School (see Lemke 2001: 192). A normative infrastructure does not evolve out of a self-regulating market as a natural or spontaneous order. 'For ordo-liberals there is no capitalism because there is no logic to capital. What is called capitalism is not the product of pure economic process and historical capitalism cannot be derived from a "logic of capital"' (Lemke 2001: 194). Consequently, ordo-liberals demand not only an economic constitution, but 'constitutional choices' (Vanberg 2001b) in the shape of a political. According to Lemke, 'the Ordo-liberals try to show that there is not just one capitalism with its logic, its dead-ends, and its contradictions, but an economic-institutional entity which is historically open and can be changed politically' (2001: 195).

The pivotal point is that the quest for both an economic and a political constitution demonstrates that social integration does not automatically follow from systemic coordination, but that it works the other way around: it comes about through individuals' everyday negotiations. The market thus becomes a means to a normatively established end, or put differently, marketisation follows a detour through norms rather than avoiding politicisation. Although not directly addressing opportunities for public debates drawing on individualisation, civil society is a serious player in the triangle of civil society, the state and the market.

A more practical alternative to self-regulating market models are basic income models where a universal minimum income is provided by the state to all citizens regardless of employment status (Offe 1995: 79). Yet, the basic income model also relies on a functioning market economy, including a labour market, as it is financed by taxes that have to be levied on some kind of income, production or consumption (Offe et al. 1996: 211). The fundamental difference between the self-regulating market and the basic income model is the stance they take towards employment. Whereas neo-liberals believe that full employment can be achieved by individuals competing for employment opportunities in an unhampered market, advocates of the basic income model assume an 'end of work' (Offe 1995: 77; Rifkin 1995) and subsequently see a return to full-employment policies as unrealistic (Offe et al. 1996: 210). Neo-liberalism tries to tie employment closely to market mechanisms, while basic income models try to uncouple income from employment. It aims to ease the pressure to compete in the labour market where less and less employment opportunities appear to be available.

Alongside Robert Theobald, Claus Offe, André Gorz, John Keane, Jürgen Habermas, Stanley Aronowitz, Ulrich Beck, Jeremy Rifkin is the most prominent advocates of a basic income model. In his book *The End of Work* he argues:

> Since the advances in technology are going to mean fewer and fewer jobs in the market economy, the only effective way to ensure those permanently displaced by machinery the benefits of increased productivity is to provide some kind of government-guaranteed income. Tying the income to service in the community would aid the growth and development of the social economy and facilitate the long-term transition to a community-centered, service-oriented culture. (1995: 267)

Rifkin hints at what most of the advocates of a basic income model put forward, namely at a redefinition of work society in general which can only come about through public discourse on the normative understanding of work. This would consequently shift and broaden the definition of work as mediated solely by the labour market. A basic income model, as suggested, has to be flanked by at least two other measures: the establishment of what Beck calls 'civil labour', or what Offe and others describe as 'informal sector' (what Rifkin circumscribes as 'social economy') in addition or in contrast to a pure market economy. The argument in favour of a basic income model is summed up by Offe when he writes:

> A traditional strategy for full employment, be it through 'more growth through more market' or 'growth through state intervention', appear illusory. A return to the apparently 'normal' model of a society of work and wage labor insulated by a welfare state is a) economically undesirable, b) ecologically indefensible, and c) socially unacceptable. (1996: 208–9)

A basic income model seems bureaucratically less complex than current welfare regimes, but it addresses similar issues. It attempts to tackle the problem of deregulation, envisages to balance out income inequalities that are based on gender, age, health, single-parenting and other factors. Above all, it challenges the 'work-centeredness' of late modern societies (Wilson 2004: 107).

The fundamental problem of this approach is its heavy reliance on exactly that of which it assumes the end, namely work. The tax income by which the basic income has to be financed depends on an economy that is able to produce, which in turn assumes consumption that again requires income. Even if a social economy was established, its infrastructure has to be financed. Equally, the reduction of working hours does not dispel the doubts that a basic income model could enable a smooth working of the economic cycle. The crux of the matter, however, is more complex. Instead of allowing a public discourse about the normative understanding of work, proponents of the basic income models, similarly to Keynesianism, shift systemic problems from the market, as the mechanism for income distribution, to the state. Once again, the 'detour through norms' takes a shortcut through the state apparatus blurring the market's dependency on the economy and the state. Thus, the result is again systemic coordination rather than social integration, while the integrating effect of work is shifted on to the state. The crucial question that remains unaddressed by basic income models is that social integration here too is fundamentally dependent on systemic processes. The dysfunctions of the market are once more systemically cushioned, while the deficits of social integration remain intact.

In the final equation, any model of the interplay between the economy and society that gives priority to either the state or the market as a coordinating mechanism puts systemic coordination above social integration. No matter which way we look at the various approaches discussed, they provide the fundamental institutional framework for the development of 'organised individualisation'. They all have a tendency to turn individualisation into an organising principle for systemic coordination rather than sparking a pluralistic process of politicisation resulting in legitimation and social integration.

3. Integration through Work: Detour through Norms or Shortcut through Markets?

While the distinctions between the various spheres of society appear to be rather clear-cut, we can gain more insights into the individualised conflict between systemic and communicative ambiguities by looking in more detail at the issue of work and the differentiation between instrumental and communicative action. The three interdependent spheres of society (the market, the state and civil society) are affected by work. This at times complex and contradictory interdependence lies at the heart of what we call 'work society'. In work societies, work is the 'glue' holding together the social fabric. From a Habermasian perspective, questions arise: can work become subject to communicative action? If work is to be understood as an integrating force, does it automatically generate systemic integration only? That would have to be the consequence of a narrow definition of work solely as instrumental action. What matters in relation to our discussion of individualisation is that in late modern work societies individuals become the focal point for an individualised negotiation between instrumental and communicative action specifically. Work, specifically, can be a socially integrating force if the normative understanding and definitions around work are subject to politicisation. Yet, work facilitates the development of 'organised individualisation' if its instrumental aspects take priority over the negotiation of its normative understandings.

The changing nature of work and its social consequences, its shaping of both society and individuals, has always held a key position in sociology. For Marx, Weber and Durkheim 'share the view that labour is the fundamental social fact. They construe modern society and its central dynamics as a "work society"'

(Offe 1985a: 129). These thinkers not only saw work as the determining factor of modern society, but they simultaneously sought the emancipation from its potentially instrumentalising consequences. Marx, for example, suggests to either humanise the sphere of work or to accept its de-humanising character by reducing it technologically to a minimum. Marcuse argues along similar lines when he writes: 'total automation would be the optimum' (1955: 156), while Durkheim considers work a twofold force of systemic and moral integration that needs to be developed equally.

Work societies can be characterised by the prominent position work holds for the material and social reproduction of individuals' lives as well as society at large. They are, however, more than that. We do not only work to 'earn a living', but work has become a 'way of living'; it provides structure, rhythm and meaning to individuals' lives. Work connects us in various ways and on several levels to society. It is part of our daily interactions, albeit an increasingly complex one. Ulrich Beck highlights the centrality of work when he writes: 'Just name any value of modernity, and I will show that it assumes the very thing about which it is silent: participation in paid work' (2000: 63). Work integrates individuals systemically on the basis of contributions to the material reproduction of society; it equally integrates individuals socially by defining their status and membership on the basis of a normative understanding of work and employment:

> At the level of social integration, work can be normatively sanctioned as a duty or, … at the level of system integration, it can be installed as a necessity. In the first case, work is the pivotal point of a correct and morally good life; in the second case, it is the mere condition of physical survival. (Offe 1985c: 141)

Yet, in his article, *Work: The key sociological category,* Offe questions the 'comprehensive determining power of the social fact of (wage) labour and its contradictions' (1985c: 132). He asks: 'Is [contemporary] society objectively less shaped by the fact of work' (1985c: 134)? He claims that work has become 'less significant and [is] no longer a point of departure for cultural, organisational and political associations and collective identities' (1985c: 136). Offe makes a strong claim by arguing that the concept of work has not only lost its centrality in overall society, but equally in individuals' lives as it has been marginalised as just one part of their lives, as

> experiences, orientations and needs other than those based on work are becoming more prominent … the attempt to interpret the life context as a whole in terms of the centrality of the sphere of work is also increasingly implausible because of the time structure of work and its location within the biography of persons. (Offe 1985a: 142)

In principle this line of argument follows Habermas's theoretical shift of the paradigm of social theory from work to communication. Consequently, communicative action and the rationalisation of the lifeworld, instead of instrumental action, become the focal point of possible emancipatory energies in the social as well as material production and reproduction of society. Hence, at least theoretically, the emancipatory potential of modern societies no longer lies exclusively in the sphere of work, but, as I would argue, in the politicisation of work. And that presupposes that late modern societies are still work.

The endless discussions about employment figures, industrial relations legislation and many more work-related issues clearly indicate the relevance of work for overall society. It is precisely the implicit normative definition of the good life as a working life and the systemically imposed necessity to work in order to be socially recognised, that define contemporary society as a work society. In fact, normative and systemic issues around work intensify as they become part of an individualised negotiation between instrumental and communicative processes. While work might have been an unambiguous key category for the classical theorists, I contend that in late modern societies work is still very relevant, but has become itself an ambiguous category. The ambiguity of work lies fundamentally in its systemic and normative features. Work has not been replaced by communication as an integrating force, but potentially could be made subject to politicisation. Here again, we can see an increase in the tensions between systems and lifeworlds. It is up to individuals to deal with the ambiguities; this is what defines the relationship between individualisation and work in late modernity.

The ambiguities of contemporary work society become even clearer when we investigate the paradox between a systemic 'end of work' and an intensifying normative 'universalised work ethic'. Both create subtle instrumentalising pressures for individuals who might say to themselves, 'I should work, in fact I want to work, yet I cannot find work/I cannot agree to working conditions. Is this my individual fault? What have I done wrong?' This ambiguity characterises the individual conflict between instrumental and communicative action.

Contemporary 'work society' fears the worst: the end of work. And undoubtedly, a work society without work is a society in crisis: it has lost its centre, its anchorage and reference point (Beck 2000: 16). Yet, a 'universalised work ethic' seems to indicate that perhaps our lives are more than ever organised, defined and structured around a normative understanding of work that goes far beyond the actual workplace. Reflecting on the contemporary meaning and relevance of work we cannot but get caught in a paradox (Liessmann 2000: 85) between an 'end of work' and a 'universalised work ethic' that gives rise to the question whether we can live in a work society without work.

The apparent 'end of work' arises mainly from systemic, that is, technological and organisational advances. The core of this argument points to the fact that 'from the very beginning of the Industrial Revolution, machines and inanimate forms of energy have been used to boost production and reduce the amount of labour required to make a product' (Rifkin 1995: 128). It is capitalism's inbuilt dynamic to reduce costs with the help of technology that automatically reduces the need for people to do the job. Thus, 'as machines increasingly replace workers in the coming decades, the labour of millions will be freed from the economic process and the pull of the marketplace' (Rifkin 1995: 291). Currently, these changes are triggered by another phase of industrialisation originating in digitalisation and globalisation. These processes open up new avenues in the capitalist pursuit of maximum productivity. This leads Rifkin to predict that

> the cheapest workers in the world likely will be not as cheap as the technology coming online to replace them ... Perhaps as little as 5 percent of the adult population will be needed to manage and operate the traditional industrial sphere by the year 2050. (1995: 9)

This facilitates a hyper-differentiation, not only of the global or national economy, but also within corporations in terms of work-organisation. As a consequence, 'new forms of working and employment, referred to as 'flexible', have gradually emerged over the past twenty years' (Vielle and Walthery 2003: 5). Despite widespread attempts to institutionally cope with or avoid a possible 'end of work' through various forms of either state-regulation or marketisation, be it basic income models, work on call, self-employment, part-time or tele-work, various technological, organisational or managerial advances, these measures do not seem to increase employment opportunities overall, but to distribute work and income differently (Offe 1995: 79). Above all, these measures do not necessarily indicate a shift from work to communication as an integrating force. The final equation is rather simple: more and more goods and services can be produced technologically, while the need for human labour appears to be in constant decline, generating deficiencies in social integration through work. It is then individuals' responsibility to deal with the systemically imposed consequences.

As a first point of critique, we have to acknowledge that the 'end of work' argument concentrates one-sidedly on work as a cost factor. Work is seen merely as one of the means of production, a commodity (Stiglitz 2002: 10). This ignores the normative relevance of work as a socially integrating force that, despite its apparent end, seems to be without alternatives irrespective of theoretical claims of a shift from work to communication. Work is still seen as an important integrating force which manifests itself, for example, in the fact that there is less work available, while individuals show an increasingly unconditional willingness to obtain work (see e.g. Wagner 2000: 216).

It is equally important to take notice of work as a crucial, normatively defined activity. Work is not norm-free. Not only the term work, but a general 'work culture' or 'work ethic' have become universalised to include a new kind of achievement principle. The normative meaning of both 'work culture' and 'work ethic' now stretches beyond the actual sphere of work. To start with the obvious, hardly anyone would doubt that someone who gets paid for a certain activity works (Offe 1985c: 129). But there is also unpaid work and it is in particular the latter that is responsible for a general spread of work as a late modern modus vivendi. We seem to increasingly work, either to be more able to work and to prepare ourselves to find work or to keep qualifying for the work we are already doing. In both cases, a lot of what might be called 'emotional work' is equally required, namely to either cope with unemployment or to come to terms with the various kinds of burdens to stay in or qualify for employment. These differentiations already allude to the fact that the concept of work encompasses more than an individual systemic function in the material reproduction of society that earns us a living. It also demonstrates that the classical definition of the work society might be too narrow to define late modern work societies. This, however, does not mean they are no longer work societies.

Speaking of a 'universalised work ethic', Weber's *The Protestant Ethic and the Spirit of Capitalism* (Weber 1974[1930]) comes to mind. While Weber referred more or less to the actual sphere of work, it actually goes beyond it: we work on relationships; we are supposed to work on ourselves; after work there is still housework waiting for us, while leisure time too is filled with work on various projects.

Work is omnipresent; its expanding meaning introduces a new achievement principle to all activities in life (Meier 2000: 75) that is not only concerned with the efficiency of a particular function in terms of costs, time and tasks, but puts the onus to achieve completely on the individual. Put differently, the achievement of both systemic and normative integration has become an individual task. On this basis, almost any kind of activity becomes comparable, quantifiable, competitive and thus subject to an economic logic that drives imperatives for a particular individual conduct of life (Liessmann 2000: 88).

Only on the basis of those assumptions does it actually make sense to work on and 'invest in' oneself, relationships, children or the structuring of one's time and tasks. Work becomes an equivalent for meaningful activity. Activities are broken down into units that can be measured, optimised, prioritised, controlled and calculated. Consequently, whatever we do can be considered worthwhile or too costly not only in terms of money but also in terms of emotional work. The maxim for any kind of activity seems to be what Max Frisch put into a simple equation: 'Whatever is profitable is reasonable' (1990: 465, translation NE). One can easily see how the gates open for a commercialisation and commodification of various areas of everyday life.

Testimony to its normative force, this universalisation appears as 'natural'. We have either grown up with it, have grown accustomed to it and that is simply how life is. The universalised work ethic has become a 'normal' way of living. The issue is, of course, not instrumentality, that is, the use of particular means to achieve an end; it is that the 'universalised work ethic' establishes usefulness and utility as the ultimate standards for what it means to be a fully recognised individual. At the same time, the opportunities to work and define work's normative meanings seem to vanish. Yet, the threatening 'end of work' and a 'universalised work ethic' are not the only dilemma. What is of equal importance is that, on the one hand, the pseudo-negotiation of systemic and normative imperatives of work are presented as individual freedom, while on the other hand, the freedom and opportunities to negotiate the normative meaning of work are scarce. In both cases, however, the responsibility to negotiate both lies with the individual.

Work cannot be perceived as either systemic or normative. The ambiguous and contradictory qualities of both interact and intensify with increasing individualisation. Work is both systemically and normatively relevant:

> A critical concept of work must grasp categorically the difference between an instrumental act in which the working subject structures and regulates his own activity on his own initiative, according to his own knowledge, in a self-contained process, and an instrumental act in which neither the accompanying controls nor the object-related structuring of the activity is left to the initiative of the working subject. (Honneth 1995b: 46)

What Honneth implies here is that Habermas's definition of work as instrumental action only is too narrow (1995a: xviii; 1995b:46). It is worthwhile to note that instrumental action also follows norms. The question remains, however, what kind of norms there are and how they are legitimated, which will not only take the discussion back to the question of politicisation, but will demonstrate the instability of the boundaries between systems and lifeworlds as the gap between them closes and the frictions grow.

For Honneth, work is part of the struggle for recognition in the sense that social recognition is granted on the basis of a normative understanding of work. As outlined in Chapter 2, social recognition is granted for the making of unique and useful contributions to society. What exactly is useful or not is decided on the basis of a society's normative infrastructure. Hence, for Honneth, work is subject to communicative processes through evaluations by at least a small group of members of society who approve or disapprove of individual activities. Thus, even if work is an instrumental act, it always carries normative connotations and, however fragmented and pluralised, refers, for example, to status or class. Consequently, from Honneth's point of view, the sphere of work has emancipatory potential in the sense that individuals claim social recognition for their contributions, if not from the whole society or class, then at least from a particular group. Thereby, they potentially challenge and possibly change the existing normative definition of work as to what is a useful contribution to society. Through the struggle for recognition, work becomes part of an individualised negotiation and contestation of systemic and normative processes of society.

The important point is this: to what degree work can be a source of systemic or social integration depends largely upon the legitimating power and control over a society's normative infrastructure, in short, on opportunities for a politicisation of work and work-related issues in civil society. It is the potential politicisation of work that defines the character of work as an integrating force in contemporary society. Work could be a normatively integrating force, if the norms and values defining work emerge from public debates and contestations. This means the individual struggle between systemic and normative aspects of work might flow into public discourses about work. On this basis, work could indirectly become the source of social integration. This does not contradict the Habermasian view that work itself as an emancipatory source is exhausted (Habermas 1989: 52). But the theoretical shift of the emancipatory potential from work to communication has to be accompanied on a more empirical level by a politicisation of the economy and work, for example, by providing individuals with the opportunity to negotiate the normative underpinnings of work. Above all, it potentially unlocks emancipatory potentials that lie in the abilities and capacities of individuals to have normative debates in civil society, rather than turning individualisation into a self-referential systemic organising principle sustaining the state and the market without nurturing civil society as the source of legitimation.

The aim of the discussion of politicisation, marketisation and integration through work is to point out the various aspects of the ambiguity between normative individualisation as a legitimating and thus socially integrating force on the one hand, and the risk of individualisation becoming an organising principle to sustain self-referential systems of the state and the market on the other hand. Most importantly, however, I wanted to demonstrate that an individualised negotiation of the intersection between systems and lifeworlds carries both emancipatory potential and instrumentalising risks. Although it seems contradictory, both aspects are crucial for the reproduction of complex societies. For that, however, the shift from work to communication has to take a detour through norms. The state and the market can become socially integrating forces only if they are subject to politicisation, thus giving social integration priority over systemic integration and avoiding legitimation problems in late modern societies. Individualisation then is neither just structurally enabled nor merely systemically compelled, but defined by its very own open-ended communicative processuality from which new structures might emerge. With the various ambiguities around politicisation, marketisation and work society in mind, the question that now remains is how contemporary capitalism contributes to the development of 'organised individualisation'.

Chapter 4
The Individualisation of Organisations

The tensions between politicisation and marketisation have consequences for social interaction on institutional, organisational and individual levels. On all three levels individualisation can be described as 'organised', as social interaction becomes subject to systemic rationalisation. In addition, what characterises so-called network societies is the decentralised self-referential production, processing and distribution of knowledge on the basis of science and technology. Above all, the economic control of access to knowledge leads to the development of an access economy. This not only deepens the ambiguity between politicisation and marketisation, but establishes networks as an organising principle that shifts the responsibility for integration to individuals.

As a consequence of an intensifying marketisation, corporations become the primary form of organisations in contemporary society. It is at the intersection of individual and organisation where the individualisation within organisations becomes most obvious through a profit-driven organisation of social interaction.

Finally, I contend that the boundaries between individual and organisation are blurred by what I call 'integration management'. Systemic processes come under the guise of lifeworlds which on the one hand open up opportunities for a politicisation of some aspects of work, but on the other hand, install organisational imperatives for an individualised pseudo-negotiation of the intersection between systems and lifeworlds. This results in an individualisation of organisations, which in turn is a major cause of organised individualisation.

1. Networks: Coordinating Markets or Forums for Public Debates?

The looming 'legitimation deficiencies' discussed in Chapter 3 find a continuation in the increased relevance of science and technology in late modernity. Scientific and technological progress underpins to a large degree the development of network societies. New technologies become a dominating force of purposive-rational justification rather than a resource that informs public debates. What I want to emphasise with the following discussion is that the coupling of marketisation, science and technology not only leads to the rise of 'network societies', but creates subtle instrumentalising pressures for individuals to rationalise their own social interactions (networking). On the one hand, science and technology can inform and spark politicisation; on the other hand, networks are the decentralised organisational structures of late modern markets that potentially marginalise normative discussions.

What Weber describes as the clash of value spheres not only manifests itself as the differentiation of various logics of action, but more importantly as the possible domination and control of purposive-rational over communicative forms of legitimation and integration. In reference to Weber, Herbert Marcuse pointed out that the potential domination of purposive-rationality is strongly connected to the development of modern science and technology when he wrote:

> The reason envisaged by Weber thus is revealed as technical reason, as the production and transformation of material (things and men) through the methodical-scientific apparatus. This apparatus has been built with the aim of calculable efficiency; its rationality organises and controls things and men, factory and bureaucracy, work and leisure. (1968: 205)

Although Marcuse had quite a different concept of science in mind (see Habermas 1971: 87–8), his analysis of Weber can to a degree be regarded as a precursory description of what we today describe as either 'knowledge', 'information' or 'network' society. The purposive-rational logic not only of the economy, but also the state increasingly becomes the main source *not* of legitimation, but justification. 'Technological development thus follows a logic that corresponds to the structure of purposive-rational action regulated by its own results, which is in fact the structure of work' (Habermas 1971: 87).

Again, fundamental issues concerning legitimation in late modern capitalism emerge. State intervention and regulation no longer merely aim to cushion the social dysfunctions and harshness of the market, as is partly the case with Keynesianism, ordo-liberalism or basic income models. Instead, as the discussion on marketisation in Chapter 3 has made clear, the state is increasingly concerned with sustaining the systemic continuity of a flourishing economy as the basis of a well-functioning society. The overall goal is what is usually referred to as 'trickle down economics' where a strong economy is assumed to generate not only a smoothly running economic cycle, but is also supposed to engender social integration.[1] The crucial point is that in order to justify state-regulation or intervention, the state does not draw on norms and values emerging from politicisation. Instead, scientific evidence is increasingly used to validate technological and organisational advances. To be sure, scientifically backed state-intervention or marketisation cannot be equated with politicisation as a form of negotiating and interpreting norms and values. A possible politicisation, drawing on the emancipatory potential of an individualised negotiation process is thus not only marginalised, but increasingly replaced by scientific and technological expertise that demands an individual response and in that sense is not liberating. The 'detour through norms' is sidestepped by scientific and technological justifications. These not only guide the state's and the economy's actions, but also work as strong expectations (systemic imperatives)

---

1   This is also the general assumption behind 'welfare to work' programs which means employment is considered the best means for social integration.

for individual behaviour. The use of science, thus, becomes hegemonic and ideological (Habermas 1971: 104).

Modern societies of course cannot do without science and technology. The question is whether we use technology and science to maximise economic productivity and to organise markets, or whether they are also put to use as a means to inform individuals and to support civil society as a forum for public debates. The tension between politicisation and technological progress becomes even clearer with the following statement by Habermas who critically refines Marcuse's argument and addresses technology's monopolising and instrumentalising tendencies.

> It is true that social interests still determine the direction, functions and pace of technical progress. But these interests define the social system so much as a whole that they coincide with the interest in maintaining the system. As such the private form of capital utilisation and a distribution mechanism for social rewards that guarantees the loyalty of the masses are removed from discussion. (1971: 105)

Trying to ensure economic prosperity with the aid of science and technology also impacts on the role of the economy itself which is no longer to simply ensure the material reproduction of society on the basis of a linguistically defined normative infrastructure. Material production *for sale* becomes the main focus (Polanyi 2001[1944]: 56). Or as Manuel Castells puts it: 'Industrialism is oriented toward economic growth, that is toward maximising output' (2000: 17). Two points follow from this:

1. Scientific knowledge translates into technological and organisational advances that help to reduce costs and boost productivity. One of the major consequences of this is the already discussed 'end of work' argument.
2. The production, processing and distribution of knowledge itself becomes a source of productivity (Habermas 1971: 100) that is not tied back to a public discourse about norms, but concentrates one-sidedly on systemic continuity.

The important characteristic of late modernity is that the source of productivity is no longer primarily to be found in material production and the sale of goods, but mainly in the instantaneous generation, provision, administration of and access to knowledge (Castells 2001: 52). Moreover, science produces knowledge, not as a source of understanding and informing public debates, but for profit. In doing so, individualisation nurturing politicisation is marginalised and as a consequence, systemic integration again seems to gain the upper hand over social integration. Above all, however, science and technical reason become an organised structure that no longer enables individualisation as a negotiation process, but turns it into an organising principle. The struggle between systemic and social integration becomes an individual struggle, while society overall appears to be steered by the invisible, systemic hand of network capitalism.

In more detail, the use of science and technology not only becomes hegemonic and ideological, but systemically self-referential. Referring back to Luhmann's systemic approach helps to sharpen at this point: various self-referential systems and sub-systems make their autopoietic selections, while the pivotal question of why these choices are made seems to dissolve into self-referential systemic selection processes for their own sake (quasi-legitimation). It is information technologies in particular that are not only the result of scientific development, but have themselves become indispensable for further scientific advances. Science itself has become dependent on the scientifically enabled reduction of complexities (Bell 1973: 30). In striving for and depending on economic prosperity, both the state and the economy tend to become self-referential systems facilitating a normative orientation that is not subject to politicisation, and in that sense might well create individual responsibilities in the form of systemic imperatives without communicative control and access over norms and values. This is the basis for individuals becoming active hubs for systemic coordination with individualisation as the organising principle; that is, individuals not only respond, but by responding actually reproduce and maintain systemic imperatives that are beyond their normative control.

To be sure, the production and communication of knowledge are essential components for any society to function. Yet, while it was the scientifically based development of production technologies that fundamentally characterised industrial society, in late modern societies it is the technologically enforced production of knowledge itself that starts to become dominating. Science in combination with technology has become an important source of orientation, not only for the function of the economy, but for all areas of life including governments. Science and technology potentially replace and marginalise individual contestation and questioning. The result is that social interactions in civil society, the state and the market are driven by a scientific 'expertism' rather than a democratic organisation of consent. Scientifically proven measures can hardly be denied their implementation and it is taken for granted that in modern economies technologies are subject to ongoing scientific development, constantly triggering rapid changes in the production process and work-organisation. Combining science and technology, organisations frame the handling of hyper-differentiated societies as networks which emerge as liquid structures of social relations organising not only the production, but also the accessibility of knowledge according to its purposive-rationality.

The material reproduction as the basis of life has of course not disappeared, but has drastically changed with the rise of service industries over the last 30 years. The production and processing of knowledge and related services have become one of the steadiest sources of productivity. In general, it is intellectual property that has become the source of profit-making, rather than material property (Rifkin 2000: 5). Castells describes the various consequences of this:

Capitalism itself has undergone a process of profound restructuring, characterised by greater flexibility in management; decentralisation and networking of firms both internally and in their relationships to other firms; considerable empowering of capital vis-à-vis labor, with the concomitant decline in influence of the labor movement; increasing individualisation and diversification of working relationships; massive incorporation of women into the paid labor force, usually under discriminatory conditions; intervention of the state to deregulate markets selectively, and to undo the welfare state, with different intensity and orientations depending upon the nature of political forces and institutions in each society; stepped-up global economic competition, in a context of increasing geographic and cultural differentiation of settings for capital accumulation and management. (2000: 1–2)

Economic processes in industrial economies were spatially and temporally dependent, if not limited. In network societies, the scientifically driven development of information technologies is central to contemporary global capitalism, shifting economic exchange processes from real space into the virtual space of fibreglass cables and satellite transmissions. It provides the technology for network-based forms of the organisation of markets as well as corporations. As a consequence, economies throughout the world have become globally interdependent, changing not only the economy, but also the relationship between the economy, state and civil society and thus social integration. 'Networks, rather than countries or economic areas, are the true architecture of the new global economy' (Castells 2001: 61). Individual action and its temporal-relational dimensions become subject to powerful processes of acceleration, commodification and compression that Barbara Adam describes as processes of 'temporalised reflexive modernisation' (2003). This deeply affects individuals as their everyday life gets caught up in networks that are both part of an access economy and a potential forum for public discourses that are, however, highly fragmented and pluralised.

The question of hyper-differentiation resurfaces here, although under the banner of an economically controlled access to knowledge. The outcome is a decentralised network architecture, described by Negri and Hardt as *Empire* (2000), that can hardly be controlled by states, nor can it simply be based on politicisation as it is highly fragmented, made up of thousands of autonomous computer networks generating an infinite number of possible connections (Castells 2000: 6). The internet is the most obvious example, as

it is creating a whole new generation of products and processes by shifting from Operating System technologies, centred around the PC, to information-sharing technologies, decentred around electronic networks powered by co-operative servers. (Castells 2001: 62)

The outcome is a global economy at the heart of which lie financial transactions 'from everywhere to everywhere, and from whatever to whenever' (Castells

2001: 54). Castells describes this as an 'Automaton' (2001: 57) that can hardly be controlled or directed, but which fundamentally conditions our lives. 'Organised individualisation' is a manifestation of the intersection and tensions between the 'automaton' and the individual.

Yet we should not forget that these technically mediated, economically driven and hyper-differentiated relationships are still concrete social relationships. There is no *deus ex machina*, but social dynamics between individuals who put technology to use. Technology may just as much empower as it is able to instrumentalise individuals and it is not always easy to see not so much the difference but the ambivalences, the contradictions and paradoxes that characterise individuals' attempts to negotiate the demarcations between systems and lifeworlds in late modern technologically and scientifically driven networks.

Moreover, to portray global financial trade and marketisation as the sole winners means to turn a blind eye on other aspects of this process. For example, new information technologies have enormously pluralised the range of participants not only in economic terms. Today, basically everyone with access to a computer can be a stockbroker from the comfort of her/his his living room. People can buy and sell shares, shift capital from one corner of the globe to another within seconds, which might not only cost someone else their job, but potentially their own, while it might at the same time increase their bank account balance. While there is undoubtedly a strengthening of market processes, a general pluralisation, fragmentation and thus hyper-differentiation not only of the economy, but of available information equally occurs. Castells describes what could be called the proliferation of ambiguities and the various factors that come into play in a knowledge economy where the market is certainly not the only fragmenting force.

> While capitalists, and capitalist managers, still exist, they are all determined by the Automaton. And this Automaton is not the market. It does not follow market rules – at least, not the kind of rules based on supply and demand which we learned from our economics primers. Movements in financial markets are induced by a mixture of market rules, business and political strategies, crowd psychology, rational expectations, irrational behaviour, speculative manoeuvres and information turbulences of all sorts. All these elements are recombined in increasingly unpredictable patterns … . (2001: 57)

While an informed civil society might benefit from new information technologies, it is still the commodification and control of access to the means of communication that increasingly determines participation in the negotiation processes in civil society. Once again, the struggle between systemic coordination and social integration comes to the fore.

In a technologically driven information, knowledge or network society, it is the charge of an admission, subscription or membership fee that controls access to services without which products are almost useless (Rifkin 2000: 5). As a consequence, economic success depends less on a one-time sale, but on the establishment of economically binding access relationships or memberships that make the individual a member of wider networks. Leasing, renting or subscriptions are economic memberships that are characterised not by short-term seller/buyer, but by long-term provider/user relationships that secure economic success through the commercial control of access to information, knowledge and networks. 'Successful businesses are built on trust between company and customer, employer and employee, and employees and their colleagues' (Kent and Anderson 2001). To be clear, the membership rules do not emerge from processes of politicisation, but are based on economically feasible exclusion or inclusion on the basis of gaining access to knowledge, information or purchasing power. Individualisation as a form of contesting and challenging norms and values is sidelined by non-negotiable membership rules. All three forms of integration discussed in Part I play a role here. Membership defined on the basis of access means organisational integration. It also means normative integration, although the norms are beyond public control; moreover, it means systemic integration as memberships are part of a wider systemic network.

Networks are essential characteristics of access economies. They are the organisational structures for gaining access to other players in the market. Networks emerge from bits and pieces of companies or government organisations, from individual skills and the ownership of specific technological devices. They are combined to exploit a market opportunity, to mutually benefit from organisational as well as technical know-how. Perhaps they stay together for a couple of years or just for one certain project, before they dissolve and never exist again in the same formation (Rifkin 2000: 28). Furthermore, the access economy translates into the work-organisational development of project management. Individuals are, so to say, the smallest unit, yet are a fundamental hub in the systemic coordination of a huge organisational web. The access economy refers to the mode of organising economic relationships regarding the coordination, cooperation and communication between various market participants, for example, producers, suppliers, consumers, employers, employees, unions, nation-states or trade organisations. The most important point here is that individual capacities play a central role in the coordination of the increasingly complex access and knowledge economy as means for systemic coordination and reproduction on an organisational level.

We have already discussed that one problem of this unpredictable pattern of network capitalism is the lack of opportunities for politicisation. In the introduction to *The Coming of Post-industrial Society*, Daniel Bell writes:

> Looking ahead to the next decades, one sees that the desire for greater participation in the decision-making of organisations that control individual lives (schools, hospitals, business firms) and the increasing technical requirements of knowledge (professionalisation, meritocracy) form the axes of social conflict in the future. (1973: 8)

This social conflict centres around the legitimation of and the access to the normative infrastructure of a global network society where individuals can, want and have to be more than active hubs for the coordination and reproduction of systemic imperatives at the hands of a rather anonymous and decentralised 'Automaton'. However, the rules and norms of that network are currently not subject to politicisation, but rather, with the aid of science and technology, are establishing a scientifically justified normative infrastructure in conjunction with marketisation and corporatisation. For instance, mobile phones enable everyone to be something like an 'embedded journalist', embedded in everyday life that can instantaneously be shared with the rest of the world. The decisive point is, however, that the means to do so are widely controlled by the economy and depend on whether one can economically afford access or not. While all of these are certainly huge gains in terms of an access to, but also the commercialisation of, information, normative control mechanisms are not impossible, but lacking. As Bell writes: 'Technology assessment is feasible. What it requires is a political mechanism that will allow such studies to be made and set up criteria for the regulation of new technologies' (1973: 27). Some thirty years of rapid technological development later, Castells further elaborates this argument:

> All in all, objections to capital controls derive from three main arguments. The first is a market fundamentalist argument about capital's fundamental right to unfettered freedom. This is losing ground in the face of widespread evidence about the damage caused by freewheeling capitalism, something that our forebears understood in the 1930s and 1940s. That damage is now amplified by network technologies and global contagion. The second argument refers to the need for a concerted international action ... to set up a new regulatory framework ... Third is the question of the technical feasibility of such controls in the age of electronic networks. My colleagues who are computer scientists voice the opinion that a global regulatory environment can be enforced technologically, precisely because of the extraordinary versatility and accuracy of new electronic technologies ... The Automaton could be dotted with electronic codes and instructions that would keep him (it's certainly not female) active but on a leash. (2001: 69)

What does all this means for individualisation? The bottom line seems to be the following: While networks constantly shape, dissolve and reshape, we are not taking a 'detour through norms', but are well and truly bypassing any process of politicisation on the digital highway of industrialisation at an unimaginable speed of scientifically driven technological innovation and change. Yet, the organisation of networks puts individual skills and abilities right at the centre of those networks in order to sustain and coordinate them which fundamentally characterises 'organised individualisation'.

What is specific about the individualisation of social organisation is the ambiguity of knowledge acting upon itself as the main source of productivity, but not as a source of informing possible public discourses. In principle, however, the networks serve as both a source of productivity and a space that not only informs, but provides a forum for public debate. However, as has been pointed out earlier, legitimation is sidelined by scientific justification and technological reason. While it might translate into economic progress and also informs individuals, the crucial argument here is that individual skills and abilities are organised and put to use through various layers of network organisation. This is what I describe as 'organised individualisation', where systemic coordination and active reproduction is wrongly portrayed as liberating and self-realising processes of negotiation.

In sum, access to the formation and legitimation of the normative infrastructure becomes a critical issue in post-industrial societies (Bell 1973: 13). Scientists, engineers or technocrats and the various players of civil society compete for opportunities to either legitimate or justify norms and values. While the former results in politicisation, the latter seems to establish the opposite, that is, quasi-legitimation and pseudo-negotiation of an already scientifically justified normative infrastructure. Thus, it is not so much 'technological determinism' but scientific justification and technological reason that leave us with an individualised systemic organisation of society. And so the lack of opportunities for politicisation and the dependence on technological quasi-legitimation is increasing the risk of organised individualisation being mistaken for normative individualisation, and further blurs the boundaries between systems and lifeworlds.

Habermas captures the nucleus of the proliferation of ambiguities for individuals when he writes that 'with the institutionalisation of scientific-technical progress, the potential of the productive forces has assumed a form owing to which men lose consciousness of the dualism of work and interaction' (1971: 105). More knowledge than ever potentially empowers individuals in finding some middle ground between systems and lifeworlds. And yet, individualisation is scientifically justified and organisationally arranged through networks. Thus, the dominance and dependence of late modern societies on science and technology fosters the potential development of social pathologies like organised individualisation where individuals are responsible for the realisation of norms and values without control over their definition or interpretation.

2. Corporatisation: Primary Form of Organisation or Negotiation?

While marketisation describes the growing importance of markets as the primary institution of our time, corporatisation refers to corporations becoming the primary form of organisation in contemporary society. Hence, the focal point of this section is certain aspects of corporations and how they become defining features of corporatisation.

In reference to Weber, most organisational theories regard organisations as goal-oriented and purposive-rational (see e.g. Adorno 1972: 441; Drucker 1995: 46–48). Building on Luhmann's differentiation between binary codes, programs and organisations as discussed in Chapter 1, Nassehi defines organisations as follows: '[O]rganisation systems continue themselves by connecting decision to decision. Therefore organisations can be designated as decision machines' (2005: 185). In a similar vein, Stewart Clegg states that 'organisation, just as any other locus for the accomplishment of agency, is better seen as a locus of decision and action' (1989: 197). Jocelyn Pixley similarly points out the relevance of decision making in particular for finance organisations and the uncertainties they have to face (2002: 200–201; see also Pixley 2004). Three basic insights can be gained from these brief statements. Firstly, modern corporations are economic organisations. Their overall purpose is to organise economic activity. Secondly, the achievement of purposive goals is based on decisions, not normative negotiation. Thirdly, action requires an actor. Hence, corporations are loci of organisational decision-making and actions that organise economic activity.

In a rather reductionist manner, corporations are often considered as pursuing one goal only, namely profit-maximisation. While this is a taken-for-granted statement, the question is: why are corporations the primary form of organisation in late modern societies? Do corporations exist because they are the most efficient means to organise economic activity? In the literature on corporations, economic activity is regularly referred to as transactions that occur on an institutional level (the market) as well as on an organisational level (the corporation, firm, business or company). There is, however, a pivotal difference that has to be taken into consideration, as Calhoun points out: 'Markets differ from corporations … in that they lack administration' (1992: 217). Clegg points out that '[f]rom the perspective of 'planning,' whether state or corporate, the notions of market and organisation seem antithetical to each other; opposed principles of management' (1996: 2). More precisely, within corporations, transactions are organised through management, whereas the market does not actively organise, but provides a space and rules to coordinate economic activity mainly through the price mechanism. The locus of action again is crucial, even if markets are described as self-regulating. Hence, when the economy is described as a coordinating mechanism, two fundamental means of coordination have to be differentiated: the market using the price mechanism as its organising principle, and corporations adhering to management in order to coordinate economic activity. Either way, coordinating or organising economic activity comes at transaction costs defined as costs of running the economic system (Coase 1967: 336). I am well aware that this approach is not new (see e.g. Commons 1951; Hayek 1945) and probably nowhere near an all-encompassing account of more detailed discussions. Nevertheless, it provides the theoretical means to deconstruct assumptions that widely underpin contemporary discussions of organisational change and economics, as both the market as well as organisations try to rationalise and thus organise social interactions in terms of transaction costs.

From that point of view, 'the main reason why it is profitable to establish a firm would seem to be that there is a cost of using the price mechanism' (Coase 1967: 336) and that transaction costs can be avoided or reduced by managerial work-organisation. Hence, 'by forming an organisation and allowing some authority (an 'entrepreneur') to direct the resources, certain market costs are saved' (Coase 1967: 338). Williamson thus states: 'I submit that the modern corporation is mainly to be understood as the product of a series of organisational innovations that have had the purpose and effect of economising on transaction costs' (1981: 1537). Economising transaction costs thus is a driving force behind work-organisational changes which in the final equation results in the economic, profit-driven organisation of social interaction within organisations in reference to the market.

We can look at corporations from the point of view of markets or we can look at markets from the viewpoint of the management in corporations. These two perspectives characterise at least two conceptual approaches to corporations. In the first case, neo-classical theories like Coase's (1967) treat corporations as mere 'production function' (Williamson 1981: 1539):

> Neoclassical theory's objective is to understand price-guided, not management-guided, resource allocation. The firm does not play a central role in the theory. It is that well known 'black-box' into which resources go and out of which goods come, with little attention paid to how this transformation is accomplished ... Management has no real influence ... Production takes place in firms. (Demsetz 1997: 426)

The assumption is that the corporation comes into existence only when the cost of managing production is less than the cost of using the price mechanism of the open market. Corporations are simply regarded as organisations that aim to minimise transaction costs for economic activity in a self-regulating market[2]. How corporations and in particular managers go about it seems to be neglected by Coasians. The biggest weakness of this approach, however, is that it cannot account for the emergence of markets. At the same time, it is able to provide an explanation for work-organisational changes. Work-organisational changes could be seen as the result of competition between the price mechanism and management aiming to reduce transaction costs. It seems as if 'organisational theorists ... have been preoccupied with hierarchy to the neglect of market modes of organisation and the healthy tension that exists between markets and hierarchies' (Williamson 1981: 1539). This tension is central to work-organisational changes.

Furthermore, there is more than a 'healthy tension' between markets and hierarchies. In a hyper-differentiated society, organised as networks at the heart of which lies a knowledge and access economy, both market dynamics and work-organisational changes condition each other. Moreover, as the market is not a human actor, but a mere institutional space providing exchange opportunities,

---

2   Economic theories at that time were mainly built on the theoretical assumption that markets are 'perfect-in principle'. It is a rather recent development that economic theories as well as business oriented research increasingly conceptualise markets as imperfect and make market failure part of economic theory (see e.g. Schauenberg 2004).

corporations and more specifically managers create the market, thus generating a field of economic activity. That being so means that the market is neither self-regulating, nor is the corporation a 'well-known' black-box. Instead, corporations have to be seen as systemically mediated social relationships, thus creating the market through social interactions with other participants in the market.

> They [corporations] complement each other rather than ... competing with each other. Firms, the sole producer of goods and services for sale to others, require conceptual 'places' (i.e., markets) in which entitlements to these goods and services are exchanged, but even the service of exchanging is produced by firms. Markets reveal exchange opportunities but do not produce goods or services; they cannot substitute for firms in this respect. (Demsetz 1997: 426)

Neither the neo-classical approach of self-regulating markets nor the organisational focus on hierarchy takes this interdependence into account. In network, access and knowledge economies, it is precisely managers' dealing with a possible lack and uncertainty of information, its asymmetrical distribution, that defines managerial action in respect to both the market as well as work-organisation.[3] Again, this approach is not new and has one of its foundations in Knight's theory of corporations (1964[1921]) which until today triggers fierce debates between the Coasian and the Knightian concept of 'the firm'. Following from that debate, corporations can be described as organisations that coordinate economic activity by making goal-oriented decisions on an ongoing basis in order to economise transaction costs through the market as well as within the corporation. By doing so, they not only create the market, but also encroach upon social interaction, in particular individualisation, as a target for profit-driven rationalisation. The 'healthy tension' between market and organisation is put on individuals and thus demands the negotiation of systemic and normative processes.

What enables corporations to do this is another taken-for-granted assumption for which Bowman coined the term 'corporate individualism' (1996: 49–51). Regarding corporations as individual personalities nullifies the distinction between individual and corporate organisation and equates to a large extent human and corporate individuality. The business enterprise, the firm, the corporation or company become entities with individual-like rights, although they have considerably more power than individuals in the negotiation or implementation of norms and values. Corporations are treated, talked about and regarded as if they were 'personalities', 'natural persons', 'autonomous actors', 'disembodied entities' to which individuality can be attributed. While they are also legally accountable, the degree of social responsibility seems to be a fundamental point of

---

3   It is in particular game theory and principal-agent models that deal with the issues of uncertain information, distribution of information as the basis for managerial decision making (see e.g. Schauenberg 2004).

difference to human individuals. They own property, litigate, make contracts and enter a variety of relationships with other corporate as well as natural individuals.

> This tendency reflects a culture that is at once pervasively individualistic – and thus underrecognises the social dimension in the creation of both markets and corporations – and at the same time support a maximally 'disembodied' ontology that allows people to accord some manner of unitary individual existence to bodiless social creatures. (Calhoun 1992: 217)

To be certain, corporations are able to concentrate and stabilise power relationships that are beyond public control and in comparison to which the individual seems powerless, unless attached to an organisational network of some sort (in the case of work, for example, unions). 'Corporate individualism' fundamentally shifts the balance of power between individual and organisation towards organisations, putting them into a position where they can organise individualisation. This deeply affects the roles of individuals as negotiators of a society's normative infrastructure. The negotiating process itself becomes dependent on organisations that operate according to norms and values that are beyond public control. Individualisation thus is no longer the organisation of consent between equals, but becomes 'organised individualisation' on the basis of pre-arranged, organisationally given norms and values. The decisive point is not the dependence of individualisation on a larger institutional landscape or general organisational structures, but its dependence on an organisational structure that is by default beyond the reach of public scrutiny. The individualised negotiation process thus carries a considerable imbalance of power to conciliate differing views.

The notion of 'corporate individualism' seems to gloss over the fact that corporations are social artefacts. Hence, rather than constructing and perceiving corporations as independent entities and actors, one should not lose sight of the admittedly ambivalent fact that systemic transactions are still social interactions. Once more, it is the fundamental differentiation between communicative and instrumental action that comes to the fore in various ways here. It is not one or the other, social or systemic, but social interaction can be systemically mediated and potentially instrumentalised. Hence, corporations must be understood as composed of concrete social relationships, that are, however, highly mediated or indirect (Calhoun 1992: 230). The argument put forward here fundamentally rests on the assumption that markets and corporations emerge from social interaction. Individualisation is here distorted, targeted, economised and rationalised as transaction costs which fundamentally enables a view of the individual as an 'entrepreneur of the self' (Gordon 1987: 300). Transaction costs, similar to work, make individualisation measurable, quantifiable and subject to rationalisation. Hence, corporations are not black-boxes, but very concrete spaces that rationalise social interaction.

If we regard corporations as manifestations of social interaction, however systemically mediated, so too are markets. The market as the primary institution of our time does not invent itself. As Clegg states: 'Rules can never provide for their own interpretation' (1989: 201). The question then is who interprets these rules? If concrete social relationships as the foundation of markets and corporations are to be taken seriously, it is insufficient to look at corporations as merely economic organisations without looking at the individuals that act in or upon them. Individuals not only act in and on behalf of organisations, but also control and determine to a large extent how concrete social relationships unfold in a corporate environment. More to the point, individual and organisation meet in the ambivalent role of the manager.

The debate about the exact role and function of a manager has many origins. Once again, I confine my argument to the Coasian and Knightian theories, while being well aware that there is an infinite amount of literature on managers and management that could also be taken into account. According to Coase, the manager 'has to carry out his function at less cost, taking into account the fact that he may get factors of production at a lower price than the market transactions which he supersedes' (1967: 338). The manager's task is limited to economising transaction costs by deciding whether it is economically more reasonable to use the open market or management to coordinate economic activity. This only works if information and knowledge are freely accessible, which in an access economy is not the case for everyone. In contrast, the Knightian approach suggests that 'because of uncertainty, good judgement is the best tool available for forging profitable production plans' (Boudreaux and Holcombe 1989: 151). While managers certainly aim to economise transaction costs, they surely do so under conditions of uncertainty and a constantly changing influx of information which plays an enormous role in gaining economic advantages in the market.

Since the beginning of industrialisation, there have been endless accounts of optimising management techniques. The history of management trends and organisational studies is almost endless and it is beyond the scale of this project to discuss them all (for a more in depth discussion see e.g. Clegg and Hardy 1996; Fletcher 1997). The most famous one is probably Taylor's 'scientific management' (1947), the crux of which is the belief that maximum efficiency is obtained by breaking down a task into its components and finding the best way of doing it. It is, however, the so called 'Human Relations' (HR) approach initiated by Elton Mayo during his famous Hawthorne studies in 1924 to 1932 (1949) that can be seen as the precursor of what the interviewees in Chapters 5 and 6 refer to as 'people management'. Mayo's findings show that productivity improves when employees and management discuss working conditions. Whether in fact working conditions improved was secondary. What made the difference was that employees would be given the feeling of being listened to, of being part of a team rather than perceiving themselves as cogs in a machine. Mayo's HR approach was followed by many other concepts that built on his findings. One of them was, for example, the so called 'management by objectives' introduced by the Boston Consulting Group as well as Peter Drucker (1955). The core of this approach is that the manager and the employee agree to what the employee will attempt to achieve within a certain timeframe, and that the employee accepts and believes in the objectives. Peters and Waterman's *In Search for Excellence* (1982) extended the approach, claiming that strong cultures and guiding values tell employees on all organisational levels what their tasks are. There are certainly many more approaches that could be mentioned here (for an overview, see Gantman 2005). But the crux of those approaches is that the rationalisation of social interaction (which is the essence of HR management) and in particular communication plays a crucial role in management. In particular, the organisational rationalisation of social interaction targets individualisation as individuals' abilities to negotiation the boundaries between systems and lifeworlds.

My interest here is not so much in management techniques itself, but in how they build heavily on individuals' qualities and capacities to negotiate and contest the intersection between systems and lifeworlds not only at the workplace but in contemporary market societies in general. Individualisation becomes the driving source for realising a neo-liberal agenda on an institutional level. On an organisational level, this refers to a corporate normative infrastructure, a particular work ethic that is expressed as corporate culture and demands a specific individual attitude. The systemic dependencies become concrete corporate and organisational imperatives for individuals. Managers not only require their employees to be more market oriented, proactive, empowered and entrepreneurial, but they themselves are under the same pressures. Individuals in organisations are required to exercise more discretion on the basis of a broader corporate culture, take initiative and take responsibility for the whole organisation: 'governing organisational life to ensure "excellence" necessitated the production of a certain type of person, namely "enterprising", autonomous, productive, self-regulating, responsible individuals' (du Gay et al. 1996: 266).

William H. Whyte, who had already analysed similar trends in the 1950s, called these individuals 'well-rounded men' for they adjust and accept any situation given by the organisation they work for (1957: 129). This situation is regarded as an increase in employees' autonomy, characterised by flexibility and creativity, when in fact it is just another veil disguising a power relationship. As Whyte reminds us:

> We are giving the individual a rationalisation for the unconscious urging to find
> an authority that would resolve the burdens of free choice. We are tempting him
> to reinterpret the group pressures as a release, authority as freedom. (1957: 65)

It seems to be up to the individual to make the most of this 'flexibility', 'autonomy' and 'creativity'. In fact, what is required is the submission and adjustment to the dominant corporate culture that leaves individuals with an ambiguity between individual autonomy and pseudo-autonomy.

This entrepreneurial attitude has become the essence of a 'hegemonic managerialism' fostering 'organised individualisation'. Being an entrepreneur no longer merely refers to the *modus operandi* of a business, but actually changes into a *modus vivendi* of individuals running their lives and society according to an organisational culture. This lies at the heart of the individualisation of organisations. The individual life becomes an enterprise and very literally has to be managed. Thus, 'organised individualisation' does not highlight individual autonomy in terms of politicisation, it indicates that individuals are 'free' to negotiate only organisationally given parameters. The responsibility for the realisation of business interests is shifted on to individuals without equally shifting the control over those norms and values.

At the same time, individuals are no longer passive cogs in a larger wheel; they are *active* hubs for the coordination and reproduction of systemic imperatives whose contents are beyond their control. Individualisation is not only dependent on organisations, it is organised individualisation as individuals actively pursue the realisation of corporate values as if they were their own. The boundary between individual and organisation becomes permeable and blurred. The manager as well as the employee are no longer bureaucratically detached, but personally involved. Accordingly, the task of hegemonic managerialism is to ensure 'that these novel work-based subjects emerge' (du Gay et al. 1996: 267). As the interview material in Chapters 5 and 6 will show, this is precisely what the term 'people management' refers to. Individuals' capacities are arranged and organised into handling systemic, that is, managerial tasks. Aspects of individualisation become managerial virtues. They are no longer individual capacities, but

> 'enterprising capacities' of individuals as subjects. In other words, individuals are to be brought to identify themselves with the goals and objectives of their employing organisation to the extent that they interpret them as both dependent upon and enhancing their own skills of self-development, self-direction and self-management. (du Gay et al. 1996: 271)

The manager turns into a 'charismatic facilitator', teaching others to learn how to take responsibility for themselves and fostering an 'entrepreneurial' sense of identification, commitment and involvement between employees and the organisation (du Gay et al. 1996: 267).

The supposed managerial benefits of 'organised individualisation' are described by Champy as follows:

> No more close supervision of workers, no more focus on data irrelevant to running the business, no more energy spent on defending turf. The role of managers becomes one of empowerment – providing workers with the information, training, authority and accountability to excel … As workers take on more management tasks, managers must take on more leadership tasks – holding a vision of the business, articulating it to workers and customers, and creating an environment that truly empowers workers. (1994: 17)

This sounds too much like slick managerial talk. What this statement omits or portrays as a win-win situation for managers and employees is based on subtle instrumentalising pressures of bureaucracy through effective 'people management'. Individuals identifying with an organisation also start to supervise themselves. How much more individualised can organisations get? Focussing only on the relevant could also mean that those forces that hamper exchange processes in the market are to be cut out. Empowerment as a management technique could also be interpreted as instrumentalisation of individual abilities for business purposes. The point is not to dismiss managerial techniques, but to highlight the ambiguity that is involved here. We can doubt that individuals are easily persuaded by these techniques, but it certainly creates ambiguities they personally have to deal with at the workplace: ambiguities which indicate the blurring of the boundaries between systems and lifeworlds on an organisational and individual level.

3. Integration Management: Systems under the Guise of Lifeworlds?

What exactly happens when the boundary between individual and organisation becomes permeable and blurred? As with communicative and instrumental action, structurally enabled or compelled individualisation, hyper-differentiated systems and hypertrophied lifeworlds, the answer to this question cannot be clear-cut. Rather, it highlights the ambiguities and ambivalences of the situation. Possible negotiation involves questions of power, individual responsibility and various forms of integration.

First of all, corporations are a field of direct power, and the power lies mainly with the manager as opposed to markets where the power of managers is rather indirect. Power is fundamentally relational (Simon 1985: 27). One person alone cannot decide to hold power. Being relational, power is also fleeting. It has to be organised and sustained on an ongoing basis. Following Gramsci's notion of hegemony (see e.g. 1971: 57), this can be seen as the organisation of consent. Ideally, this could be done democratically, which is, however not the case in corporations, unless they are subject to a process of politicisation. In work organisations, the reproduction of power occurs through 'standardised reporting, co-ordinating or control mechanisms ... [that] tend to reproduce existing configurations of power within a given organisational field' (Clegg 1989: 227). In particular, in goal-oriented organisations like corporations, power is a means for the controlled realisation of goals 'through individuals', as one of the interviewees will describe it. Power, thus, constitutes instrumental action.

> Surveillance, whether personal, technical, bureaucratic or legal, is the central issue. Its types may range through forms of, for instance, supervision, routinisation, formalisation, mechanisation and legislation, which seek to effect increasing control of employees' behaviour, dispositions and embodiment, precisely because they are organisation members. (Clegg 1989: 191)

Being a member of an organisation seems almost to negate a specific use of various aspects of individualisation and thus is an important feature of 'organised individualisation'. In this sense, the demonstration of power has a clear function:

> It is to resist the evident fact that the member of an organisation is simultaneously and ineradicably a speaking subject, a labouring subject, and an embodied subject. Both meaning and body, fused in the person, are capacities for resisting the encroachment of organisation control on individuals' discursive and bodily capacities, which require some disciplining if any control is to be achieved. (Clegg 1989: 194)

It is this organisational disciplining that not only mediates or constrains individualisation, but makes use of it. Hence, although power is relational, it configures, rationalises and standardises individualisation towards the achievement of organisationally defined goals. The employment relationship thus is a relationship of economic domination and subordination and as such it constitutes an organisational cornerstone. Standardisation through corporate culture in particular has become a crucial concept, not only in terms of mass production, but also in regard to power and control over individuals at the workplace. It can be understood as a process of rationalisation, as it facilitates calculability, measurement, predictability and control. In the sphere of large-scale production, standardisation has become a major principle for cost reduction and flexibility. But the same principle of standardisation as applied to processes of production has been extended into administrative and organisational spheres. Individuals are no longer mere appendices to machines. Their individuality and way of living is required to become an appendix not necessarily to one particular organisation, but a certain organisational culture. I capture this trend with the term 'corporatisation': the control of individuals' inner processes through the already discussed 'universalised work ethic' on a general level and through a particular culture at a specific workplace. Standardisation enables managers to gain control over organisational activities as standardised activities become predictable and measurable. But it does not stop there. While procedures can be standardised, measured and quantified, the challenge seems to be to achieve the same for individual behaviour, which at times can be spontaneous and unpredictable. The claim is that 'standardisation reduces the need for managers and extra levels in the hierarchy because rules and standard operating procedures substitute for direct supervision – that is, rules replace face-to face contact' (Jones 2001: 74). This can certainly be regarded an example for a profit-driven control of social interaction in the sense of economising transaction costs.

The term 'culture industries' as introduced by Horkheimer and Adorno (1991: 98) describes the extension of the principles of mass production, that is, standardisation, into the sphere of art and culture as consumer goods. Corporate culture refers to the set of norms, values and rules within an organisation.

> Values are the bedrock of any corporate culture. As the essence of a company's philosophy for achieving success, values provide a sense of common direction for all employees and guidelines for their day-to-day behaviour. (Deal and Kennedy 1982: 21)

Those values, norms and rules aim at the employees' commitment, loyalty and attitude towards work. Corporate culture is not only the standardisation of manufacturing or administrative processes, but the attempted standardisation of attitudes, social behaviours and thinking and feeling. Management techniques that take the whole personality into account dissolve the boundary between individual and organisation and shift the task to distinguish between systemic activities and normative negotiations on to individuals. In business terms, this is expressed as follows:

> The guiding aim and abiding concern of Corporate Culture ... is to win the 'hearts and minds' of employees: to define their purposes by managing what they think and feel ... The strengthening of Corporate Cultures, it is claimed, provides the key to securing 'unusual effort on the part of apparently ordinary employees'. (Peters and Waterman 1982: xvii)

If one looks at culture in general as a 'way of life', it becomes immediately clear that corporate culture is a very abridged understanding of culture which Lasky, for example, describes as one of the aspects of *The Banalisation of the Concept of Culture* (2002). The culture of a society might be everything we as members acquire through processes of socialisation and what becomes a taken for-granted world. Corporate culture turns culture into a management tool using specific corporate jargon, rituals and symbols. More specifically, what I aim to demonstrate with my argument about 'organised individualisation' is that corporate culture converts culture and individualisation from a *modus vivendi* into a *modus operandi* within and dependent on an organisation in order to standardise, homogenise and regulate individuals at the workplace and indirectly the work they do. Culture becomes a means for rationalising social interaction. It is cost effective as it reduces the amount of time and resources that have to be put into face-to-face control; and it saves time, as employees behave and think automatically in a desired way.

With the concept of culture returns the question of social integration and membership. We are born into a culture and therefore gain membership by birth in, for example, a family, a society, a nation or a religion. In traditional societies, this coincides with a workplace. In contrast to the affiliation of an individual to a particular family or to a nation state, membership in an organisation is no longer a 'natural fact', but depends on the organisation itself and the definition of the membership role (Deutschmann 1987: 42). Whereas usual processes of socialisation are based on communicative action, that is, learning by negotiating and re-negotiating culture, 'organisational socialisation' (Fogarty and Dirsmith

2001) is characterised by learning a pre-given and, for most people, non-negotiable corporate culture. In other words, employees must identify with an organisation's values and norms that are designed to produce standardised responses to a variety of unforeseeable situations. Again, the individualised ambiguities of a shifting boundary become clear, as it is up to individuals to respond, while the response itself is already defined organisationally.

The increasing emphasis on culture within organisations indicates that, besides the actual processes of production and administration, human beings are increasingly looked upon as a resource. This finds expression in terms like 'behavioural accounting' more commonly called 'human capital'. What these terms refer to is

> accounting for people as an organisational resource. It involves measuring the costs incurred by business firms and other organisations to recruit, select, hire, train, and develop human assets. It involves measuring what it would cost to replace an organisation's human resources. It also involves measuring the economic value of people to organisations. Thus, human resource accounting means measuring the investment made by organisations in people, the cost of replacing those people, and the value of people to the enterprise. (Flamholtz 1989: 470)

Employees, that is, individuals, are treated as a resource for profit making and it is in this context that individuality at the workplace is subject to power, control and standardisation as a major part of the instrumentalisation of aspects of individualisation. 'Organised individualisation' is very much about the organisational control of individuals' capacities and qualities. However, following Arendt's belief in plurality based on the unpredictable human capacity to act spontaneously, this control can never be total.

Alongside corporate culture as a means of rationalising individual behaviour, power manifests in contractual relationships that also define corporations. Corporations are a concentration of contractually coordinated social relationships. What is characteristic about contemporary power relations in corporations, and what turns individuals into active hubs for systemic coordination, are what du Gay and others describe as processes of 'contractualisation' and 'responsibilisation' that in particular find its expression in project management:

> '[C]ontractualisation' typically consists of assigning the performance of a function or an activity to a distinct unit of management – individual or collective – which is regarded as being accountable for the efficient performance of that function or conduct of that activity ... these units of management are in effect affirming a certain kind of identity or personality. This is essentially entrepreneurial in character. (du Gay 1996: 155–56)

And he continues:

> In keeping with the constitutive principles of enterprise as a rationality of government performance, management and related techniques function as forms of 'responsibilisation' which are held to be both economically desirable and personally 'empowering'. (du Gay 1996: 157)

The notion of 'empowerment' is particularly interesting, as it reveals the paradox of power at the contemporary workplace. On the one hand, 'contractualisation' and 'responsibilisation' delegate the authority to act to the individual; on the other hand, it is precisely the delegation of authority that enhances the power of the organisation (Clegg 1989: 201). Here the individual is no longer a competent, self-determined actor, but becomes truly an agent through the assignment of agency through the subtle inculcation of a corporate culture that is an unarticulated part and parcel of work contracts. What is tagged 'empowerment' cannot obscure a factual disempowerment. Contractualisation and responsibilisation both diminish the opportunities for politicisation where individuals could collectively negotiate their working conditions or shape industrial relations legislation. While the bargaining power on the individuals' side is individualised, atomised and thus considerably weakened, corporations as collective organisations gain bargaining power. This shifts the balance of power considerably not only at the workplace, but for the whole of work-society and the forms of integration it can develop. In particular, it affects the role of unions and the labour movement in general (see e.g. Wilson 2004). Most importantly, it means that the collective forms of negotiation are turned into an individualised negotiation of the boundaries between systems and lifeworlds that allows considerably more power to organisations as 'corporate individuals'. The Habermasian tug-of-war between lifeworld and system in that sense is dealt a blow in favour of systemic forces: individuals are supposed to be better off fighting for themselves and then get the short end of the stick. To be sure, what this means is that the relationship between individual and society based on communicative action and various aspects of individualisation works only if the collective and relational organisation of power is part of the equation.

The individual life has to be run like an entrepreneurial project (Gordon 1987: 300). 'Organised individualisation' thus means that aspects of individualisation are used to organise economic activity, while at the same time they are portrayed in the vein of individualisation as a process of liberation. Being absorbed in a seemingly all-encompassing project of self-entrepreneurship once again brings up the question of social integration. Individual integration into contemporary society depends to a large degree on corporations and their management, which seems to encompass most dimensions of an individual's life. Managers are aware of this: 'not only has today's management … to care about the money. It has also to generate some sort of meaning' (cf. Brooks 2000: 151). A few characteristics of the link between corporations, management and social integration can be pointed out that are closely related to what I have already introduced as 'people management'. Symbolic management refers to everything from the installation of equipment (Hewlett&Packard 2002: 10) to Christmas celebrations and architecture. It aims at the construction of a 'pseudo-lifeworld' specific to the corporation, that is, a set of norms and values the corporation claims to stand for in order to reach certain clients as well as employees. It thereby attempts to combine the otherwise, at least theoretically, separated areas of work and lifeworld. The uncoupling of system and lifeworld seems to turn into a coupling of systems and lifeworlds. The blurring of boundaries between systems and lifeworlds thus is a process of de-differentiation along the logic of economic action. The world of work is infiltrated with typical elements and symbols of the lifeworld, such as billiard tables, pinball machines, fireplaces or libraries. Thus, symbolic management aims at generating a lifeworld specific to the corporation (Ebert 2001: 89–90).

In the same vein, the contractually established relationship between manager and employee comes across as a 'friendship-like' relationship of trust and responsibility. It refers to managerial endeavours to implement methods aimed at creating feelings of belonging and individual recognition. New methods of organising the corporation's workflow, like project management or the emphasis on a reputedly flattened hierarchy, are increasingly common. The core of the matter is 'managing' individuals and their social interactions.

These developments change the role of the manager considerably. The manager is no longer a pure rationalising agent, but a lifeworld-manager, a people manager creating forms of normative commitment within the corporation. A business-like attitude is demanded for the handling of emotional and social concerns. These forms of integration and commitment control both manager and employee. Whyte gives a fitting description of what people management means: 'Business is people, and when you help people to rise to their fullest you make them fulfil themselves, you create more and better goods for more people, you make happiness' (1957: 76). The ambivalence of this statement lies in the fact that this is true, while it equally expresses an increased instrumentalisation of relationships.

There can be no doubt that corporations and managers influence social relationships and shape social interaction. Thus, they must be considered to have some impact on social integration up to the point of a colonisation of the lifeworld (Chapter 2) where individualisation is no longer the foundation of system formation, but turns into an organising principle with individuals as active hubs for systemic coordination. However, social integration in the context of corporations and various management techniques is 'based on relationships over which participants have little control, of which they may not even be aware' (Calhoun 1992: 232).

While Part I of this study was mainly concerned with the proliferation of ambiguities characterising individualisation as a negotiation process of an increasingly blurred boundary between systems and lifeworld, I have explored in Part II the potential of an individualised negotiation process under contemporary conditions of network capitalism. We have seen that individualisation can spark and flow into public debates and discourses about norms and values resulting in normative guidelines for the state as well as the economy. How and whether this process of politicisation evolves and might be institutionalised is a matter of politicisation itself, as legitimation and social integration cannot be organisationally arranged or prescribed. The various constellations of civil society, the state and the market do not do justice to an individualised negotiation process. Instead, tensions emerge between politicisation and marketisation on an institutional level. In particular a self-referential organisation of the state and markets cannot replace politicisation as a source of social integration.

The various models of political economy regard work and employment as crucial components for social integration. However, they aim to achieve it not through public discourses of work and employment, but through marketisation at the institutional level followed by corporatisation on the organisational level. Together, they constitute the conditions for 'organised individualisation'.

Corporatisation triggers a shift in the balance of power mainly on the basis of 'corporate individualism'. As corporations are non-democratic organisations, the power over the definition of norms and values between individual and organisation eludes public control. Furthermore, standardisation, responsibilisation and contractualisation can be singled out as manifestations of a contemporary managerialism that defines 'organised individualisation'. The individual becomes an 'entrepreneur of the self' depending on organisational directives and imperatives. Individuals seem to be subject to economic rationalisation as they start to rationalise themselves.

We have now arrived at the individual level at the workplace, more precisely at the observable role of the manager. The following chapters will show that the theory of 'organised individualisation' is well illustrated and supported by empirical material.

Chapter 5
Managing Individualisation at Work

Throughout the theoretical discussion contemporary individualisation has been described as the individualised negotiation of the divide between hyper-differentiated systems and hypertrophied lifeworlds. The negotiation process is not only shifted on to individuals, but also leaves it up to them to deal with a fundamental ambiguity between an individual gain of autonomy and an increased risk of instrumentalisation. On an institutional and organisational level, marketisation and corporatisation in particular seem to turn the negotiating capacities into an organising principle for systemic coordination. The individual at the workplace seems to be at the centre of a tug-of-war between systemic and normative processes, between systemic coordination and normative negotiation. This struggle within the individual fundamentally defines the ambiguities that the concept of 'organised individualisation' captures. Managers foster and facilitate individualisation at work by creating the subtle expectation of individual responsibility for the organisation without control over its normative underpinnings. And that is where 'individualisation' is at work.

The theoretical argument presented leads to central questions: Do managers really see the individual as a work-organisational resource and do they try to make individualisation an organising principle at work? How relevant is the individual at the contemporary workplace? The following statements firmly establish the relevance of individuals for corporate success. Herman, a very successful 38-year-old CEO, got right to the bottom of it when he said: 'In order to be successful today, you need to be able to work through individuals'. This attitude is the succinct nucleus for the establishment of individualisation as an organising principle. Likewise, Rory, who heads quite a young and trendy internet business, assigned a central position to individuals when he stated in managerial fashion that it is 'the collective nature of individual success that adds up to the success of the business'. And again Herman joined in along the same lines:

> In order to realise a productive organisation, you have to breed individuals that work on their own … they have to know their 'solar system', [they need] orientation … and they have to know their role and function within it and their instructions.

These statements certainly support the proposition that the individual *is* at the centre of managers' attention as a work-organisational resource. Yet, more questions arise: How does one work through individuals? How can one get individuals to equate individual- with business-success? What underpins the need for businesses to 'breed' individuals? What is a 'solar system' at the workplace and what is its purpose? It is along those intertwined questions that we will investigate the ambiguities of 'organised individualisation', not theoretically but empirically.

Needless to say, the following material cannot be considered to be 'representative' in a statistical sense. Instead, it is concerned with currently emerging trends and experiences. The material in this and the following chapter issues from 20 in-depth interviews with managers from internationally operating corporations. Fourteen out the 20 are CEOs or hold a top management position (for example, head of regional management Asia-Pacific), while six hold positions in middle management. Four of the interviewees are female and this obviously does not allow any comparison between male and female managerial styles. The industries covered are manufacturing, consulting, pharmaceutical, IT, travel, banking, insurance, car industry and retail.

1. Autonomy: 'as if they worked independently'

To a great extent, the interviews deal with the relationship between the individual and the organisation. Autonomy plays a crucial role here in various ways. On a theoretical level we have seen that it is a fundamentally relational and permeable space for negotiation in which individuals use their abilities and the social opportunity to express needs, desires and wishes. The crucial question is whether an existing field of power allows individuals to transcend that very structure that has been acquired through socialisation by relying on reflexivity, competent action and interaction. It is individual autonomy that allows individuals to contest, question and negotiate existing routines. Precisely by feeding the results of those contestations, thoughts, actions and interactions into a process of politicisation, individuals rise to their full capacities as human beings. They thus contribute to the formation of norms and values on the basis of which social recognition is granted. The question that needs to be addressed is: how autonomous are individuals at the workplace to change or go beyond a given structure along the lines of which the wider contemporary work society operates?

The following statements by Ted and Herman, two of the interviewed managers, depict a fundamental ambiguity referring to autonomy at the workplace:

> They [employees] like to feel as if they worked independently. Even though they like to be part of teams, they really want to be feeling as if, even if they are not, they want to be feeling that they are making their own decisions. Very important to them. (Ted)

The pseudo-character of individual autonomy here is glaring. While individuals might feel responsible, they might not be in control over what they are responsible for. But this statement also demonstrates the shift of the struggle over individualisation to the individual. While individuals want to act voluntarily and do the right thing, they also have to do what the corporation wants them to do. Hence, the instrumentalisation of individual autonomy can, on the one hand, result in organisationally dependent pseudo-autonomy as a part of 'organised individualisation', while on the other hand, it gives individuals at least within a particular framework the choice to do things their own way.

How permeable the boundaries between the individual and the organisation are becomes clear from the following statement by Herman, who himself comes across as a very responsible person. As long as employees use their autonomy for business purposes, 'I keep telling my people that they've got autonomy up to the point of killing themselves. They've got to decide that for themselves'. This certainly represents an extreme understanding of individual autonomy and it is rather questionable whether it can be called autonomy at all. What these statements really mean is this: Feel free to do the utmost for the corporation, but if you do, be aware of the fact that it is your 'free' decision that you do so, and that the responsibility for any consequences is yours. Individualisation at work is thus a struggle within the individual that is subjected to various pressures that might result from prioritising conflicting spheres of action, like for example, family values versus business interests or quality time with the partner or children versus twenty-four hour availability for the good of the business.

Edwin, who is 55 years old and has 36 years of managerial experience in the travel industry, articulated the impression of some sense of autonomy when he stated that thirty years ago 'decisions were being pushed upon the workers rather than being made at a lower level', while today 'decision-making is really left at the lowest supervision level'. This pushing of decisions from high levels of hierarchy to lower levels seems to parallel the shift of the boundaries between systems and lifeworlds on to individuals. The intention behind this development might well be to give individuals more autonomy. This, of course, is a Janus-faced arrangement. The advantage of granting more autonomy from a manager's perspective is that 'people take responsibility for themselves' (Herman). And it is exactly that type of individual autonomy that managers try to 'breed' (Herman) when they say: 'I trust and empower people' (Paula). And yet, while it gives individuals certain freedoms from rigidly prescribed rules, they come under pressure to take responsibility and make decisions along normative lines over which they have no control whatsoever.

This paradox of power at the workplace becomes an obvious platform for individuals' struggle between individual autonomy and organisational dependence, the pseudo-negotiation of the non-negotiable. Autonomy emerges as an ambiguity, a double-edged sword. On the one hand, handing down responsibility and allowing individuals to make their own decisions can certainly be interpreted as an increase in individual autonomy. On the other hand, however, as Edwin noted:

> Nowadays, there is much greater pressure put on the employee to perform than 20 years ago, 15 years ago, even as little as 8 years ago. Everything is really results-oriented.

These pressures lie at the heart of the struggle over individualisation at work, where individuals constantly have to decide: how much do I want to, and do I really have to immerse myself into the work processes? The answer to that question is certainly influenced by various pressures. One of the more immediate pressures is that the increase in individual autonomy is not only restricted but linked to an emphasis on result orientation and has nothing to do with the definition of goals. Ted, a 38-year-old specialist in human resource management, gave an example of the importance of goal-oriented outcomes:

> I think what's happening more and more and more is that we are now identifying that it's outcomes that should be the focus, not inputs. Someone wants to come in midday and finish at ten at night because it really suits their lifestyle, it really fits in with their creativity … If it can be done and if that person generates outcome over and above what you expect from them, let them do it, let them do it.

Clearly, the corporate strategy here is to give as much individual autonomy as possible within the parameters of predetermined goals. More precisely, while the setting of goals might be slightly 'democratised', achievements and performances are certainly not negotiable. For the individual, an unarticulated expectation might be generated to put business interests first, while on the surface there seems to be an interest in making the individual feel comfortable. Over the last decades, input, that is, training, inductions or any kind of further education has become a cost factor and is thus automatically subject to possible cost cutting. What counts is performance and outcomes. Thus, individual 'autonomy' is granted above all to enable employees to achieve results over and above expectations and to save on training and supervision, while the imperative to comply to rigid organisational dependencies is not softened, but made perhaps more subtle. It is in precisely that sense that individual autonomy runs the risk of being instrumentalised by enabling 'individual entrepreneurship' or 'individual agency' within the corporate framework where individualisation becomes the underlying organising principle. And yet, as the discussion of other aspects of individualisation will show, it works both ways. Both sides can, to a degree, benefit from this development. While certain opportunities for normative negotiations seem to open up, expectations and individual responsibility without normative control on the basis of pseudo-autonomy equally increase.

The fact that managers actually make a connection between reflexivity and autonomy becomes clear from Martin, a 34-year-old ambitious young financial controller in the manufacturing industry, who stated: 'I've got to have someone who thinks for themselves. I call it an autonomous type of worker'. This refers, however, not to the individuals' ability to process information, to monitor and examine their own behaviour and to go beyond a taken-for-granted way of thinking. What it refers to here is rather the expectation that individuals use their capacities to streamline business operations.

When asked, basically all of the interviewees articulated the view that good employees are ones that 'think for themselves' or are 'self-directed' as opposed to 'micromanaged'. Freddy, a 34-year-old, rather introverted, research and development manager with an engineering background explained for example:

> I like people who are fairly self-directed. So I like to be out there saying: 'This is the broad goal, this is what I want you to try and do', and then I like the individual to be able to determine what they need to do themselves ... But you get other team members who don't like that. They like to be micromanaged, they like to be told: 'This is what I'd like you to do today' and I find that more difficult and they find me less satisfying as a manager.

Without using the term reflexivity explicitly, Freddy gave a more detailed account of how he wishes his employees to use their ability to think independently and autonomously.

> I like to say to somebody ... this is the problem I've got. This is where I want you to get. And this is how I think you can solve that problem. I really hate it when people take my solution for three months and then come back and tell me that it doesn't work and that all they've done is continuously work the way I've told them to do it. I really like to say: 'This is how you should solve it.' I like them to go away and think about what I said as a starting point and then come back to me and tell me that I don't know what I am talking about, that's not going to work, this is the way it should be done. I want them to think about the solution. I don't want to be taken too literally. Normally when I suggest a solution, it's really just a way of getting them to think about a problem, to kick it off. So I like people to be fairly *self-directed* and we maintain regular contact but not every hour every day ... on a weekly basis I'd like to get an update and see how things are going.

Thinking independently and being self-directed, sounds very much like an 'autonomous type of worker' and also seems to define a whole new sense of achievement for individuals. And yet, one can also ask: where does the broader direction for being 'self-directed' come from? Is the individual at the contemporary workplace really engaged in developing or negotiating a direction? Freddy's statement tells us something else. Thinking independently, as described by him, means thinking independently within a given set of rules and with a clearly formulated and defined goal. To a degree and taking into account the very character of the workplace, it can hardly be any other way. Yet, in a corporate context, thinking independently is desired in regard to the way of getting there, not in terms of what ought to be achieved. Martin, the controller, spelt out what thinking independently as a work-organisational principle means and why it can be satisfying from a managerial point of view:

> You know, it's assumed that you [employees] know how to add up, it's assumed
> that you know how to work your way around a balance sheet and a cash flow,
> it's assumed that you understand basic statutory reporting, you know, those are
> all givens. Anyone can do that with enough experience and the right education.
> What you're [the manager] employed to do is, firstly, to ensure that … things
> happen, secondly, that your staff do what they're asked to do without being
> asked.

And he continued:

> I mean to me that's probably the biggest success of a manager ensuring
> everything is done without actually ever having to ask if it's done. 'Cause you
> know that you've got it so smooth that people just do their job … And I'm not
> being egotistical. I'm actually quite proud of the fact that I can make an office
> run without actually having to say anything.

This is a clear account of 'organised individualisation'. Martin, as the manager,
aims to organise things in such a way that individuals themselves coordinate and
reproduce the system. Although he talks as a manager, surely the same must
be the case for managers themselves, which highlights the characteristics of
individualisation at work even more. However, from a strictly managerial point
of view, to be an autonomous, independently thinking worker means this: Do not
use highly paid managers as a resource to tell you what you have to do; take the
responsibility and work it out by yourself. That saves time and money and frees up
resources, including time for more important things, and this might even reduce
the number of managers needed. There is a strong sense of instrumentalisation, of
economising social interaction. Being able to solve a problem independently from
rigid directives is important for individuals' self-esteem and achievement. It carries
a positive sense of recognition and trust in intellectual abilities and capacities. In
reference to Giddens's understanding, the corporation becomes an organisational
structure for individuals that also enables them to use their intellectual abilities and
capacities. This very clearly defines ambiguities for individuals. While they might
feel empowered and enabled to do a job, they might just as well feel restricted,
constrained or limited in their range of actions.

Having been at the helm of a global insurance corporation for 15 years, Karl,
now 44, connected the issue of autonomy and reflected on another aspect of
corporate culture that will be dealt with in more detail in the next chapter:

> Once the vision is shared by everyone, everyone is perfectly capable of thinking
> independently, but most companies spoil 90% of their employees. Everyone,
> I mean in principle almost 100% of employees can work independently, are
> proactive, are open and honest … .

The contradiction is obvious. Thinking independently is dependent on a shared vision. In a corporate context, however, this ambiguity is twisted in a particular way. Thinking independently here refers to individuals thinking along a corporately determined set of performance criteria. The principle is the same again: minimal input in terms of time, money and direction; maximum output in regard to problem-solving, profit-making and efficiency. The individuals' ability to think critically or creatively is potentially turned into a management tool. It is not necessarily restricted by a given set of rules, but is nevertheless dependent on the structures. Self-realisation and organisational objectives seem to coincide.

It is, however, not only the case that managers try to instrumentalise individuals' intellectual capacities for business purposes, but part of the ambiguities around 'organised individualisation' is that they themselves fall prey to pseudo-autonomy. Most of the interviewed managers admit that they can simply not stop 'thinking business'. It is in fact the business that imposes itself upon a manager's thinking. Thinking about work and work-related problems becomes a compulsion. The blurring of the boundaries between the individual and the organisation is illustrated by the following example:

> Some people separate their work and their private life as quite distinct things and they can do any job tomorrow, it doesn't really matter to them. I think people who get into research often identify themselves with what they do. So I identify myself with what I do and … I'll be at home on the weekend and while mowing the lawn I'm still thinking about my work and I guess it has to affect your private life because in your private life you're still thinking about your work and never really leave it behind. (Freddy)

That in itself seems like a normal processing of work issues that cannot simply be switched off, and yet it might be an indicator for how much work is part our self-understanding which does not have to be understood negatively. Lars, after more than 20 years in the same managerial position in the manufacturing industry, explained:

> You know, I can never stop thinking about the problem. It doesn't matter if it is technical or commercial problems or organisational problems. Fortunately, we have a little weekender down the coast and for me there is nothing better [than] to go down there and potter in the garden and so on. But what I'll be doing is solving all the issues.

It seems that 'thinking independently' within a given corporate framework is fine, as long as the framework is not questioned. In that sense, even critical thinking is welcomed as long as it optimises the realisation of the corporate strategy. Once 'thinking business' is perceived as part of individuals' self-identification, it has taken hold of reflexivity. This also highlights a work-life collision that actually surfaces in most of the issues defining individualisation as an organising principle. In any case, the individuals' ability to critically reflect and think upon their environment is restricted to their private life. A genuine politicisation in terms of challenging work conditions, a corporate line or product is reduced to mere problem-solving which amounts at best to a pseudo-negotiation of the non-negotiable and puts individualisation at work along a predefined strategy.

However, it is not just individuals' pseudo-autonomous thinking along a corporate line, either as an employee or as a manager that makes for business success. What counts on the ground is action: organising purchases, production and sales of goods, services and access. But it has to be the right action, that is, profit-driven action. In other words, managers and employees equally ought not only to think the right things, but also let the right actions follow. And that means from a corporation's point of view that employees do their work in the best, quickest and cheapest possible manner. That is what they are given individual autonomy for. What is important to Ted as an HR manager in that context is: 'I just want to have the autonomy to do it my own way'. Consequently, one might be able to say: I did it my way. But ultimately it is more like: I did it my way, but without any say!

In this context, it makes sense to speak of agency, of individuals as agents, as both managers and employees act on behalf of a corporation's interests. Rory, a CEO in the travel industry, confirmed this: 'It's about developing strategy and giving people the room within their own levels of confidence to develop solutions to meet that strategy'. To be clear, management provides a strategy, but how people make it happen is up to them. That is the essence of agency. This means, however, that employees have little or no autonomy to determine 'what' the strategy is, but that they do have a degree of autonomy in regard to 'how' they should put the strategy into practice as long as it is in the most efficient way. There is a strong sense that corporations are building their business on a sense of agency as an aspect of individualisation. Moreover, individuals' desire to actually express themselves through deeds is something management is well aware of as Ted from the HR consultancy explained:

> Most reasonably well educated driven individuals want to be able to … generate their own outcomes in their own way. Because I think they see it as more valuable that they've got more control over it. It's not just the hours thing, it's the way it's done.

Backed up by 29 years of international experience, Paula's statement is a good example illustrating different degrees of responsibility, control and agency that still come without any autonomy in determining the goal itself. While some companies for which she has worked as a manager said, 'you've got to save a million dollars in expenses and so … you're not going to conferences, you're not doing this, you're not doing that, you can't do this, you've got to get permission for that'. Other companies simply told her: 'You've got to save a million dollars in expenses, go and do it! And they empower you, you decide how you're going to a save it'. Management is thus well aware of the importance of a sense of individual autonomy. The following two examples from two old-school managers, Lars who works in the car industry, and Craig who runs a big retail business, show how sensitive and significant it is to strike a balance between individual autonomy and power. They want people to think and do the right things regarding the business, but do not want to appear as authoritarian, overbearing or controlling. Lars has come to the following conclusion with respect to agency and individual autonomy:

> Well, I think the most important thing is that in peoples' area of expertise they make decisions relating to that area of expertise. That's the most simple thing. And … that doesn't mean people cannot be critiqued or questioned on it.

Others like Craig are equally wary of the sensitive interconnection between control, autonomy and agency:

> I tell you I was interested in every facet of the business. I would call into a buyer's office to see what's happening and they would be more than pleased to tell me. I never ever interfered with what they bought because they are the buyers, they've got to know and … I would praise them. I would never ever say you've got to do this or you've got to do that. One thing I learned a long time ago is: Don't tell people what not to do. You can't tell them what to do either … that's the more important thing.

There is, however, some understanding of the limited nature of this kind of agency as, for example, Karl's statement demonstrated: 'You need autonomy. You've got to have an area where you can do what you want and you can decide. Of course within boundaries that are given, but you can decide'. Martin gave an example from his managerial career where he felt too much control as inhibiting and was asking for more independence:

> I haven't had enough responsibility or the responsibility has come with baggage and the baggage has been a boss who comes in every five minutes 'What are you doing?' At the end of the day, if you employ someone to do a job, let them do the job.

Ted made it clear how the connection between autonomy, agency and pressure comes down to a strong result orientation at the heart of which lies the assumption: 'you have no right to interfere in my work as long as I achieve and even less if I overachieve.' This attitude is underpinned by individual entrepreneurship, as becomes clear from Ted's remarks about the owners of the business he works for:

> I prefer to have the freedom. … Occasionally these guys [the owners of the business who employ him as a CEO] have commented and I keep saying: 'Hang on, I'm the one generating income for you. I am doing it. I am overachieving

budget in every way. Don't start putting brakes on me 'cause I will get the shits and if you just want to measure me on the number of hours I'm sitting on my desk making phone calls, then I've joined the wrong place. You look at my bottom line, you look at what I'm generating, you look at how much effort I'm making, how many meetings I'm making, that's fine, you can do that as well, but just charge me on the revenues 'cause I'm working smarter as I'm getting older and I've also got to stay fresh …' And you know, my revenues are growing round about 20% per annum, year on year on year on year, you know, I still got my challenges, I still worry about where's the money coming from next month and it's a lot of pressure because you got a family relying on it and all the rest of it. But now I'm used to it. I'm prepared to accept the pressure of that in return for the autonomy and being my own boss. I run my own business here effectively. I would say I am 85% free to do my own thing, my own way in my own time.

Although Ted feels free to do what he likes and enjoys that kind of freedom, he is also under subtle pressure to use that freedom more efficiently. It is, however, up to him to draw the line. The imperatives are rather clear-cut: you get more autonomy to achieve and you had better overachieve. In addition to that, you are also responsible for your over- or under-achievements. Put bluntly, when you overachieve, we take the profits; if you underachieve, ultimately you get the sack. Agency in this sense cannot be understood as a means for expressing one's needs, desires and wishes at the workplace. Quite the opposite: the expectation is to express and realise the corporation's interests and goals without having any say in determining those goals unless you own the business. It is along those lines that 'organised individualisation' emerges as the individuals' struggle over the use of their abilities and capacities. The crucial aspect here is that the individuals' ability to act, to simply do things, is constrained and guided, but also facilitated by a corporate strategy, while at the same time, the contestation of the underlying normative patterns is beyond their control.

It goes without saying that autonomy in the sphere of work is defined and embedded in a field of power relations. Within that field, individuals are competent and knowledgeable agents, but not self-determined actors. However, can managers' actions also be reduced to mere agency? To a degree, that is certainly the case. They are the agents of markets, shareholders, owners and also their employees. But the difference between employees in non-managerial positions and managers is that the latter can determine, to a large degree, the framework for their employees, the rules within which agency is given or expected. In that sense, managers have a degree of self-determination and not just agency, as Rory seemed to understand:

I think the opportunity I have, perhaps over and above everyone else is, that I can influence the direction of the business and pose my own thoughts on that and … trust your own judgment, prioritising.

Managers' autonomy to reflect on and determine the direction of the business and their own way of working is perhaps the strongest manifestation of 'organised individualisation' at work in terms of power. However, a manager's autonomy and power are also tied to certain criteria such as achievement and success. Asked how important success is in regard to a manager's power and autonomy, Herman responded:

> It is absolutely crucial as it covers your back in order to be able to do what you want to do, that means you always have to pay attention … monetarily, you need a certain fundamental independence in order to be able to really do what you want to do. … You have to learn that success in the business is the one thing that earns you reputation and credibility and from that point of view it provides you with autonomy. … Independence in business terms, that's just how it is, means to be successful.

After a few seconds, he added the following afterthought: 'What I like about it? It's the possibility to have an impact, in negative terms: power'. What this tells us is that 'autonomy' is organisationally arranged and defined.

The question of power is a crucial part of the question of autonomy. Power can drastically restrict, but equally facilitate individual autonomy. And this is the case no matter how much talk there is about 'flat hierarchies'. As Freddy admitted: 'Organisations are hierarchical whether or not you describe them as flat, there are always those who are in control and those who aren't'. However, the sheer imposition of power is not welcomed by employees. They want to feel as if they are in control and that is what flat hierarchies really are about. But not all managers see a need to disguise their power. For example, Karl, the insurance manager, made a clear case about what it means for him to be in control:

> Sometimes you simply have to say: 'That's how I want it because I own this company or because I am the boss and that's how it is'. That's how I say it, I am honest about it. And that's not to be discussed because I want it just the way I say I want it. And I try to say this as rarely as possible. I don't tell people when they have to come in in the morning … actually I had to do that once too. 'Someone has to be here at nine o'clock. Even if you think you're a genius and even if you only manage to leave at 10pm, you've got to be in at 9 because you have to be available', and that's something I would not discuss. That's got nothing to do with freedom. But I try not to say it, but let's not kid ourselves here and I believe this is right, I've got the power and people are free to say: 'That's unacceptable, I can no longer work here' or 'o.k., not a problem, I can put up with that because otherwise things are fine'.

Put crudely, the choice given is: like it or leave it. If you like it, it means you have to comply; if you leave it, you have to find employment elsewhere. Surely the exercise of power is based on a work contract and membership. While Karl's statement appears like a rather unrefined way of using power that brings Weber's 'whip of hunger' (1961: 209) to mind, Herman presented a more differentiated view:

> Usually I'd say power manifests itself by not being used and it grows by not being used. Hence, it is only a quasi-threat but I guess as we all know to a certain degree that's what characterises power. How power manifests itself today? I believe power manifests itself today through other abilities, like to integrate and moderate.

But it is not only about managers having the power to define situations or to integrate or to moderate. As much as people usually complain about those who are in power, Herman shed some light on the ambiguity of power. Power also provides security for employees' agency:

> For me personally the feeling of power also manifests itself through continuous requests to decide this or that and if you basically say: 'What would you do? Why don't you decide for yourself?' that's when you feel you've got power and that it provides an essential sense of security for others, that's very important.

Hence, agency within certain boundaries is backed up by the manager and in that sense enables individual autonomy in terms of agency. The relational character of power is quite obvious. Herman explained in more detail how that works:

> You back people up by offering yourself as a resource or the ability to make good for mistakes or to deal with mistakes within the broader environment so that things don't escalate … and these are principles of power that over time increase power and basically that's what keeps you in your chair, yeah, because in a sense you're carried from below.

It is not so much a sense of autonomy that emerges here, but the interplay between a manager's power and the ability to build up a trusting relationship with employees, to 'organise consent' although not democratically. Interestingly enough, however, this reveals a correlation between a sense of autonomy and obligation that runs deep when it comes to employee loyalty and commitment.

To have agency at the workplace is certainly positive and the point here is by no means to dismiss it. And yet, what creates a real sense of autonomy is not agency, but self-determination. This seems to be a privilege that mainly managers or self-employed people get to enjoy, while others dream of being their own boss. In that sense, self-determination is a highly longed for value that many employees and managers dream of, although it certainly does not mean less work. Bob, for instance, has made the move from being a top manager in a large company to founding his own company.

> It's much more invasive now with my own company. And the reason being is
> that you tend to … I guess be more involved in it. So, it is much more invasive,
> there is no doubt about that. Is that a good thing or a bad thing? Well, it's hard to
> say. I found it much less stressful, so that's a good thing, potentially much more
> profitable, that's a good thing … it can be much more flexible, that's also a good
> thing because we've got a young son … Yeah, there are very few downsides
> actually.

What seems to be decisive is the degree of tension, friction or stress that emerges from the juggling of various value spheres in an individual life. For Nancy, responsible for HR on the management board, self-employment is an aspiration that is clearly connected to the entrepreneurial idea of the self as well as a project-like approach to the lifecycle. She wants to

> be self-employed as a psychologist. I'm talking 15 years down the track, to have
> that option to be able to choose the hours I work and maybe work two days a
> week when I'm 70 if I want to, that's what I want.

Alongside differentiations of autonomy and instrumentalisation, agency and self-determination, the presented statements also indicate that people are to a certain extent aware of the different degrees of autonomy and actually perceive it as contested terrain. How could they otherwise long for more freedom in whatever form? However, it is also obvious that self-determination and the question of autonomy in general are connected to the management or organisation of time. Whenever the issue of self-determination came up in the interviews, time awareness was not far behind. As the last two statements already point out, time-management plays a huge role in this respect, but also in regard to continuity.

What emerges from the above is that there is an ambiguous increase in individual autonomy in terms of reflexivity, agency and interaction. However, it is a contingent and above all arranged, prescribed or 'organised autonomy'. The presented material indicates that creating a sense of pseudo-autonomy allows management to get the best out of individuals for the benefit of the corporation, while individuals have to balance other expectations by themselves. As a matter of fact, individual autonomy as an aspect of normative individualisation in the contemporary sphere of work is subject to a struggle between different normative underpinnings or Weberian value spheres within the individual.

2. Continuity and Fragmentation: Having a Normal Life

Another aspect of individualisation which supports the conceptualisation of individualisation as 'organised individualisation' is the individuals' ability to create a sense of continuity. As has been said, continuity is a multi-layered concept referring to individuals' ability to continuously re-create a sense of coherence and sameness for themselves, but also for others. They do so not only over time, but also in terms of constantly changing possibilities of identifications and experiences which is an important aspect of personal identity formation. In the hyper-differentiated context of networks, knowledge and access economy, the multiplicity and discontinuity of experiences has risen infinitely and thus makes personal identity formation a difficult task.

The rapidly transforming sphere of work is not exempt from hyper-differentiation, but might even be one of its main sources. The exceptions, however, are the economic goals of profit-maximisation. They constitute the core of systemic continuity. These transformations play a crucial role in individuals' everyday experiences of others and themselves. Notwithstanding the continuous transformation, the contemporary workplace is still an important reference point for individuals. The material presented in this section suggests that a highly competitive knowledge and access economy, as Gordon, CEO of a global manufacturing business, put it, 'is disruptive to, sort of, having a so-called normal life'. The frictions between systemic imperatives, requirements and demands seem to create ambiguities and conflicts on an individual level between systemic continuity and a fragmenting experience of the self. How do people in corporations experience, express and deal with this kind of hyper-differentiation?

The answer might partly lie in what has already been described as flexibilisation to which managers and employees equally adhere: 'You've got to be flexible in order to get business', said Deborah, a 54 year old managing director, before she quickly added: 'When you have to change focus, you have to change focus fairly quickly and fairly readily in your daily work'. She went on, repeating: 'Oh, I think it's critical to be flexible, it's critical to be flexible, it's very critical to be flexible'. The constant organisational demand for flexibility has become a standard feature of individuals' everyday life!

Flexibilisation seems to be contagious as the demands to be flexible spill over from one value sphere to others, from the economic sphere into the public, political and private spheres. The economic rationalisation of social interaction challenges the alignment and integration of a growing number of personal experiences into a coherent self-image. Flexibilisation, it seems, 'liquefies' the sphere of work as a reference point for personal identity formation and yet individuals consider it crucial to be flexible. Nothing ever stays the same. As the individual becomes an appendix to organisational demands, the sense of personal coherence and continuity is sacrificed for systemic primacy. While the creation of systemic continuity for the business remains an important task, the impact of producing social discontinuities that challenge the formation of a coherent personal identity is mostly disregarded.

How do the interviewees experience this aspect of individualisation at contemporary workplaces? A good starting point is the occupational roles that are used to provide clear-cut occupational identities, but which are now dissolving:

> Well, you no longer need sales reps but integrators and communicators and
> that's the multitasking ... You shift from offering products to offering services
> and that simply means that other abilities are needed. I also got rid of terms like
> sales rep, for example ... now there are business managers so that they are aware
> of the fact that they are responsible for everything. The catchphrase is CRM
> [Customer Relationship Management]. You've got to be the customer's channel
> for communication, organisation, integration. And then they've got to bring in
> experts and motivate them instead of being the expert on everything themselves.
> (Herman)

It all seems to be there: responsibilisation, integration management,
communication. When people face questions about what they do for a living,
the answers are less clear-cut. The interviews revealed two main answers to that
question. It was either 'I am a project manager and at the moment my project is
xyz' or 'I work for XYZ and they do this'. This suggests that clear-cut occupational
identities are less likely today and thus the construction of 'life-narratives' (Sennett
2006: 5) seems to be more challenging.

In general, flexibility and the discontinuities that come with it are understood
as a precondition for success. As such, flexibility emerges as an unquestioned
premise of today's sphere of work. Bob confirmed that in saying:

> Now some people try to promote it [flexibility] as like a universal thing that
> needs to be applied to all workplaces, should all be contract based, you know,
> this sort of thing, and you can see that it's not for everybody. Some people feel
> very uncomfortable.

Bob's viewpoint contrasts with most managers. For them, work structures
and employees are never flexible enough. While employees do not resist change
generally, they tend to consider it difficult to cope with. Andrew's outlook as a
manager in the IT industry on flexibility and the willingness to change shed some
light on that:

> A lot of people resist change ... I enjoy and embrace change ... I really enjoy
> change, so as a consultant I would work on a six-month assignment in a
> company, build up relationships and expertise ... bang ... move on! And I enjoy
> that degree of change. But a lot of people don't and you try and introduce change
> into an organisation and it is very interesting to see the impact that that has.
> Many people go on stress leave. You change a software system that someone
> has used for ten years ... all of a sudden something is different ... They don't
> take it very well.

Both flexibility and the imperative for change come across as an external,
uncontrollable fact of life that has to be accepted. Deborah, who is 54 years
old and has been at the helm of her organisation in changing roles for 20 years,

although with some doubt in her voice, said: 'I always like it [change]. If you stay somewhere for too long you become stale'. She further explained that she thinks that she had to learn to constantly adapt to a new and changing environment. She clearly felt uncomfortable with that question and, as if she wanted to reassure herself, she added that you've got to like change, otherwise 'you've got a problem with life in general'.

Because of economic pressures, Rory had to implement massive changes in his organisation as a CEO over the last two years. He said:

> The business has been through a substantial amount of reorganisation in recent times and as a result of that ... there are ... a lot of people who are a bit tired, worn out through change and there we've got to reinvent for them the objectives of the business.

The systemic continuity in terms of a successful continuation of the business comes first, and employees simply have to adapt to given facts. The urge for systemic continuity in the economic sphere subtly encroaches upon individuals' sense of continuity and coherence that all of a sudden seem to depend on systemic continuity. Freddy's organisation, which, as is commonly the case in businesses, has a policy of constant improvement and restructuring in place. He explained how he tries to deal with constant flux:

> I think if you're in good times at work there is no need to really switch off, but in bad times, you know, there might be restructuring going on or *change* going on and you're not adapting very well to it. I think the best thing to do is to switch off sometimes when you get out of it. Otherwise the tension builds up too much and ... particularly, if you're in an environment where we are continuously restructuring, sometimes I look forward to it and I think this is going to be great and there is other restructuring, you don't enjoy it ... and you can't do all those things continuously, you really have to put it aside saying 'that's the job'.

This statement gives the impression of a rather narrow escape route from systemically imposed change. Freddy's first-hand experience seems to suggest that constantly adapting and pseudo-negotiating the lines between the individual and the organisation stretches peoples' capacities to create a sense of continuity. From a managerial perspective, the demand for flexibility generates an artificial justification of uncertainty with which individuals are expected to cope. You are expected to live a normal life, while the artificially created uncertainties do not allow you to do so. Yet, if you fail to live a normal life, it is usually interpreted as 'You are not coping very well'. The managerial demand for and power over constant change becomes a strategic means to keep individuals 'busy' with adapting to change, rather than enabling them to contest or question underpinning goals and values.

The managerial premise is that change is a good thing, but hard to implement. Bob described employees' usual reaction to change:

> What it means is that people that want to change things are actually to be treated with, I wasn't gonna say … contempt is not the right word, suspicion, concern. So if you wanted any change by definition: 'Is it working right now?' 'Yes.' 'So why do you want to change it?' 'Cause it could be better!' And people say: 'No, no, no, it could be worse!'

Generally, managers appear to perceive their staff as likely to ward off change and discontinuity as long as things seem to work, while they themselves seem to be driven by an urge for constant improvement that ensures the continuation of the business that might come at the cost of social discontinuity. Ted, from the HR consultancy, put the managerial take on change in a nutshell: 'The fact that something isn't broken doesn't mean it doesn't need improvement'. Again, this suggests that managers use their power strategically to keep individuals uncertain and, by doing so, shift the boundaries between the systemic and normative process onto individuals. The onus to keep up with systemic change is put on individuals. The power to actually create uncertainty becomes a strategic management tool on the basis of subtle instrumentalising pressures, while individuals feel as if they are not able to cope with change for which they themselves are actually not responsible.

With respect to continuity, another controversial aspect is certainly the management and flexibilisation of time. How intertwined flexibility and time-management are becomes evident from what Ian, a 41 year old manager in manufacturing, has to say. He takes quite some pride as he organises his staff in what he considers the most flexible manner, namely, 'on a minute to minute, hour to hour, day to day basis, sometimes depending on what the load and the schedule is'. While Ian is proud of the fact of a flexible work-organisation, Freddy is more sceptical. In his opinion, it leads staff to

> believe that they'd been asked to do more and more in less and less time to the point where the time they've been asked to do things is just humanly impossible. They are happy to do the work and they enjoy the technical content. They're just not enjoying the time demands.

Yet, with a belittling tone, he gave the following example of a particular employee: 'Things that we would expect he would be able to do within a month he really wanted six months to do and he actually expressed that he wanted six months to do it'. One could say that this employee failed to successfully negotiate the boundaries between systemic demands and his everyday life. Or is it that he actually wanted to negotiate and express what he really thought, rather than pseudo-negotiate what is, in an unarticulated manner, non-negotiable anyway? The unwillingness to adapt, to shift the boundaries between the system and lifeworld is perceived as unreasonable. Here, the friction between systemic continuity and personal discontinuity becomes quite obvious.

But the concern about time pressures and the subsequent hyper-differentiation resulting from disruptions, fragmentation and discontinuities is something that even some of the managers approach critically. Karl, the insurance manager, for instance, made the following point about workaholics:

> Workaholics, I think they've got a problem, a personality problem, you know, an inferiority complex or something or other is not right. If you work more than 50 hours per week, you've got a problem, you can't organise your work properly.

Some managers even try to make a point about time management to keep the boundary between the organisation and the individual clear. Drawing on what seems to be a managerial network or friendships centring on his consultancy, Ted told another story about his friend who is also a CEO:

> A quarter to six he goes around his office asking his staff: 'What are you still doing here? You've got kids, get out of your chair. If you haven't finished, get in earlier tomorrow and finish it. If you can't finish your job in the amount of hours this corporation is giving you, then we need to start looking at your performance. I don't want you to be here 8 or 9 in the evening. Exceptions, always. Sometimes you just need to do stuff. But it is the exception, not the rule.' And he used to go around and kick everyone out of his office and get in his car and drive home.

While managers in general appear to push for change and constant improvement, they also complain about inhuman time pressures (maybe not to their employees, but certainly to people conducting interviews about their work). Managers themselves, although they advocate flexibility, feel pushed to the limits in regard to time pressures and the impact of the business on their private lives. It simply becomes difficult to fit it all into one life. Gordon, the captain of a global manufacturing business, is happy to let steam off when he reproachfully fleshes out what actually is disruptive to having a so-called normal life. The following statement made it quite clear that it originates in the attempt to manage conflicting value spheres in a global knowledge and access economy:

> The hardest thing I find, quite honestly is … I virtually find them [his employees all over the world] going 24 hours a day sometimes with conference calls and video conferences, you know, last night, for example, I was filled with calls up until about 11 pm with guys needing answers on questions and there is a hell of a lot of travel. I mean I travel constantly. I mean, I get to the office at 7.30 and go home at 7 pm. What I find is now, you know the impact on your family, fortunately I don't live very far from here. You know if I've got a situation where I know I will be working till 9 o'clock or 10 o'clock with conference calls I might often go home for lunch and just have lunch with my wife. I spend some

> time with her then, rather than miss her the whole day. Because sometimes I get up and she's asleep and I come home and she's asleep and the same with the kids. It's not a good quality of life … I'll be flexible and try and spend different times of the day and I've taken her on trips with me although that generally never works out well, because the trips are so gruelling that they just don't like hanging around in hotels all day long waiting for you and when you come back and you're tired and grumpy. So, it's not very effective to have your wife travel with you on business. The better thing is to at the end of a business trip maybe once a year take a holiday with them somewhere and I'll do that. I mean this last trip I got back two weeks ago and I was away for two and a half weeks and there probably was only one occasion where I was in one hotel for two or three consecutive nights, the rest of the time you're in one hotel for one night, you're having business meetings, dinners and you're travelling as well, so it all cumulates and when you get home it takes about a week to catch up!

It becomes quite obvious who has to be flexible and that it is the general sense of a 'quality of life', the family life, the free time that suffers. Being at the same level of international top management as Gordon, Herman, although in a slightly different personal situation, takes the same line when it comes to *individually* coping with the fragmenting effects of the business world. When asked how the constant change in business affects his life, he responded:

> Greatly, especially in terms of thinking. Where am I at? Where do I want to be? What's left to achieve? … If you haven't really settled and you are constantly on a contract, well, that exactly prevents you from settling. It constantly gives you reason to ask yourself: What am I going to do next? … You never build a home … you don't even think about renovating a garage, that's simply out of the question. Why should I do that, because in two to three years' time I'll move. That's incredibly annoying, that influence on the private life. And it's a very unsteady way of living and that's really annoying because long-term planning is an impossibility, it comes with uncertainties and that influences your private life enormously. Your wife too cannot necessarily do what she wants to do.

While the business is supposed to grow steadily drawing on individuals' as resources, it results in an unsettled way of life that forbids long-term planning and is all about dealing with uncertainties. The individual dependence on organisational issues has a stark impact on a personal sense of continuity. Clearly, in the name of profit, in the name of a strong and prosperous business, systemic continuity leaves a sense of personal limbo. One of the biggest ambiguities of 'organised individualisation' becomes obvious here. Individualisation as a self-determined or somehow more liberated way of life is strongly tied to and dependent on the organisation. Everyday life becomes fractured, is under organisational siege, under duress. A personal sense of continuity is defined in reference to the business and takes a special effort, if it ever can be achieved outside the corporate context.

Nancy, the head of HR management of a global car supplier, also found the expenditure of time at work overbearing: 'You know, at some point I'm not going to work 60 hours a week whatever it is I'm doing'. While continuity is defined in business terms and individual continuity accordingly appears to be dependent on the organisation, Nancy does not consider it to be a lasting and thus normal way of life. Yet, whatever thoughts these individuals have, they revolve around the organisation they work for. The rationalisation of their personal lifeworlds is determined by the rationalisation of their businesses. The divide between business and individual has become permeable, blurred and shifted into the value spheres of their homes – if they are able to build one at all.

As a consequence, life- or career-planning is deeply affected by the purposive-rational decisions defined by and fostering the business. Individuals do not just reject, but also embrace and actually internalise these imperatives as the organising principle of their life. Ted, from a consultant's perspective, not so much sees it in his own life, but confirms this attitude in regard to young career starters. He gave an example by referring to a conversation he had with one of his young clients who said:

> If you're going to talk to me about a particular role, [if] you want me to talk to them [potential employer], you must understand I will get bored in 18 months to two years because they will not have the opportunity or ability to develop faster. I'm not blaming them, I'm just saying upfront that I will probably move in two years' time because I just want to move on.

The pace of individual change is made dependent on organisational change and the capacity to change. Not only has the hyper-differentiated systemic world colonised her lifeworld, but now her hypertrophied lifeworld 'hits' back on the business by demanding more opportunities for organisationally defined individualisation. Being flexible, being on the move, living on the edge, these seem to be the values of an increasingly flexibilised sphere of work instead of a personal sense of continuity. What is continuous is constant change, not only in organisation terms, but also personal achievement. In this case, the boundaries between the individual and the organisation can hardly be identified. The typical characteristics of a generation of upcoming managers for whom this has become a normal way of life, as Ted sees them, are:

> Early 30s, marketing professionals with science degrees and often have finished MBAs or half way through them, so well qualified, sharp young people, happy to move every two years, change companies. It's starting to happen more and more.

But Ted also made it clear that there are a lot of unreasonable expectations that seem to be based in what was discussed earlier as 'universalised work ethic'. How individuals define them is clearly dependent on organisationally defined milestones in life along which individuals again rationalise their own life in reference to corporations. This 'worldview' becomes clear from the following conversation Ted had with another young career woman:

> And I asked her: 'Why did you do the MBA at 22?' 'Oh, I felt it looked good on my CV.' 'Is that it? What about learning, growing up, understanding what the business is about?' 'Yes, all those things', she said, 'of course as well'. 'If you had a commerce degree, why did you need a MBA straight afterwards?' 'Because I want to be a general manager at 33.'

In contrast, Ted continued by pointing out how people who are at another stage of their life perceive possible career changes. They seem to be more after a balance between systemic requirements and personal continuity and stability which at the same time does not mean less organisational dependence:

> Now, on the other hand, the more established people say, guess now we're talking about the next, not next generation, but career generation like me, 38, two kids, another one on the way, houses bought, settled down. So guys my age … are thinking a lot more long term. They're starting to think: 'I'll look at this role if there is a better than 50% chance of career progression to the next position in about two years' time. Much longer than this I probably start getting itchy feet if I don't really see the product pipeline of this corporation coming through with a new product on the global level … I probably won't join them.' So they're starting to look at a little bit more strategic issues, bigger long term stuff.

This suggests that 'organised individualisation' plays out differently in connection to the lifecycle. While people at an earlier career stage seem to be happy to accept or even desire and embrace discontinuity in their lives, people at a later career stage are at least looking for a sense of security, certainty and personal continuity in regard to family and quality of life. Thus, how individuals look at the possibilities to negotiate work and life is contingent and dependent on where they are at in their life cycles. Yet, in both cases, there is an ambiguous dependence on corporations to provide not only change, but also stability.

As with individual autonomy, the ability to create a sense of continuity and coherence as an aspect of individualisation is subject to a struggle between the different normative underpinnings of the lifeworld and the system. On the one hand, efforts to keep the business prosperous are predominant; on the other hand, individuals strive for a 'normal life'. Management certainly has the main goal to ensure systemic continuity to keep the business going and to increase profits, while efforts to form a personal sense of continuity and coherence become secondary and contingent. This is most evident in terms of flexibility on the part of the individuals that emerges as a universal premise and thus produces discontinuities with which individuals have to cope by themselves. While this is portrayed as opportunities for negotiation or self-realisation, it actually prevents individuals' ability to construct a sense of continuity as a coping mechanism for the discontinuities generated by the system. It thus becomes pseudo-negotiation of and within systemically pre-given frameworks. Social discontinuities in terms of family life, life trajectory or everyday life are – if not embraced – at least often accepted and tolerated. To be certain, on the one hand, systemic continuity can contribute greatly to the formation of personal identity; on the other hand, the predominant logic of flexibility instrumentalises the ability to create a sense of individual continuity and coherence.

What the interview material demonstrates is that 'organised individualisation' at least partly arises from a tension between continuity and fragmentation that is either perceived as disruption or as the essence of having a normal life.

3. Recognition: Kicking Bums and Patting Shoulders

The role of recognition has been discussed as yet another important aspect of individualisation. In a modern society, social recognition is not granted automatically on the basis of ascribed status, prestige or an otherwise fixed normative infrastructure and hence cannot be taken for granted. Instead, it is the individual struggle for social recognition that takes priority in contemporary society. It is the assessment of an individual's contributions to society, a group or an organisation and its values on the basis of which social recognition is granted. It is precisely in that sense that work and employment could, in principle, function as central sources of social recognition. The crucial questions are whether the contemporary sphere of work is indeed able to provide recognition and what kind of recognition it provides.

Just as individual autonomy runs a risk of being instrumentalised, recognition too is contested. Individuals, on the one hand, strive for social recognition on the basis of their activities at the workplace, the meaning of work and their normative connections to a wider social context; on the other hand, it is also used as a management tool and hence is dependent on organisationally defined norms and values that are not the result of public discourses.

How do managers actually understand recognition? Martin defined the core of social recognition when he stated that, besides all the purposive-rational business decisions, 'you've got to treat humans as humans'. This is elaborated in more detail by Andrew who highlighted the general relevance of recognition at today's workplace:

> If you're going to kick someone for doing something wrong, then you should be patting them on the back when they do something right. A management style that you see a lot of is the kicking in the bum. Very rarely does an employee get recognition that they're just doing a very good job and they're putting a lot of effort in, and people are. A pat on the shoulder or a 'Thank you' goes a very long way.

Although using different words, Craig made a similar point: 'You haven't got the right to criticise your staff if you're not prepared to praise them when praise is due'. The underlying, more generalised and abstract meaning behind those statements has clear implications for the way individuals see themselves and are seen by others. Karl, for example, described how he sees his employees, namely as 'strong personalities, individuals, you know, mature people. They can think independently, they can decide for themselves and that's how you've got to treat them in a company'. There is a sense of respect in those comments that is also articulated by Ted when he said about his organisation: 'Our key value is that we treat people with a great deal of respect'. Respect is certainly the key aspect of social recognition. The question however is: respect for and on the basis of what? Andrew's further comment shed some light on the very basis of recognition: 'I think if you give people a bit of variety, a bit of self-worth, they feel that they're playing a part, it's very important from any employee's point of view, that they believe that they are making a difference'.

It is the feeling of making a useful contribution, of 'making a difference' through which individuals gain a sense of self-worth and self-esteem. This is, however, dependent on an environment that assesses contributions and consequently approves or disapproves of them as useful or useless. What is and defines a useful contribution, and in what form recognition in consequence is granted or is defined entirely depends on the organisation. The struggle for social recognition is individualised as individuals want to feel as if they are truly making a difference. The norms and values, according to which their contributions are assessed, is organisationally given and defined by a rather small number of people, that is, managers.

The most obvious kinds of recognition in the sphere of work are connected to financial rewards and inducements. And yet, when asked, most interviewees seem to be after something more than just material gain. Andrew gives an example of another type of reward and recognition. Being asked what kind of rewards besides money he liked best in his career, he told the following little story:

> I must say that the favourite was probably X and the least favourite was Y-insurances. X, it was because I was also involved with the business. Now as you know, X are in the business of putting bums on planes and sending them all over the world, well, they did that for me. They decided that the product that I had developed was going to be used by Z, so they put me on a Qantas plane, first class, seat 1b. I sat next to Olivia Newton John, flew over to Europe. Now that wasn't just the reason why I enjoyed it, but that meant a lot. Y-insurances? They could offer me a death policy. That didn't excite me!

Recognition here is granted for special achievements in the form of 'special treatment', a 'touch of fame', feeling a bit like a 'celebrity', in any case, some sort of motivationally uplifting experience.

However, broadly speaking, it seems that the biggest reward is a 'good quality of life', which includes self-fulfilment, job satisfaction, responsibility, trust and being trusted, and a job that is widely recognised as making a useful contribution. All of this seems to be captured in the central notion of respect. Martin, the chief financial officer, explained managers' train of thought on the issue:

> At the end of the day I don't believe money, finance should be the motivation for an employee's performance and I know some people believe that, you know, pay me a bigger bonus and I work harder. My view is if you work hard then the bonus will be self-fulfilling. If you do a good job that will be recognised. I mean managers aren't stupid. If you work hard and you do your job and in fact if you exceed the expectation, you're rewarded. It may not happen straight away, it may not happen in the magnitude that you're anticipating, but over time, you know, most managers are like elephants, they remember things for a long time.

After a little pause, he continued, making various differentiations:

> Let's be honest. We don't work for the fun of it. We work to pay bills, to be capitalist bastards so we can go and buy another video recorder or a top line car, let's be really honest. Look, job satisfaction would be number one for me. I've left a role that paid very well, very well, but I wasn't happy in the role, I was bored. And I remember my boss saying, sheepish you know: 'You're one of the highest paid staff in the organisation.' I said: 'But I'm bored.' And he said: 'How about we give you more money?' 'You're not listening to me', you know, 'I'm not here for the money'. And I was thinking, oh, that was a good day, it added value, if you want to use that word. And to me being able to add value, being able to influence decisions, being able to see that influence come across in the way an organisation operates has much more job satisfaction than someone paying me some extra Dollar at the end of each day. Look, I'm not saying money is not important, it's probably fifth on the list. Behind that I would have to say good working environment, you know, whether that'd be the people you're working for, the physical office, the interaction between your colleagues, your peers, your subordinates, your directing managers, that's vital, again, it comes back to the job satisfaction side. I'd then say probably responsibility. I really enjoy having responsibility. You know, I'm not necessarily saying I get it right every time, I don't. But someone turning around saying we *trust* you to do this, now go away and do it, that is a real buzz and if you're able at the end of the day to say I did it, here is the outcome, here is what you get for trusting me … that responsibility is important. Then I'd probably say money.

So, money is important. But it is actually the meaning of work, adding value to the quality of life, being able to satisfy needs, and again being able to make a difference, having responsibility and being trusted as a person with certain abilities, that seem to be the really crucial issues at work. Starting with the core element of respect, recognition emerges as a bundle of various issues such as: job-satisfaction, responsibility, trust, self-fulfilment and self-worth. While none of these features of social recognition can be measured or matched accurately – if at all – in monetary terms, human relations and transaction cost approaches try to economise exactly that.

The previously quoted Freddy has experienced how an individual sense of achievement can also turn into its opposite: a demoralising experience of disrespect, of misrecognition:

> So when we restructure there tends to be new blood [new employees] pulled in. And you have the old people sitting there thinking 'I worked my butt off to get us here. This guy has been brought in and put above me and has not put his sweat in.' So, often people either resign or move.

Jamie, who has only recently joined the management board, points out yet another form of recognition that results from the feeling of having a challenging job or task at hand. Most people are granted recognition for jobs with high levels of responsibilities, skills or knowledge.

> I guess, hopefully, I'll soon be in a position that I, whatever it is, I don't really mind as long as I still find it challenging. I mean I don't want to be in a job where it becomes mundane, becomes routine and boring. I think that would be an indication for myself to move on and find something else. So hopefully, I'd still be employed further down the track and I'll be doing something that I find challenging and hopefully still enjoy. (Jamie)

Interestingly enough, her sense of recognition starts with the fundamental question of having a job at all, and if that is the case, the job hopefully is a source of recognition too in terms of some variety, change and joy that altogether make it a positive and rewarding challenge. Andrew from the IT business makes an even stronger point about challenges, which he described as problem-solving:

> I enjoy working and I enjoy problem-solving. I think … the thing that I like doing the most when I am relaxing is doing cryptic puzzles and solving logic problems. That's what I enjoy. So, I think problem-solving is what I enjoy, I am getting personal reward by solving problems.

The personal reward is the feeling of being smart, of being up to it, again of being able to make a difference. The result is job satisfaction and equally the simple fact that others, be it the environment or the wider public, notice and approve of something as an achievement, although it is usually an improvement for an organisation. Andrew referred to this as his 'personal reward and satisfaction level' when he talked about a former managerial position and why he left it:

> My personal reward and satisfaction level was not there. I was … on very, very
> good money. Peer level and management level loved me, my staff, my direct
> staff before I fired them loved me, but the satisfaction and the reward and the
> challenge was not there. The challenge, we have a problem and it is a massive
> problem and these are the issues, please, make it go away, fix this problem and
> sit down and work with all the people and to see how it can be done and discuss
> it and sell it to your staff and management. Present the big picture, this is how I
> see this problem being solved and running with it right through to completion.
> And it doesn't matter whether it is a technical or a business problem or people
> problem, it's irrelevant. It's the personal reward you get by doing a job: well
> done.

The 'personal reward and satisfaction level' are his words for making a useful contribution and these are the standards for being respected. But he would not gain any of that in his last position. And he explained why:

> After 12 months in this particular company there were no challenges mentally
> for me and the company financially was having terrible problems and personally
> I didn't feel like that firing people was a very good way of spending my day and
> to be honest after 25 years this is the only job that I dreaded going to work, I
> didn't enjoy going to work. And I must say that in all my career I never felt that
> until recently. So, I knew that there was something wrong …

It would be rather simplistic to reduce social recognition just to making a useful contribution and being respected for it at the workplace. Andrew hinted at something 'bigger' that motivates him:

> I go to work, I get paid but that's not what drives me. So, as long as I am in a
> position where my basic costs are met and the lifestyle is [what]… I want my
> family to have … then the rest is my personal interest by what I get out of the
> company. Unfortunately, at this particular company I didn't get a lot of self-
> reward. I would … save money for the managing director, the managing director
> was happy. But from a personal satisfaction point of view it wasn't there. And
> that's why I think … the need probably not to go to a large corporation … I think
> my challenge would be to work at a hospital, or a university, a pharmaceutical
> [company] or something where the company is a good company, they provide
> good services and value and to help them to provide that better. How nice is that?

What this statement shows is that there does not necessarily have to be a conflict between the economic and the cultural value spheres, but they can work hand in hand as Andrew's examples demonstrate. There is however a subtle, but important difference. The value to which a corporation adheres can be defined through the organisation alone or can be connected to a wider and broader definition of a society's normative infrastructure. In the latter case, the potential for job satisfaction seems to be unambiguously higher. While the individual's job satisfaction level is dependent on the organisation, the level of social recognition that can be gained seems to be dependent on the social organisation of consent. The subtle difference that emerges in regard to social recognition lies in a distinction between recognition based on an organisationally defined normative infrastructure and recognition based on a normative infrastructure that is subject to politicisation. As becomes clear at the end of the last quote, this finds its expression in what a company does. There are obviously different sources of recognition, such as corporate success that earns people a living, making the general manager happy as well as self-reward, job-satisfaction or serving the wider community. This by no means excludes any kind of profit-orientation, but the basis on which recognition can be granted can either be systemic or social. The normative underpinnings are different and quite often clash within individuals.

But Andrew's last point about working for a 'good' company leads to another important aspect of social recognition: a sense of meaning that can be gained from either a particular task, a certain product or even a corporation's reputation. Social recognition seems to be about a deeper sense of meaning that managers themselves are looking for and at the same time regard as something they have to provide, at least to a degree, through 'integration management' to their employees. Gordon, for instance, said: 'Well, the core value to me is to provide meaningful and satisfying jobs to the staff'. But this is a complex undertaking, as the generation of meaning greatly depends on the kind of products or a corporation's reputation. As Freddy explained:

> For me personally, I don't know, certain products to me are worthwhile working on and others aren't. For me working on a medical device is worthwhile, to help people working on a package machine is not … so an attractive workplace for me is a place developing a product that I think actually has some value to people, you know, it doesn't just make money for the shareholders. Even though my background and interest is technical, I like to work on products that add some value back to society I guess.

This quote shows clearly the difference between adding value financially and adding value socially. It also demonstrates that systemic, organisational, scientific, technical or any kind of purposive rationality does not have to be self-referential. Instead, it can be guided and steered by norms and values that define a greater good than merely organisational profit-making and which are not the result of purposive rational, but communicative action. The meaning of work in terms of 'adding value back to society' and the identification with it refers to a broader sense of making a useful contribution not only for yourself or the organisation you work for, but also for society in general. Thus, the sense of a 'useful contribution' is not only restricted to a certain product or the aforementioned personal feeling of reward, but in Herman's understanding, for example, is connected to a broader understanding of what I have previously described as the politicisation of the economy and work.

> It [my identification] is even more important than the company itself, its values and its culture, much more important than that. For me personally and in particular in this industry, life-saving therapy, we are dealing with human beings. If you can't deliver then that has got a different impact than not being able to supply some muesli-bar and having to tell some dude he won't get any tomorrow. In that sense I've got quite a different kind of responsibility … and that's important to me. It means a lot to me even to the degree that all the negatives that come with management, you know, the usual politics, organisation, a bit of bullying here and there, it even makes up for that.

And he added with the same enthusiasm: 'I couldn't and wouldn't just want to do some job, I'd always be whole-heartedly in there'. Ian, working in the manufacturing industry, made a similar point:

> See, I worked for the nuclear industry and it's really hard to talk up the nuclear industry, but … if you can make somebody live longer or solve a … problem because of the work I've done, yeah, that makes me excited, yeah, that's what engineering is all about.

Recognition in the form of meaningful work, making useful contributions and having responsibility is of course a huge motivating factor, as Sascha, the CEO of a long established global family business, explains. But for him, too, it is the connection between economy and society, a sense of social responsibility and accountability grounded in the public discussion and perception of norms and values that seems to be more satisfying than mere number crunching.

> The motivation in the end is the result of being proud of the products and the reputation of the firm. Having said that, the reputation doesn't only result from the product, but also from a company's credo. For example, we were one of the first companies that reached an agreement with unions in terms of no child labour, no hard labour, supporting collective wage negotiations, just wages, fair working hours, we were globally one of the first to do that. (Sascha)

Ian, from the manufacturing business, uses the reputation of his organisation and the resulting recognition to motivate his employees:

> We're getting a reputation for our capacity internationally. We have parts in … one in five automobiles worldwide, we really need to build on that foothold and generate that culture … I have always been of the belief that people want to do the best they can and people get a buzz out of being a part of a team that works,

and being part of an innovative product, something new, something they can say they had a significant part in.

Generally speaking, people are searching and striving for social recognition based on their work. The interviewees express that the financial success of the corporation is not so much secondary as less rewarding. However, one has to bear in mind that these are managers who do not need to worry if there is enough food on the dinner table.

Paula has a more down-to-earth and less enthusiastic approach to her managerial position. She likes her job, but she makes the point that for her it is not her all-and-everything. It is generally speaking more important to her to be recognised as

> a good person. I mean this is the absolute truth. If I won lotto today, I wouldn't work. I don't have a need to work. If I won lotto today, I would go and open a soup kitchen and have probably more satisfaction than I have now, or maybe not, I don't know. I'm not in it. But status is not important. If people say: 'Gosh, Paula, she's really a great person or she does this for people and that', that's more important to me than sitting in a nice office and blah blah blah. I like it, but it's relative.

But even though she says work and the recognition that results from it are not that important to her, she still wants to be socially recognised as making a useful contribution to society with, as she says, opening a soup kitchen (which, of course, involves work as well). Again, the source of recognition based on a politicised normative infrastructure of the whole society, in contrast to an organisationally defined normative infrastructure beyond public control, come into the spotlight. This became even more obvious when Paula talked about her family which is proud of her being a female manager. 'My kids are proud of me. I'm the only woman in the picture. My daughter noticed. They'd like me home more, I think, but yeah, they're supportive and proud, you know, 'My Mum is a manager''.

While so far it is actually social recognition that employees and managers try to gain from work, there are numerous examples where management tries to cultivate a sense of recognition at the workplace in terms of a profit-driven rationalisation of social interaction, a more subtle kind of 'kicking bums and patting shoulders'. But how are individuals supposed to work this out without being torn between a genuine normative process of negotiation and a strategic and managerial use of social recognition? The material presented so far suggests that recognition too can become a marker of the individualised frictions between systemic and normative processes. This is well illustrated by Jamie, the young financial manager, when she spoke about an award that she has recently introduced in her organisation:

> We do like a few things to generate morale and we've recently started an award, it's just a trophy that everybody sort of keeps for a week if they get nominated and basically if you do something that somebody recognises they can bring it to

the attention of the management staff and then we'll award it at a staff meeting, and that's just sort of like a morale booster.

And she continued speaking about the effect of such boosters on the employee:

We had a quality audit recently and basically he [the employee] was new on site and he got asked a certain question and I think he impressed, he managed to impress the auditors so we were like: 'Ah, that's good, he's new and he managed to remember everything we told him in the introduction period, that's good'.

However, she also explained the strategic purpose of the award from a manager's perspective:

So, in a way we're saying the company values these things and then we're saying: 'And aren't you great because you can do it?' So it's got a two-front approach. The politics and procedures, one has to have those things because they just help you manage. If you haven't got anything like that then the manager is doing the whole job of telling the employee what they can and can't do all the time. Whereas if you've got that in place you just let the employees read it and do it then we can concentrate on higher level stuff.

Recognition in the form of an award demonstrates that it does not have to be a financial reward, but it also exploits the individuals' needs for social recognition in order to implement and communicate a corporate strategy. Nancy, the HR manager, who works with a similar award system, put it like this:

No, there is no money attached to it at all, but somebody wins that thing every week for doing something over and above the call of duty and they're handed this at a meeting and they get a certificate and they wave this thing around and go: 'hurray!' and it's just a little nicety that shows these things are valued by the company.

It is one thing to treat employees and colleagues with respect, and it is another thing to manipulate their struggle for social recognition for business purposes by granting recognition for strategic purposes.

What all this indicates is that recognition plays an enormously crucial role in contemporary workplace relationships. However, individuals have to constantly deal with two kinds of recognition that seem to mark the intersection between systems and lifeworlds. There seem to be two different normative underpinnings on the basis of which a sense of recognition can be gained.

Both types of recognition and their normative underpinnings coexist but also collide, fight each other and it is the individual at the workplace who is caught in between. In a very literal sense, normative individualisation comprises the struggle for recognition as adding quality to one's life. The urge to do so as part of becoming who we are is instrumentalised by corporations. They use the fundamental desire to be recognised as a huge motivational factor to realise their corporate strategy and thus turns social recognition into a part of 'organised individualisation'.

The material presented so far depicts a struggle over various aspects of individualisation at work as a struggle within the individual that is dependent on an organisational context. It is this dependence that fundamentally defines 'organised individualisation'. From the interviews, this dependence emerges along the lines of three main aspects of individualisation dealt with in this chapter: individual autonomy, continuity of identity and social recognition. Individual autonomy is dependent on a pre-given organisational set of norms and values that are beyond public control and thus non-negotiable. 'What' and 'how' things are done is not the result of a negotiation process between the individual and the organisation, but dependent on an organisationally defined normative infrastructure. Continuity is mainly defined through organisational stability and prosperity to which individuals are expected to contribute as a form of self-realisation. Individualisation becomes 'organised individualisation', as individuals become an appendix to the organisation, while they are left to believe that they can negotiate their relationship with the organisation. Finally, recognition too is shown to be dependent on organisations. All three aspects of individualisation are potentially used as management tools and thus define to a large degree frictions that individuals have to cope with and that define 'organised individualisation'. How exactly individualisation is 'organised' on a practical level of everyday experience is the question that lies at the heart of the next chapter.

Chapter 6
Organising Individualisation at Work

In the previous chapter the focus was on the individual being the centre of managerial attention as a work-organisational resource, and how ambiguities emerge from the relationship between individuals and organisations. Now we turn to 'individualisation at work', exploring managerial measures taken to 'organise' individualisation and managers' own experiences as 'organised' individuals. Both perspectives allow a further investigation of the ambiguities that define the shifting boundaries between systemic and normative processes and the various pressures put on individuals by corporations fuelling the development of 'organised individualisation'. The central question addressed in this chapter is, therefore, how do marketisation and corporatisation, network society, knowledge and access economy translate into work-organisational changes that turn individualisation at work into an organising principle? Three main developments can be found in the interviewees' statements: people management, corporate culture and project management.

1. People Management: Walking on Water, While Running on Trust?

The aim of this section is to understand people management as a key factor defining contemporary transformations of work. It plays a central role in shifting the boundaries between systems and lifeworld on to individuals by engaging them not just functionally, but also personally, in the handling of systemic processes.

People management has a long standing history, originating in Elton Mayo's 'Human Relations' or 'Human Resource Management'. The interviews reveal the more recent significance and developments of this approach. As Paula confirmed: 'If I think of managers, you know, 10 or 15 years ago, there were some managers that were brilliant business managers … [who] can produce great marketing plans, you know, and do the numbers in a flash but weren't good people managers'. She continued by saying that today, 'Managers have to be good people managers, not just good business managers'. But what is the point of people management? What is its purpose? To be clear, people management is a management technique. And Paula straightforwardly admitted: 'Honestly? Managing people is making people think they can walk on water. I think managing people is making people believe they can do whatever it takes to be successful'. The aim, however, is not simply to make 'people think they can walk on water', but, put crudely, to rationalise social interaction. This is not just the case in terms of network capitalism, but, as a consequence of that broader environment, in terms of the workplace. Nancy, an

HR manager, explained in a more straightforward manner what she thought people management was all about:

> It [people management] is about looking after people. It's about maximising the benefit of what you can get from people to further the organisation. And you can best further the organisation by looking after people and getting the best out of them.

While these are statements about the aim of people management, Herman, a CEO working in the pharmaceutical industry, gave a more differentiated insight into how people management works:

> It [people management] has got to do with moderating, the evaluation of information, motivating teams and above all with getting people to do things. Nowadays, you achieve things through the individual. Motivation is the big issue here and there are various possibilities to do that. But you get people to do their job by treating them respectfully, the right kind of leadership and that's what's really changed.

To be sure, moderation, evaluation, information, leadership and teamwork are all dependent on social interaction. It is, however, systemically or managerially mediated interaction that, in Calhoun's words, creates and establishes 'indirect relationships' (1992: 221). Yet there is a fine line between moderating and achieving through the individual, and manipulation. If people management is an 'art of manipulation', the question is why is it so important to do it with respect? Is there something like respectful manipulation? This seems to be a contradiction in terms.

People generally want to be treated with respect; people generally want to be recognised as individuals with certain intellectual or other abilities and capacities. And yet people management might just be the expansion of principles of capitalist rationalisation into yet another influential work-organisational resource, namely the individual. Ted, working in the HR industry, explained why business management, or simply 'doing the numbers', was not enough:

> I think the human side of the business is absolutely vital. You have to engage staff. They have to feel some ownership ... these days. If they don't have that sense of ... responsibility for the business or belonging that will affect the way they deal with clients.

As the above quote shows, people management targets the 'human side' of the business, which appears at first glance to stand in contrast to the more usual systemic focus on business processes. However, it merely highlights two things: that systemic processes are fundamentally built on social interaction, and that the ambiguity between systemic and normative processes is a real issue addressed by management. These are the fundamental issues people management deals with. It aims at engaging staff so that they feel (but do not have) some sense of 'ownership' and accordingly have (and not only feel) responsibility for the business as if it was their own. The tensions between membership, control and responsibility are the defining features of the individual as an 'entrepreneur of the self' who does not 'own' the means to fundamentally define what he or she is responsible for.

People management is thus not about creating opportunities to negotiate the divide between systems and lifeworlds, but about a particular kind of individualisation dependent on and defined by the organisation. However, social interaction at the workplace is fundamentally subject to power relations, and the power to define values and norms lies – despite various legal, political or organisational safeguards – mainly with management. Moreover, power in regard to people management has many faces, such as teambuilding, communication, workshops or personal development. Usually managers build on various forms of authority, including coercion, persuasion, legitimation or competence (Pusey 1991: 128). In the final equation, individuals are regarded as 'human capital', as a resource that has to be managerially optimised. While social interactions can result in the formation of norms and values, people management is built on a given corporate value system and instrumentalises social interaction in order to make employees think and act along the corporate line. Hence, people management is an extension of the access economy into the organisation and individual layers of the economy. It is about gaining access to or unlocking the qualities and abilities of individuals for business purposes. The organisation of the qualities and abilities of individuals, on which people management is built, is a cornerstone of 'organised individualisation'. What provides the key here is the idea of 'contractualisation' under the guise of trust.

Before the question of trust can be addressed, another question needs to be clarified: Do managers really perceive their employees as resources? At first sight, people management gives the opposite impression. It seems to be – and indeed, is perceived by managers themselves – as a way of caring about employees and their personal growth as individuals. 'It [people management] is all based along the lines of helping people improve, to get somewhere. Helping people reach their potential' (Nancy). She continued:

> At the moment we have a project on for developing the performance of appraisal schemes which naturally leads into developing the individual and recommending training courses for him or her.

The twists and turns of what 'helping' or 'developing' means becomes more obvious with the following quote:

> I'm interested in people. I'm interested in seeing people develop, seeing them getting the best out of themselves as well as getting the best out of them to an end, to the company's benefit (Nancy).

This is quite ambiguous. On the one hand, people management is about personal growth as individuals acquire skills; on the other, it is all about economic growth. Importantly, the responsibility for both rests on the individual. Corporations try to build their success on the generally widespread belief in and emphasis on individual development, personal growth and self-realisation. Consequently, individualisation is 'organised' by management predominantly for business purposes.

It is hard to tell the difference between what is good for the individual and what is good for the business. Why can it not be the same? Doing a good job, being successful and being recognised for it certainly contributes to a good individual quality of life. It is statements like the following by Andrew, the IT manager, where 'caring', 'personal growth' and 'looking after people' turn into rather dubious managerial claims: 'Employees are treated as resources. Their issues and concerns, their likes and dislikes are never really of interest to management. Management are trying to do the most that they can with the least cost'.

There is clearly a sense of disrespect, flowing from the managerial manipulation, evident in this statement. The nurturing of individuals seems to be a means rather than the aim here. As an HR manager, Nancy was convinced that:

> If you can prove that you're looking after people, then they'll be happier and they will trust you more. And a happy person is a productive person. I believe that people are naturally productive. You just have to find the right environment where they can blossom. I mean, some are more productive than others and some have greater ability. But the point is trying to get the best out of what you've got.

What makes someone a happy person? Can trust develop in an environment where social interaction is essentially based on an uneven distribution of negotiating power between employees and managers? In what sense are individuals supposed to 'blossom'? What all of this indicates is that productive, not necessarily happy employees make the manager happy; the business, and not the individual, is supposed to blossom. This is the essence of 'working through the individual'. In essence, happiness and trust become managerial 'keys' to build corporate success on individual abilities and qualities; something the following quote suggests:

> As a manager you have to be able to look at what's happening in your work environment and I look at the quality of people, the training of the people, the understanding of the people, the history, the background. You have to basically analyse each individual and know their strengths, their weaknesses and their view of how they approach their work (Nancy).

In order to 'analyse each individual' and, in essence, rationalise their social interactions, managers want

> to be able to conduct psychological appraisal to be in a stronger position to make recommendations of how people can develop, achieve potential … as well as working out who will fit best in what team, however, for whatever reason. A lot of it is aptitude, not just ability. And those things can be picked up from psych-tests far better than any kind of gut feeling with an interview in my opinion (Nancy).

Many of these issues will re-emerge in a later discussion of corporate culture, but the bottom line of all these statements is clearly articulated by Nancy: 'A human being is human capital to the company because it's an essential part, same as any other, same as the financial resources'. Hence, people management is the management technique that optimises and organises individuals as human capital.

Trust: What a Contract Cannot Define and Money Cannot Buy

The question is, however, how to get the best out of individuals? Are the rational means of signing a contract of employment and a regular wage not enough to get the best out of people? It would be too simplistic to portray people management as merely seeking to manipulate employees. It is certainly more subtle and complex than that. Put in more managerial terms, the question is: how do you optimise human capital? Edwin put his finger on a crucial aspect of the problem. 'If you can stir someone's motivation about believing in the company as part of themselves, you will always get the extra mile from them'. In that sense, people management is supposed to get what a contract cannot define and money cannot buy. It goes beyond the rational management behaviour of dealing with quantifiable 'hard factors', and instead addresses qualitative or so called 'soft' or 'human-oriented factors'. One of these soft factors that the interviews brought to the fore was trust, which confirms what Jane Mansbridge has written regarding trust: that it 'greases the wheels of commerce, politics and social life' (1999: 290).

Trust, of course, is a complex concept (see e.g. Markus 2003) and while it is not our aim to define or explore its nature here, various layers and aspects of trust will help to decipher some of the more subtle ambiguities emerging from individualisation at work. In the context of my discussion, trust is an important issue in terms of both social integration and systemic cooperation. It is very much concerned with the welfare of other individuals. And yet it is precisely the concern for – and the emotional dependence on – others in dealing with individual skills and abilities that reveals the vulnerability of any kind of social interaction built on trust, including in the workplace. These complexities are of central concern in regards to people management.

> Well, for me trust is something you earn. It is not something you're automatically given. There is an inherent amount of trust and responsibility that when you employ someone that you trust they will do the job to the best of their ability. You trust that they will undertake the task that you have requested and that

> they're in the job. Over time I think you just get to understand that they do
> the job properly, they do the job without stuffing it up, they do the job without
> complaining, without moaning that it's too hard, too easy or whatever and after
> a period of time you and the individual understand each other in relation to, first,
> what's required, and second, how to do it… It comes … to that monitoring from
> a distance. (Martin)

The important point emerging from this description is that trust is connected with the issues of expectations and control. This very much gives the impression that trust in the workplace is a requirement for systemic cooperation, rather than social interaction or some kind of negotiation process on equal terms. The concept of 'monitoring from a distance' reveals the vague and ambiguous pressures that emerge from a fear of failure, probably on both the manager's and the employee's side, although for different reasons. The manager, however, has the power to pressure employees if there is a risk of them failing to cooperate.[1] This relationship has been described by Martin as 'pseudo-trust'; in essence it boils down to control. Against this one might say that real trust has to be built on reciprocity on equal terms. We could therefore ask to what degree – if at all – a relationship based on an employment contract can be built on genuine trust. 'The basis of trust' argued Barbalet, 'cannot be knowledge or calculation' (1996: 78). Thus the connection with control alludes to trust as a means to systemically organise processes at work that reach into a dimension of individuals that is normally out of reach to purely rational processes. It is here where the boundaries between systems and lifeworlds become blurry and ambiguous.

The managerial understanding of trust could be called expectations in a field of relational power. If a manager can no longer trust an employee, the manager has the power to act to rectify the situation; if an employee can no longer trust their manager, it is considerably harder for them to do anything about it. It comes down to questions of empowerment, agency and self-determination. It is in this sense about dealing with the 'freedom of others', as managers would like employees to 'freely' choose to do what is best for the business, while manipulating their freedom to question and contest the normative underpinnings. Paula, responsible for sales in her organisation, made the following comment:

> I'm the kind of manager who is hands off … In other words I don't look over
> other people's shoulder all the time … I trust and empower people … I personally,
> to be honest, tend to employ people who like that style of management if I have
> a choice.

What this proposes is that managers give autonomy and agency (empower) to their employees, and on that basis expect and rely on employees to do their job.

---

1   Barbalet points out that trust is the 'emotional basis of cooperation' (1996: 77) and that coercion usually comes into play if people fail to cooperate (1996: 78).

But they do not totally trust them. Why otherwise would the 'trusting' relationship need 'monitoring' even if from a distance? There is a sense of pseudo-trust that is supposed to enable agency, organisationally instilled 'inner-direction' (to use Riesman's term), that requires a less rigid form of control and orientation as the individual has internalised the principles of the business.

How do managers create a sense of trustworthiness[2] on the basis of expectations? Communication seems to play a crucial role in this, yet not in terms of negotiating norms and values, but in terms of creating trustworthiness. The development of trust, as revealed by the interviews, hinges on a differentiation between formal and informal ways of communicating. On the one hand, Martin, who belongs to a younger generation of managers, said he builds trust by communicating

> very informally, for example, by turning around and saying to someone 'How was your weekend, how is your day?' You're effectively communicating in a social format, but on the other hand, you're also turning around saying, you know, let me built trust, let me shape communication. So not everything has to be about work for you to communicate with your staff.

And at another point in the interview he said:

> And again if you turn around and you say to those people, right, you know, first, 'How can I help you?', second, 'What resources do you need?', and third, 'How are you going on a regular basis?', then you maintain, first, the relationship, second, you earn a little respect or give respect which is very important, and third, the probably most important aspect of it ... they feel that you're monitoring their position without looking over their shoulder.

At first glance, one can clearly see a sense of care and concern for the relationship between Martin and his employees. However, while the intention might be good, respect (recognition) and trust still turn into means of controlling the fulfilment of expectations. The boundaries between communicating socially and communicating about systemic imperatives are there, but blurred. Above all, the manager can build trust from a safe distance, while the employee is expected to give for the benefit of others (Mansbridge 1999: 291), in this case for the corporation. The following example given by Andrew, the IT manager, suggests that he is aware of different layers of trust and that the blurring of formal and informal boundaries can create problems.

---

2   In reference to Hardin, Mansbridge described trustworthiness as 'optimistic trust' assuming that there are no bad intentions and that there is a basic sense of respect in dealing with other individuals (1999: 295). Individuals are happy to give although it might make them vulnerable.

> One thing I try not to do is to get too involved in the private lives of the people
> that work for me. Not that I'm not interested, it is that, then when you have to
> stop being the friend and start being the manager that things tend to, you know,
> break down. For instance, if you have to sack people. How would it be if you
> worked with your wife and you said: 'Sorry, you know, I have to sack you. But
> by the way, what's for dinner?' 'Rat poison!'

The boundaries between systemic and normative processes seem to be clear
from a manager's point of view, while for the employee this might not be the case.
The informal and friendly language of trust changes rather quickly when difficulties
arise and the willingness to cooperate is at risk of failing. If a staff member does
not do a job properly, and as a consequence loses a manager's 'trust', the friendly
chat about the weekend turns into an unambiguous managerial demonstration of
power as the following statement by Martin indicates: 'You're on review. You're
on probation. You're not doing your job properly. It's been formally documented
with HR. HR has got a copy, the big boss has got a copy. You've got three months
to pick your socks up or you're out'. And further:

> I think there is an inherent style of management that's coming through at the
> moment and that is if you employ someone for a job then make sure they do it,
> don't cover for them, don't let them slack off. If you believe the individual is
> not doing his job properly then it's up to you to do something about it because
> they're not going to volunteer 'Boss I'm doing a really crappy job. I think you
> should fire me', you know.

Basically the message from management is: 'I trust you as long as you do the
right thing'. There is an expectation to do the right thing, but no opportunities to
negotiate it. Thus, the individual reaction and negotiation of trust at the workplace
is mediated not only rationally, but also emotionally in terms of dependence and,
perhaps, fear. Deborah, drawing on her experience in the extremely competitive
aviation industry, summed it up in one sentence: 'They [employees] get targets
and if they don't achieve they're gone'. As long as expectations are met, as long
as things run smoothly 'managers are friends' and 'trust' employees; as soon as
trouble emerges, that is, as soon as expectations are no longer met, so called trust
becomes irrelevant.

Yet managers need more than their employees merely meeting expectations,
they need their trust in order to run the business. People management on the
basis of trust is also about making sure that the social dynamics at work do not
impair the realisation of goals and expectations. It is also about communicating
and imprinting an attitude to employees. The following story told by Andrew,
drawing on his experience as a consultant, highlights how people management
and business management actually reinforce each other, and that each is deficient
without the other:

The first time that that happened to me [that he did not pay enough attention to people management] I did not engage with the employees. I was involved at the management level. They said we would like this software solution to be retired and we want this software solution to be implemented ... What was missing was the selling of the new solution to the users of the product ... I felt that ... that's something I should have done. So what happened was there was a big resistance ... which caused the company literally six months additional cost to sell it to their own employees. So in future engagements I learned very, very early in the piece to engage the major stakeholders in the process. Even though they weren't specifically required to get me to the end solution they would be the main users of the product, they are the ones that have the most knowledge around the business needs that the solution is following. Engage them, understand what their specific needs are. It might be a simple change that's required like moving one field from the right hand side to the left hand side, changing a colour. But something like that can be important to the user. So it all comes to communication involving people into the process. They feel that they own it, they are part of the process, so they are more supportive.

Andrew also gave an example of how trust, in terms of management communicating aims and developments, could be earned; this could mean that not all trust in the workplace is pseudo-trust.

If you came in saying: 'Look in 12 months' time we gonna be looking at implementing a new product that does this. Over the next few months you'll notice some people come in, they may be talking to you.' ... If you keep that communication going it's very successful.

This comes back to people wanting to be recognised and treated as human beings, rather than being regarded as merely a human resource. Employees want to be treated with respect, want to be included, informed and asked and not just treated as resources that can be pushed around at someone else's will. And yet we can still question whether the simple flow of communication amounts to relationships built on trust. The ambiguity for individuals is whether the strategic use of trust can generate actual trust, and that is what individuals have to work out themselves by trusting their own judgement and intuition.

Trust as a managerial tool is, amongst others, about trying to exert some control over the flow of information. This makes trust an issue not only of one-on-one interaction, but also of group interaction in teams and markets in general. That is, trust is an issue important in interaction between strangers, which not only comes back to the 'greasing' function of trust (Mansbridge 1999: 290), but also raises the question of a more 'generalised' form of trust and strategic interests (see Markus 2003). All interviewees praised teamwork and emphasised how important it is to be a team-player. At the same time, managers know that teambuilding and team meetings are management tools to establish horizontal trust between 'equal' team members, but also vertical trust between team and manager to collect information and control social dynamics; in short, to 'manage people' as a group. The question is to find the right style to achieve all of this, as Karl explained drawing on 15 years of managerial experience in the insurance industry:

> Some teams like to have meetings on a regular basis, you know, they like coming together. I've had teams where we had meetings on a daily basis … We spoke about every single case, you know, just to have a sounding board. Other teams hate meetings. Finance people usually hate meetings. I'd only organise monthly meetings with them and try to communicate informally as much as possible, you know, a lunch here, a few drinks there. There is no point in forcing people to have meetings if they don't like it, but a minimum is necessary. It's sporadic, depends on the team. The formal stuff is not that important. What counts are the personal relationships, personal trust. My line has always been: no bullshit, no excuses. I hate excuses. I want results, not excuses. If I get excuses, doesn't matter how good they are, it does not interest me and I get quite nasty.

It all sounds very focussed, 'trusting' and 'easy-going', as long as the job is done properly. And yet the question remains: why worry about these semi-trusting relationships if in the end all that matters is performance? Karl revealed why he wanted to have a working team, trustworthiness and trusting relationships: 'A strong team? You can achieve anything with a strong team, you know. Once you get a team behind you, you can turn the world upside down'. Trust seems to unlock and render sources of engagement and motivation that no rational means of management seems to be able to access. The following example given by Karl illustrates how this works:

> You know, first you need a vision. Then you need to be able to evaluate people and a team. That's not the same. You must not employ the same kind of people. You need different people with different strengths and skills. But they shouldn't be too different as they'll end up arguing all the time. They have to be a little bit similar, they've got to have something in common, a vision, a goal. A bit of difference is good. It will motivate them. If they are too similar it gets boring and they won't deliver as good as they can … And you've got to motivate the team. Anyway, it's enough if you don't de-motivate them. But you have to create an environment that's motivating like interesting projects, exciting tasks and interesting people so that people can develop. If you manage to get this sort of thing going then the guys will do anything for you.

What we can learn from this statement is that trust is not about a formal work-contract, but addresses the optimistic attitude of individuals to contribute something meaningful and useful. Individuals want to make a useful contribution. In that sense, what appears to matter is not a legally, but rather a morally binding contract. Referring back to the beginning of his managerial career at a global insurance company, Karl noted:

> There was my boss and his boss and they absolutely trusted me. They asked me to manage quite a big portfolio and the only expectation was: do your best! That was all. They've told themselves that I will soon know more about that portfolio than they do … They thought I am smart enough to work it out myself. If they had not trusted me, they would not have employed me.

They trusted that he would deliver. But the crucial point comes to the fore when he continued:

> And this kind of trust was morally absolutely binding for me, absolutely… They have morally obliged me, not with a contract, no, not even in terms of a promise. They've invested trust in me, took a lot of risks with me … They simply said: 'Do your best!' and that's what I've done (Karl).

The language itself, particularly Karl's idea of 'investing' trust, reveals the boundaries between systems and lifeworlds. Of course, there is always an element of trusting someone in advance, but in this context, the corporate language of investing in something – something that is fundamentally based on social interaction in the lifeworld – gives it a systemic or strategic slant. Obviously, trust adds a moral dimension to the formal work-contract. Yet, there might be a confusion of moral as in 'ethical' and simply 'doing the right thing' in business terms, which has little to do with morality. But this is exactly the ambiguity that individuals face and might find difficult to disentangle. While the work-contract might describe tasks and wages, trust tags on the organisational expectation and 'morally' imposed obligation to 'do your best'. To establish and impose a moral obligation that goes beyond the factual work contract is not only the core of an instrumentalisation of trust, but a cornerstone of 'organised individualisation'. And that is, in essence, how people management establishes individualisation as an organising principle in the workplace: working and achieving through individuals by instrumentalising their sense of trust as a morally binding obligation that increases individual – and in the final equation corporate – productivity. To reiterate briefly: people management emerges as a crucial management tool in the context of a network society and knowledge economy and thus is a pivotal aspect of gaining access to knowledge and information on an individual basis. While employees might think they can walk on water, managers are running the business on 'trust' in the already elaborate sense.

2. Corporate Culture: Catchphrase or Normative Control Mechanism?

At various points in the interview material presented thus far, managers have talked about 'a shared vision' (Karl) or a 'solar system' (Herman). These expressions describe what is commonly referred to as 'corporate culture'. Corporate culture is supposed to provide orientation, engage individuals in the business processes, and present an image of the organisation based on corporate values. What then were the interviewee's experiences and thoughts of corporate culture?

To start with, Quinn did not quite understand the hype surrounding corporate culture, arguing that 'one and one is always gonna be two, whether you identify with a particular corporation or any other organisation in the world'. Although critical, the statement highlights that corporate culture on some level addresses individuals' capacity to identify with what a corporation stands for. As Paula reluctantly explained: 'It [corporate culture] means joking ... because it's a catchphrase'. Bob, who had worked in several big organisations before founding his own corporation, was highly sceptical, but got right to the heart of the matter when he explained his view. For him corporate culture was

> a normative mechanism to introduce control. And it's used to weed out people that don't fit ... In fact [it's used] to impose somebody's concept of corporate identity that was intended to introduce some level of control. So, it's more of a power thing really.

Again, it is important to note that corporate culture is as much a (self-)control mechanism for managers as well as employees. Corporate culture is the 'solar system', the corporate value system on the basis of which integration management aims to create an artificial lifeworld as business environment. This becomes evident when Gordon, aged 57 and with 37 years of top management experience, stated: 'I'm ... looking at what I've got to work with and trying to balance the culture with the staff that I have against the culture and environment that I want to breed'. Rory, in the midst of restructuring processes with his organisation, agreed that it was about 'breeding' a certain environment. At the same time he explained the nature of that environment: corporate culture, for him, was about 'a positive environment. It's about shared objectives'. The crucial question is: Who defines the objectives and in what sense are they shared? Can they be understood as 'shared', as if they were the result of communicative action in the Habermasian sense? Or are they shared as in 'passed on' and 'communicated', so that everyone is informed and knows about them? The whole notion of 'shared' cannot but be relative in the context of hyper-differentiation anyway.

On a more general level, corporate culture is referred to as 'a mission statement [on] what the company believes of itself and how it promotes that' (Andrew). Or as Martin expressed it: 'To me having the right culture within an organisation is vital to its success'. While these statements are certainly not wrong, they do not give any clue regarding where the mission statement comes from, how it is realised or how or why culture should translate into business success. It is Martin's remark that gets a bit closer to the heart of the matter: 'It [corporate culture] is … the glue that holds the company together. Without it … there is no cohesion, no interaction between staff'. What is referred to as the 'glue' are systemic imperatives that provide the purposive-rational basis for organisational integration and membership. Corporate culture here provides the purposes. Thus, as theoretically outlined earlier as 'integration management', corporate culture is about integration and interaction in the workplace. The question, of course, is: What kind of integration and what kind of interaction? Does work on its own not presuppose a certain degree of social interaction and subsequently a minimal sense of integration on the basis of a division of labour?

The Instrumentalisation of Communication

While communicative processes are *the* central aspect of corporate culture, these processes are defined by the ambiguity existing between communicative and instrumental action, as elaborated earlier in reference to Habermas. Whereas people management uses communication to create (pseudo-)trust, corporate culture builds on the trusting relationship and uses communication to further instil corporate norms and values. Accordingly, the pivotal question is: Does corporate culture allow some kind of contestation in which individuals can make claims, negotiate, re-negotiate, approve and disapprove – in short, influence – the norms and values that guide their actions at the workplace? Or is communication simply a means of control to impose, gather and distribute information about business processes?

The following statement gives a clue. To start with, if we believe managers, then one of their main tasks is to communicate: 'A lot of my time is communication and getting the right communication across, that's a struggle… At my level it's strategic [communication], it is company focused, it is culture, it is a company overview' (Ian).

The fact that it is 'strategic' communication makes it sound not like a negotiation process designed to reach normative understanding, but rather an 'instrumental action' oriented to systemic success. Gordon, heading a large global corporation, pointed out that the form of communication depended on the size of the corporation:

> Small is beautiful but the other thing about small companies [is that] the communication is generally better because the manager can talk to everyone and everyone can talk to each other and there is less fear … People basically develop fear if they don't know what's happening. And I've noticed in large organisations, just because they are large, they become more bureaucratic. People down the line don't get communicated to as frequently. They start to develop negative attitudes which build up in their minds.

The issue of fear links back to the question of trust. Moreover, corporate culture emerges in this as a bureaucratised and rationalised form of communicating managerial positions, used in order to avoid the development of negative attitudes amongst employees. What it actually addresses is 'peoples' minds' rather than the hard factual numbers on spreadsheets. Andrew, coming from IT, described why the process of communication needed to be embedded in 'culture':

> In many large corporations there is still a very hierarchical structure that in itself causes a lot of overhead, miscommunication. When you try and communicate a point of view through multiple layers of management it ends up being distorted by the time it gets to the other end. Flat management styles work but tend to lose specific focus. It becomes more generic and things tend to get bypassed. What's the happy medium? That's a good question. I think it requires a company to adapt, to be able to put in place a structure and to review it on a regular basis and if it doesn't work to have the courage to change it.

Basically, the point is to replace organisational hierarchy with an internalised corporate value system. The goal is to have a culture in which corporate goals can be communicated without becoming distorted. Gordon gave an example of how and what his organisation communicated:

> We communicate a lot with staff. We have regular staff meetings each week and we have an in-house newsletter. We reinforce the core values which are research and development, innovation and commercialisation of that innovation.

Communication with staff appears to be a rather one-way-street. It is simply the means to inform and reinforce the core values of the business. Thus one of the main functions of corporate culture appears to be to reinforce business values. The corporation and its values become a 'generalised other' and the employee is supposed to internalise the normative infrastructure given in the corporate culture. Individuals in the workplace are in no position to make normative claims on the basis of which they could possibly gain social recognition. For managers, employees' normative claims are, indeed, a source of distortion. Staff meetings are there to inform, to explain and not to discuss or make normative claims. Communication does not mean individuals are able to participate and contribute to the formation of those core values. Consequently, corporate culture is mainly not a culture of mutual communication, but is about distributing and gathering information in order to coordinate and ensure business purposes (systemic imperatives). The 'control' of those coordination processes is one of the main objectives of corporate culture.

Many of the managers interviewed for this investigation believed that the relationship between individual and organisation was a flexible one. Yet Ian, overseeing global manufacturing processes, left no doubt that it was not so much about flexibility, but instead about control:

> I am of a sound belief that if you don't know what's happening, how much in control can you be? And from a management point of view, if I came across with a scenario that is top down communication … and 'do as asked', there is really no capacity to get information from the bottom up. I can't as a manager … make sound, reliable decisions without feedback. It's just impossible to do. I can make good estimates, but that's all there will be.

Thus rather than flexibility, this is about permeability and self-referentiality within a systemic environment. This resonates strongly with the Knightian view that managing is, to a large degree, based on 'good judgements'. How such judgements are shaped was further elaborated by Ian: 'If I understand the environment, I can control it better. So as a manager basically I use communication as a platform to operate'. To make this work from a managerial perspective is not always an easy undertaking and links in with the instrumentalisation of trust; as Ian continued to explain:

> At times it is a bit difficult. Some of the guys always back up and say: 'What do you really want?' … So I'm trying to bring down that façade and it is for the most of them working. I get some very good feedback just by promoting this method.

People management and the instrumentalisation of trust brings down the façade, and opens up channels of organised communication that can be used to reinforce corporate values. In this Martin pointed out how new communication technologies help this managerial approach of control by communication:

> I love email. Some people hate it, I love it. The reason I love it is it tells me if the person has read it. It doesn't tell me whether the person understands it … I've got to talk to Mr. Microsoft and see if we can actually put that into the software package: 'Do you understand what I've written?' But you know … it gives me a record of what I said, it gives me a record if they've read it.

Corporate culture is thus a management tool that capitalises on people management and uses communication not only to gain access via a trusting relationship, but in order to instil control; to organise the flow of information. This suggests that managers are not really interested in normative contributions, but above all in the gathering of managerially useful information. Andrew, the IT manager, gave an example of the kind of impact it has if managers are denied access to information:

> [I'll] tell you a story. I was a consultant with XYZ and I was being charged out at 3000 dollars a day. I was giving management consulting to the head of IT at the Reserve Bank. They felt that the amount of money that I was being charged was so high that they put a direction to the staff, that I was not to be spoken to.

They didn't want me to be interrupted 'cause they were paying so much money. I arrived on site and I felt like I was in starlight 13. People would not even look me in the eye. And it's very hard from a consulting point of view when you need to find information and people were not willing.

Consequently, cultivating a certain communicative culture is about controlling the flow of information from management to employees, and vice versa. As Gordon observed:

So we went through that business plan presentation to every staff member and explained what we are trying to achieve … We have a weekly management meeting … We link in people around the world. We have biweekly staff meetings and the email system too is good to keep people informed.

He continued along the same line: 'I mean fundamentally, we have a vision for the business and a business plan, you know. We communicate that to staff'. Obviously, the values and norms incorporated in a business plan or vision have to be communicated to staff. It is not that business plans or visions are subject to discussion. They are the normative infrastructure of the corporation (systemic imperatives) and as purposive-rational goals and decisions, they are non-negotiable. One gets the impression that management reaches out and borrows elements of the lifeworld (the ability to negotiate and communicate) that systemic processes cannot generate, and turn them into some form of pseudo-negotiation. Most importantly, however, this 'borrowing' process occurs on an individual level.

As is the case with people management, corporate culture blurs the boundaries between social integration (modus vivendi) and systemic coordination (modus operandi). The instrumentalising character of corporate culture lies in the fact that it is a management technique that cannot be installed or implemented 'technically', but must build on the ability of human beings to emotionally identify with tasks, people or organisations, and which builds on processes of socialisation (internalisation/externalisation) as a fundamental aspect of individualisation. Sascha was totally aware of the fact that corporate culture was reliant on people in this way when he observed that

Corporate culture cannot be set up in a few months. You cannot design a corporate culture on paper. You might be able to note it down on a piece of paper, but corporate culture sincerely comes out of one's heart, that people can talk to each other and communicate what the corporation stands for.

This statement reveals an interesting ambiguity. While managers are the ones that to a large degree shape a corporate culture, they seem to intuitively sense that it has to become part of individuals' identifications through a negotiation process, part of their lifeworld. Gordon argued along similar lines: 'Everyone can write a business plan and everyone can write a mission statement up on the wall, but if it doesn't connect with the hearts and minds it's useless'. This suggests almost a collapse of system and lifeworld, and thus a nullification of the need to negotiate between systems and lifeworlds. But why would management want to connect their mission statement with the hearts and minds of the employees? Bob, having just left a big organisation, explained that

> When you've got a big steam ship, you know, it's a sheer momentum of mass … So what you want to do is eliminate mistakes … You now have to change your organisation from being risk focused where you don't care about the consequences, to risk averse where you do care strongly about the consequences. And of course … in that transition you're … changing really the cultural aspects of the organisation.

Is it possible, however, to eliminate such 'mistakes' from social interaction at the workplace? So far it all sounds more like negotiation is likely to be eliminated, as the outcome might not be in line with a non-negotiable purpose. Thus, corporate culture aims to rationalise social interaction on a normative level by addressing informal, organisational and individual layers that cannot easily be controlled. Bob's following statement points out what is to be gained from that:

> How [do] you control informal action? Well, you can't. I can't see that you can. And most of the informal action does not work against the formal processes, but supplements it in a way that was never intended by the original design of the process. Because the process by definition is much more complicated than some bonchead could sit down and draw up on a paper.

This suggests that the reduction of systemic complexity is an issue here. One of the underpinnings of corporate culture seems to be to reduce and control systemic complexity. Accordingly, corporate culture instrumentalises culture as an organising principle within complex corporate (systemic) structures. However, culture is a dynamic, complex and – above all – social force. As such, it might grow to be a system, however, not one that can be sustained by machines, computers or formal structures. The ambiguity that individuals have to face here is that culture is a product of communicative processes in the lifeworld; yet the statement suggests that systems cannot do without, at least, borrowing some elements of culture from the lifeworld while excluding genuine communicative processes. Culture in this sense is simply another management tool that is not subject to negotiation, but rational assessment: 'Examining the culture to me is no different to making sure the company has got a good product pipeline, … that its financial performance is reasonably sound' (Ted).

But corporate culture also becomes important in regards to individuals' work ethic. All of the interviewed managers emphasised that what they were looking for in their employees was 'abilities 10%, attitude 90%' (Martin), which describes again a fundamental ambiguity. On the one hand, everything in a business seems to be geared towards systemic success, while on the other hand, corporations rely enormously on normative orientations, as building blocks not only of the corporate world, but also to contribute that which the corporate world cannot provide. To be clear, we are not talking about an attitude towards life in general, a lifestyle or worldview, but attitude towards work, people's work ethic. Corporate culture as an organising principle then is about communicating and thus instilling a particular attitude towards work, a specific extension of the 'universalised work ethic' on an organisational level into a corporate work ethic. How important the issue of 'attitude' is becomes clear in a statement of Herman's: 'It's about interpersonal courtesy on any level, no matter if you have to communicate on the same level, upwards or downwards. That's how you create an esprit de corps'.

Attitude is, however, not only about an individual attitude or work ethic. As the term 'esprit de corps' highlights, it is a collective attitude, a collective work ethic that is desired. The crucial point is that it is not generated collectively, but pre-given. Gordon too was convinced that attitude is an essential prerequisite for success:

> The one thing I have recognised more than anything in moving from one business to another, is the attitude of the staff has a huge impact on the business, huge impact. And if staff are motivated it is so much easier to drive a business and … you know what I am trying to create with this business is a situation where the staff will get an opportunity to have ownership and get a longer term reward financially as well as having a meaningful career which they feel satisfied with.

What this really means is: if you adopt the right work ethic, you will be rewarded financially and with 'a meaningful career', which is exactly what integration management is supposed to do. However, it is not a meaning that is self-determined and freely chosen. Above all, the aim of corporate culture is to implement a certain work ethic and to integrate employees so that their participation and contribution adds value to the business.

The following statement by Karl dispels any lingering doubt about the purpose of corporate culture and the imposition of a corporate work ethic: 'You can make a cult out of a corporation, a sect. You can turn a firm into a sect and if you don't go too far it is extremely successful and strong'. The kind of 'vibe' that 'corporate cults' (Arnott 2000) create is quite often referred to as a sense of familial bonding. When asked how they would describe the culture in their organisation, many of the managers gave similar, almost clichéd answers; Jamie, who had just become a member of the management board of the organisation she worked for, noted this: 'I would say the culture here is … one big happy family'. And yet one is left to wonder why employees are supposed to feel like family at the workplace? Quinn, 58 years old and managing an online business, explained this:

> I think the bonding comes from the fact that it's pretty full on all day for everybody, very highly pressured [and] because the pressure has been ultra

extreme, the bonding also seems to be part of that whole deal, you know, the tougher it is [the stronger the bonding].

No matter if managers call it 'esprit de corps' or 'family', the bonding experience seems to play a crucial role in coping with stress, managing emotions and providing the pressure to 'go the extra mile' in a collective sense, as Quinn argued:

> The one big plus we've got here … which is being lost in lots of industries, [is] a great bonding between the people … There is a great feeling of we're all local and we're all in the same situation whether it be good, bad or a mess or whatever. We're all in it together. Yeah, it's good, we've got a very good … staff feeling, between everybody, from the top down.

This adds a new angle to the point about 'shared objectives'. It is obviously not only about sharing objectives, but also about sharing stressful experiences. Again, it is social qualities that form the basis for systemic functionality. Herman got to the heart of the matter when he said:

> [It is] the loyalty on a more personal level … that generates the most important value for all of us: security. Hence, people who've been here for a number of years and who have lived through various crises, you know, it's like being in a relationship, that's normal.

Thus corporate culture is also a management tool for dealing with uncertainty. Deborah, managing the regional headquarters of an airline, confirmed that going through particularly tough times created a sense of bonding:

> Well, the mood was so-so. We've gone through a lot of crises. First, they [European headquarters] said we don't fly anymore. Then they used smaller planes. Yeah, we've gone through a lot of crises and that has created a bond between us here. We once had 90 staff and we are now 15 generating the same revenue.

The kind of strength these bonds develop was outlined by Karl:

> Employees are more than that [instruments]. They are friends. I can still call my former employees today. Many of them have continued to ask me for advice for years after the official work relationship had ended. And they are all entitled to that, you know. When they need to go for a beer with me, I'll still be there for them today. And when I need a secretary, I can still call today and ask: 'Can you type that letter for me?' Many teams still meet … although they've long stopped working as a team. But at a certain point in time they were a team and they still meet. That's how strong it [bonding] is.

And yet, shared experiences and friendship are only one aspect of corporate culture resulting in a sense of bonding that in the final equation serves the interests of the business. Friendship is certainly one of the strongest basis of trust. However, in the context of economic relations, friendship is highly ambiguous. As Hart, for example, pointed out, it is in the area of friendship that 'trust plays so prominently a role, relatively unmediated by the formal obligations of kinship and contract' (1988: 178). Business relationships are, however, always mediated. It might be questioned whether the bonds developing in a business environment can ever become real friendships. This does not mean they cannot, yet what might be the case is that systemically mediated processes borrow trust from individual's lifeworlds to grease systemic processes. To handle the intersection and the overlap between systems and lifeworlds is once again the responsibility of individuals.

There are other events, processes and measures that in managerial terms might be called 'coaching', while from a more sociological point of view might better be described as 'corporate socialisation' aiming to instil a certain work ethic. Sascha, heading a global family business, even equated corporate socialisation and the socialisation of his kids regarding a certain work ethic: 'Above all, the lower the entry level the better. At the most I let my kids work in the storehouse, that's all'. He simply wanted them to 'work their way up', 'get their hands dirty' so that they know 'what it means to work'. Similarly, managers want their employees to internalise a particular corporate work ethic. Craig, who has been at the helm of a retail business for many years, told the following story:

> Actually a manager who came from a competitor to us wanted to go and 'manage'. I said to him … 'No, no, no! You become a storekeeper first. And the reason we want you to become a storeman first is that we want you to know the way we operate. You can't engage a storekeeper if you don't know what his job is. Then you become a shop assistant … You might have been a manager for these guys, but you are not a manager for [us]. You've got to go through all of that. It won't take long but you have to have the right attitude. So, if your attitude is "I don't want to go through all this shit" then you're coming to the wrong place.'

While this sounds like an old-fashioned kind of induction, the following anecdote recalled by Ted, now an HR manager, is more dramatic:

> The first sales conference, first day, we all set down and there was about 130 of us… The CEO goes: 'O.K., here are the basic rules. We're gonna play up every night. We're gonna drink, we're gonna party, we're gonna have a great time. We're gonna work hard during the day. It's gonna be hard. And Friday night you just desperately want to get home and get some sleep… It will be nagging and it will be hard. But I'm gonna tell you this: every single morning we start at 8 am. The doors you can see behind you, these huge big leather covered doors, they are

going to be locked at 8 o'clock. Anyone who is outside those doors at 8 o'clock is fired. No excuses. If you are outside these doors at 8 o'clock you are outside this company.' First day next morning two guys got locked out, opened up for morning tea at 9.30 or something and there they were sitting there, you know, thinking he he he, grinning nervously hoping he wouldn't get it. One of these guys had a family. He had just joined. 'Guys give your keys to the managers. Your managers will arrange transport for you, pack your bags, you're gone.' That was it.

Like any other kind of socialisation, the learning of culture is in essence the internalisation of certain norms, expectations, rules and values. And clearly, in this context, they are non-negotiable. Andrew made a clear point about this:

> Very large corporations do that very well. They have HR departments, they have marketing departments and marketing in itself is a very interesting art form. But in order to promote myself [that is, the corporation] externally I need to ensure that internally those people can express the value propositions if they, for example, have a phone call. You could be somewhere out shopping and someone asks you 'Who do you work for?' You need to be able to come up with the corporate line.

The link to people management is obvious. Once a trusting relationship has been established, corporate socialisation maximises the benefits to the corporation, and at the same time increases the value of 'human capital'. The process of learning an organisational culture aims to establish a work ethic that self-directs individuals and furthers the business. This is what is commonly referred to by managers as 'cultural fit', and which seems to be an essential requirement for entry to organisational membership, which is the whole point of integration management. Martin, having a significant degree of responsibility over staff as chief financial officer, pointed out what he was looking for in employees:

> In general, number one, personality. Number two: cultural fit. People usually ask me what do you mean by cultural fit? There is no point putting someone into this organisation … given the size of it who will not interact well with people and his peers, his or her peers or direct line subordinates. There is no point in doing that because you just get clash after clash after clash. So, probably number one for employing someone for me would almost be cultural fit.

However, it is not only about the cultural fit of employees. It is also about commitment, as Gordon pointed out: 'We've got excellent people here… They are generally committed people and very low staff turnover and that's because of the culture'. Ted, the HR expert, explained what happens with people that do not fit or are not willing to commit themselves in a certain way:

> The sort of people I noticed being weeded out and made redundant because they were not good performers were people who weren't particularly transparent in what they did, they were poor communicators, they were people who made … personal commitments that they didn't keep.

Without the willingness to perform according to given benchmarks and corporate goals, without transparency that allows control, without openness to corporate communication and without commitment to the corporate values, employees run the risk of being weeded out. Their performance as individuals does not match the 'organised' norms and values, or they might even speak out against them. The divide between individual and organisation is not negotiated, but imposed and it is hard for individuals to resist, as any such resistance is interpreted as lack of commitment.

The blurring of the boundaries becomes more visible in the figure of the manager, as corporate culture is inherently linked with them. This is particularly so for human resource managers, as Ted explained: 'HR directors have an enormous influence on the culture'. He continued to differentiate the role of managers in regards to symbolic management as part of a corporate culture:

> I also believe that culture is a lot about symbolism … and I think that especially sales directors and managing directors … who understand how Greek theatre works are the ones who can drive a culture, who can actually have an influence on the culture. Because without their influence the culture develops itself and it's still valid, it is as valid a culture as any other culture. It's just that I think in more successful organisations … the CEO or the MD and the other directors in concert are driving a particular message and image down consistently through the organisation.

How much corporate culture depends on the manager becomes clear in Ted's addition:

> The leader can be the culture… There are cultures where people get promoted because they are white Anglo-Saxon, male and highly sport oriented or play rugby. I think you can't separate culture from CEO. It just depends on who the CEO is. If the CEO has built the business himself or someone who started the business and grown it from scratch then you could probably say it is his or her culture.

This suggests that managers take on the role of 'generalised others', representing and probably living by example the corporation's norms and values that employees are supposed to internalise. Paula, who manages the Australian market for a global pharmaceutical company, referred not only to that, but summed up the underlying issue of corporate culture, that it is very much 'like it or leave it', when she noted:

> Well, the first one [function of managers] is to set an example … If I believe …
> they [employees] see I believe in it and I believe that's a very strong thing. … I
> believe if they're not proud of working for this company … and they understand
> its values and its ethics and they're still not proud, they maybe shouldn't work
> here to be quite honest.

The whole issue of corporate culture is controversial. Does corporate culture simply squeeze extra effort out of employees? Only one of the interviewees, Karl, made a comment about that:

> I don't think much of corporate culture. It can be misused, manipulation to slave
> employees even more, you know, and I think that's negative. You've got to be
> honest. People want to work. I don't have to rip them off so that they work for
> me. They want to have a bit of fun and they like a pleasant work environment.

The presented material suggests strongly that corporate culture is about the economic rationalisation, de-differentiation or streamlining of social interaction for business purposes. Consequently, corporate culture is supposed to initiate a culture of cost efficiency, of economising the cost of social interaction and thus establishes a culture of pseudo-negotiation that not only defines, but draws on individuals' capacities to negotiate the demarcations between systemic and normative processes. At the same time, it is quite clear that corporate culture as a management tool draws on culture as a lifeworld concept. It is here where the boundaries are blurred and individualisation becomes obscure and ambiguous.

3. Project Management: If it is Not a Work Project, it's a Home Project

At various points of my discussion I have referred to Colin Gordon's notion of 'the entrepreneur of the self' (1987: 300). What this means in terms of individualisation at work becomes clear in terms of project management as the third work-organisational development to be discussed here. The concept of 'project management' will also deepen our sociological understanding of what 'working through the individual' or 'organised individualisation' means alongside ambiguities around trust and communication. In many ways, project management is where various aspects of 'organised individualisation' come together as people management and corporate culture are put into practice. It might not always be called project management, but the predominance of its work-organisational principles – that is, in which individuals are treated as active hubs for systemic coordination and reproduction – cannot be overlooked. As Freddy suggested, 'Everybody is doing projects and everybody is involved in running and managing a project'.

What is it, however, that drives the predominance of project management in the contemporary work place? What are its principles? With the following statement Freddy hinted at what has changed work-organisationally, and by doing so characterised project management:

> In the early days you might have a more [simple] functional division of labour. So you might have electrical department and mechanical department and those sort of things ... Now the trend ... is to have a multifunctional team which has all the different disciplines in the team and your alliance is not to the discipline, but to the product you're trying to get out.

What this means in more practical terms was stated by Ian, from the manufacturing industry: 'In the past 18 months we were looking at a process based manufacturing set up. We have broken down the shop into different processes'.

This indicates that the once formal and functional structures of the workplace have become hyper-functionalised as a consequence of the generally hyper-differentiated context. What I mean by this is that even organisational structures are totally subordinated to the flexibility of production processes. Project organisation is the manifestation of this hyper-functionalisation that comes with the shift from a functional division of labour to a processual division of labour, from industrial to post-industrial modes of production. Above all, it describes the organisation of networks, the access to knowledge and information. Accordingly, the work-organisational structures have become more fragmented, differentiated and flexible. Consequently, project management can be regarded as a work-organisational response to hyper-differentiation. In this, the division of labour along the lines of departments and clear-cut continuous occupational roles dissolves into a pool of multi-skilled employees. Out of this pool of skills and knowledge, constantly changing teams are arranged and assigned to equally changing targets, budgets, timeframes, market pressures or customer wishes on an hourly, daily, monthly or yearly basis. In general, however, project management appears to offer a means to cope with intensified market pressures that prompt the demand for flexibility and cost efficiency: 'The pressure creates the efficiency', Quinn from the online business concluded.

Cost efficiency is the underlying managerial principle of project management:

> [The goal] is to get the right balance that achieves the quickest outcome in the shortest time at the lowest cost with the best reliability. And often what that means is to bring everybody's head together to work out an acceptable blend ... to actually produce the required outcome (Bob).

And that is exactly what project management tries to do. But what has all of this got to do with individualisation? The point is that an increasingly fragmented, flexibilised and structurally differentiated workplace turns the individual into a work-organisational hub that has the ability and capacity to intelligently process complex information, to stitch together goal-oriented work-processes in order to achieve a desired outcome on time and on budget. On the basis of people management and corporate culture, project management positions the individual as a work-organisational hub in the corporate network that processes and handles systemic imperatives flexibly and efficiently. This, in itself, is not problematic. What is problematic in this process however is that individuals become agents, and that agency is understood and portrayed as some kind of liberating aspect of self-realisation. What lies at the heart of project management as an individualised form of work organisation is not self-realisation, but the realisation of profitable outcomes through the individual. The individual's abilities to integrate and handle a complex situation – to think independently, to create a coherent string of actions out of a complex set of tasks – is systemically instrumentalised for business purposes. Business projects become the projects of individuals. Hence, the individual as a work-organisational hub refers to the fact that aspects of individualisation (reflexivity, competent acting, social interaction, continuity, recognition, autonomy) are used as a means for systemic coordination and reproduction rather than social integration. How, we might ask, does the individual become a work-organisational hub?

To answer that question, the practicalities of project management need to be considered. Karl's example illustrates the interconnections existing between people management, corporate culture and project management:

> Let's say I want to build an ark. If you want to build an ark, you don't run around and tell everyone to organise wooden boards, hammer and nail. What you've got to do is to instil a vision of the big wide world. That's what it's about and you'll see, people will start to think for themselves saying: 'Shit man, that's what I want. Do we need a ship for that?' And I'd say: 'Yeah, that sounds right to me.' They say: 'But then we need wooden boards?' 'That's right too.' And then it just goes on from there: 'I'll organise nails.' 'And I'll go and get the tools.' Before you know it, it all comes together, once they share a vision.

On the basis of this example, it is not hard to see how individual autonomy, reflexivity and agency underpin and play into project management. The same goes for people management and corporate culture. Although project management is a highly individualised process designed for getting a job done, it does not mean that the individual has much say in the definition of the job, the task, the budget or the timeframe. The essence of 'organised individualisation' is that these things are organised. But how then does project management get people to do a job as if they were doing it for their own sake and not to the company's benefit?

Freddy, head of a research and development division, gave some insight when he described the start of a project as follows:

> The Vice-president or the CEO will say that's the target, these are the subtasks and these are the things that we need to do to reach that target and meet all the other business requirements. Based on all that input the project plan is put together and the project manager runs it according to that plan.

This is a strong reminder of what agency in this case means: pre-given targets, predefined subtasks, pre-formulated business requirements tied into a bundle called the 'project plan'. Once the project plan has been drawn up, the project manager is brought on to the scene and that is where project management starts to 'work through the individual' and where 'responsibilisation' becomes a fact.

The Instrumentalisation of Individual Responsibility

Andrew explained the next step from the point of view of a project manager:

> I am the project manager, I am responsible from my company's perspective to implement the solution within the budget and the timeframe that we have agreed to. I will then go and engage all the relevant people that I need on the project. I might need architects, I might need project analysts, and I'll need programmers. I will then need people from other companies that will also need to be part of the project. So, you work in a team environment and the project manager … has the overall responsibility … A project manager is basically the person responsible for implementing the solution for the customer.

The project manager is the hub of the project. The basis of this, however, is the individual's ability to take responsibility. Hence, as another aspect of 'organised individualisation', the organisation offloads the responsibility for a project onto the individual for business purposes. This is even clearer in Freddy's detailed account of the role of the project manager:

> The project manager is told: 'This is what you have to do, that's the hill, so make sure people get there', that sort of thing. So without thinking about why we are going there, how is that linked with the market, it's just continuously focused on driving the team to that position.

He continued:

> The function of a project manager is to provide feedback to the team in terms of: 'this is your target, this is how you are going, this is what you need to modify to get there'. So, the project manager ensures continuously the team is task driven, ensuring that they are hitting their milestones, goals and objectives and … the project manager in that instance does not have time for much else. So they don't get involved or don't have the time and ability sometimes to get involved in the technical decisions or strategic decisions.

To phrase it more bluntly: it is not the employees' job to worry about why a job has to be done, but the project manager must 'make sure', 'drive the team' so that it is done. Hence, the core of project management is the individual as a work-organisational hub, resting on the ability of individuals to assume responsibility geared strictly to the task. Thus the instrumentalisation of individual responsibility is another central aspect of 'organised individualisation', in which systemic imperatives structure individual tasks. What characterises the project manager as a work-organisational hub is the responsibility to coordinate systemic imperatives, that is, the milestones, goals and objectives; in short, to coordinate a task driven team.

While individualisation as an organising principle lies at the heart of project management, the question is: how do employees deal with the managerial expectation of individual responsibility? What does it mean for ordinary employees? In one phrase: it means flexibility on the part of individuals. Ian explained this in the following quote: 'If we're light on work in one area they [employees] can be transferred on a temporary basis to support wherever we've got the lump... They don't need a mill programmer in that team, so they don't have one assigned to them'.

Employees show their loyalty to and responsibility for their work with the unconditional willingness to be flexible. This means not only being subject to control, but also giving up control over tasks, times and places. Gordon explained in more detail what sort of flexibility project management demands and who actually benefits from it:

> I guess there are two underlying factors ... One is multiskilling and the other one is team-based management ... We are extremely fortunate because a lot of our key people have a broad range of skills. To give you an example. We just recently got a fairly large order where we're involved in the assembly and test of the next M class Mercedes and the Jeep Grand Cherokee which we're doing in the US. So we've got to build machines here ... and we're on a quite tight lead time and we were able to take people off of a totally different project which was suffering from lack of funds to support it from the customers. We took three people out of that project and put them on that other project ... If we hadn't done that or if we weren't able to do that and had to bring in people from outside, we ... just would have failed. I know that. People are quite used to switching teams and working with different teams to achieve a certain objective. And that adds to that 'life-is-interesting-aspect' of the job.

Nancy, an HR manager, gave an example of how far the 'life-is-interesting-aspect' reaches beyond the actual workplace: 'I like the sense of achievement I can get by actually following a project ... I find it very difficult to think about nothing. So if it's not a work project, so maybe it will be a home project.

Living one's life itself seems to become a project driven by efficiency, achievement and systemic coordination, yet not so much as a response to systemic dependencies, but as an active individual reproduction of those dependencies. This resonates strongly with the idea of an individual as an 'entrepreneur of the self', which is portrayed as a win-win situation; yet as a matter of fact reveals another ambiguity between self-realisation of freely chosen norms and values and 'organised' systemic imperatives. The corporation operates to optimise the cost efficiency of their human resources, while employees get an opportunity to see something different that avoids a kind of Taylorist monotony at the workplace. The issues of flexibilisation and cost efficiency are predominant. However, it seems that job variety is more of a side-effect than the actual goal of management. The managerial demand comes down to something like this: everyone is supposed to do anything instantly and anywhere. The focus is on delivering outcomes in the most cost efficient way. What makes individuals so valuable as work-organisational units (human capital) is that they have the abilities and qualities to deal with, reproduce, and coordinate hyper-differentiated systemic complexities. Individuals are multi-skilled; they can be flexible and switch from one task to another. Thus project management turns the individual into a central work-organisational means that can be trusted (people management) to meet instilled expectations (corporate culture). The need to psychologically process these experiences and create a sense of continuity and coherence did not even cross the minds of any of the interviewees.

People management generally tries to gain access to individuals' qualities and abilities for business purposes. It clearly builds on the struggle over reflexivity, agency and power by creating a sense of pseudo-autonomy and pseudo-trust. People management is an instrumentalisation of trust which veils managerial power to impose expectations and exert pressure to achieve and perform. Above all, people management tries to increase cost efficiency and productivity by imposing moral obligations on employees to 'do their best'. The proliferation of ambiguities crystallises here for individuals around the issue of trust.

Corporate culture not only builds on, but further expands people management into the 'hearts and minds' of the employees. The corporate values represented by a particular corporate culture are not – as has been emphasised many times – the result of politicisation. The aim is to instil, through various means of corporate socialisation, a corporate work ethic and thus achieve informally what no formal work organisation could ever achieve: making the handling of systemic complexities an individual challenge. Individuals' ability to participate and contribute to communicative processes (social integration) is instrumentalised and turned into systemic coordination for which corporate culture delivers the non-negotiable normative guidelines, a corporate lifeworld. In that sense, the instrumentalisation of communicative processes cuts out the individuals' ability to actually think beyond a given and learned normative infrastructure. Again, this is not a clear-cut situation but it certainly contributes to a proliferation of ambiguities on an individual level as it is up to individuals to see through systems in the guise of lifeworlds.

Project management is the work-organisational development that puts 'organised individualisation' into practice. It is a highly individualised and flexibilised way of working, utilising a basis of intensified structural differentiation, fragmentation of work processes and the ability of individuals to behave as competent and knowledgeable actors. The relevance and purpose of corporate culture as the glue that holds everything together is self-evident. And yet the pivotal point remains that people management, corporate culture and finally project management turn the individual in the workplace not into a cog in the machine, but into an active hub for systemic coordination of the knowledge and access economy that not only operates along the lines of pre-given corporate norms and values, but is 'forced' to actively reproduce and sustain them. The proliferation of ambiguities here builds fundamentally on the sense of liberation of individuals by asking them to take responsibility – yet taking responsibility is not the same as being in control. This distorts and blurs the sense of liberation that individualisation carries.

The interview material presented advances the idea that individuals and their abilities are the focal point of work-organisational and managerial developments. While the potential and space for autonomy, reflexivity and agency has increased in conditions of late modernity, so also has the risk of instrumentalisation on the basis of a proliferation of ambiguities along the lines of various aspects of individualisation. The struggle over these aspects concentrates on individual autonomy, including reflexivity and agency, as dependent on a pre-given, organisationally defined set of norms and values. The ability to create a sense of continuity and coherence is mainly used to foster systemic continuity, which tends to turn the individual into an appendix to the organisation. Social recognition is granted on the basis of an organisational set of de-politicised values and norms that are beyond public control. Overall, the struggle over individualisation establishes individualisation not as a mere response, but as an active process of reproduction of systemic dependencies, which is what I have called 'organised individualisation'. With the aid of people management, corporate culture and project management, individualisation becomes established as an organising principle and a management tool.

On the basis of the discussion and analysis of the interview material we can now say that individualisation is a central issue in the contemporary workplace. But of course things are more complex than that. While there is a degree of individual freedom to negotiate, it is not – as has been argued – the freedom to negotiate norms and values. The individualised negotiation process is distorted and more or less instrumentalised into a coping mechanism and an organising principle for the coordination and reproduction of business processes. What defines individualisation as an organising principle is thus individual responsibility without normative control. More specifically, what the discussion has demonstrated is that the negotiation of issues like autonomy, continuity and recognition has shifted onto individuals. Individuals themselves have to decide how much they engage with their whole personalities in the work process. Yet they do so under astute managerial guidance, where the realisation of business interests is presented as a means of self-realisation, while the interpretation and definition of interests is beyond the control of individuals. Thus 'organised individualisation' is not the realisation of a unitary normative infrastructure of society, but is concerned with the individualised implementation of decentralised market imperatives which are organisationally given. What is even more central in the definition of 'organised individualisation' is that individuals not only feel as if they are compelled to respond to these imperatives without having any say about their interpretation, but they make these imperatives their own. By doing so they not only coordinate, but reproduce their dependencies on systemic imperatives.

What the interview material also reveals is how individualisation is experienced and organised in the contemporary workplace. The fundamental issue here that has come to the fore mainly in Chapter 6 is that no matter how systemically mediated business processes are, they seem to draw on the resources of individuals' lifeworlds in order to coordinate and reproduce systemic processes. This seems to tell us in a rather plain way that systemic processes depend on lifeworld processes. The market, the corporation and the state cannot operate without building on individuals' capacities and qualities which drive the social reproduction of society. The understanding and use of trust, communication and individual responsibility at the workplace makes this quite clear. Thus while individualisation can be the negotiation of norms and values or the re-negotiation of the demarcation between systems and lifeworlds, the work-organisational developments of people management, corporate culture and project management have deflected the emancipatory potential of this process. The liberating characteristics of individualisation have become an unconscionable freedom to organise and experience individualisation at work.

Conclusion
Organised Individualisation

The proliferation of ambiguities throughout various levels of society is one of the hallmarks of late modernity; it is also one of the key factors underpinning contemporary individualisation. Yet as the overall architecture of the discussion has demonstrated, these ambiguities allow the contemporary relationship between the individual and society to unfold in a complex and ambiguous fashion on the institutional, organisational and individual levels. One of the main premises of this study is the inseparability, interconnectedness and interdependence of three themes: structural differentiation, individualisation and social integration. I have argued that 'organised individualisation' describes the contemporary relationship between individual and society as ambiguous. On the one hand, individualisation is driven by a sense of liberation; yet on the other, hyper-differentiation and the increasing dependence on organisations subject it to more or less obvious risks of instrumentalisation.

1. Individualisation and the Proliferation of Ambiguities in Late Modernity

While concepts like the social division of labour, the rationalisation of value spheres, self-referential systems or the uncoupling of systems and lifeworlds all allow us some grasp of the contemporary structural differentiation of society, they are equally concerned with the changing role of the individual. Hence when we talk about individualisation, the sense of liberation we associate with it is inherently intertwined with an increased structural differentiation that opens up at least some space for real individual choices. However, an increase in differentiation does not automatically mean an increase in individual freedom. So, what are the consequences for individualisation under conditions of hyper-differentiation?

As contemporary society has become hyper-differentiated, choice has turned into a compulsion and into an expectation underpinned by uncertainty regarding how to make choices. Roles and statuses are not ascribed, clear avenues do not exist to show how to achieve them, and so they are not readily available to be chosen. Individuals themselves have to define and establish the roles they would like to play, which in itself redefines the achievement principle as both the goal and the way of achieving have to be generated by individuals. Thus structural differentiation has led to an increase in individual autonomy, in individual freedom and in the possibility to generate choices while that very autonomy becomes a duty, an inescapable responsibility for one's own self.

The sense of uncertainty in this context – something we perceive to be a characteristic feature of late modern society – is thus riven with ambiguity. There can be no sense of liberation for individuals without them equally accepting a more active role in constructing both their own identity and the social world in which they live. While we might feel uncomfortable with uncertainty, it is at least to a degree the manifestation of more individual freedom. It is this fundamental ambiguity that structurally underpins individualisation in late modern society, and from which various other ambiguities spring. Late modern individualisation undoubtedly carries a sense of liberation, but as the social order becomes normatively and functionally pluralised and fragmented, it equally becomes a necessity and individual responsibility to make constant choices. Moreover, the seemingly structural constraints are equally to be perceived as possible freedoms, transcending thus the arguments of mere structurally forced adaptation or the pessimism of an 'iron cage'.

In this context, the hyper-differentiation cannot be dismissed as a fancy theoretical idea. It is an observable everyday experience that permeates society on the institutional, organisational and individual levels. On an institutional level, the structural differentiation that came to the fore with the rise of modern society did not come to a halt once distinct value spheres and their modes of legitimation and rationalisation became established. On the contrary, it turns into hyper-differentiation through a pluralisation and fragmentation within the various value spheres that break up the rather linear links of early modernity between, for example, class and political preference, social status and power, religion and a particular lifestyle, fixed roles and individuality. The question concerning individualisation today is whether it still carries a sense of liberation, or whether hyper-differentiation also increases the risks of instrumentalisation.

Probably never before, at least in Western societies, have individuals been more capable, educated, resourceful, inspired and informed to be self-responsible individuals. The question of interest here is whether this translates into an equally emancipated self-organisation of society, or whether these capacities and capabilities are sidelined and put to instrumental uses. What the interdependence of structural differentiation and individualisation as a gain in freedom really means is that any kind of autonomy or freedom can only lie in and emerge from the processual self-organising capacities of concrete social relationships. It can be protected and regulated, but cannot grow from or be prescribed through institutions or organisations. And yet it is not independent of institutional and organisational settings.

One of the major consequences of late modern hyper-differentiation is that organisations, rather than classes or status groups, become increasingly important reference points for individuals' self-understanding and integration. Thus while a particular value sphere is defined by a specific logic of rationalisation it is situated in a decentralised organisational landscape. Organisations might be part of one and the same value sphere, but their goals, practices and even values are by no means unitary. They differ, are fragmented, contradictory and pluralised.

While the general goal of minimising transaction costs seems like a common denominator, the normative interpretation and purposes that define the use to which organisations are put are likely to be contradictory. To be clear, there is no society without organisations. Individuals equally depend on them and have to choose between them in their workplace, their political parties, their yacht clubs and car services and health care centres and NGOs. Thus on an organisational level hyper-differentiation generates another late modern ambiguity, namely the free and individual choice of organisational dependence in civil society state and market. But this organisational dependence is not the same as self-organisation.

The functional, normative and organisational hyper-differentiation of the various spheres of action is only one side of the coin, albeit an important one. And surely, hyper-differentiation to a large degree means a gain in individual autonomy. Yet a fundamental discrepancy emerges. On the one hand, individuals are confronted with an increased level of choice, and not only have to, but are capable of making decisions that were previously more or less given; on the other hand, the individual choices to be made are functional rather than normative. This ambiguity between functional and normative individual choices translates in the broader social context into a conflict between marketisation and politicisation. In particular these two modes of interaction seem to compete over the control of norms and values guiding individual behaviour. At this point the nature of the organisational dependence on individual action becomes crucial.

In a context that is generally defined by marketisation and the resultant development of networks and access economies, the primary form of organisation is the corporation. What fundamentally characterises the corporation as the primary form of organisation is private ownership and private control; it establishes a normative infrastructure that is not up for individual contestation and thus diminishes the chance for self-organisation and normative individualisation. This turns the 'no choice but to choose' (Giddens 1991) into 'no choice, but to choose what is organisationally required', where the ability to make decisions and choices is instrumentalised.

However, hyper-differentiation has occurred not only within value spheres, but also within organisations, in particular in corporations, and this has triggered a flexibilisation of work-organisation that finds its expression mainly in the development of corporate culture, people management and project management. Project management itself is a response to systemic hyper-differentiation, as discontinuities of time, place and tasks require more generally defined work roles. In particular, it can be regarded as a means to enable reflex-like responses from individuals to a hyper-differentiated market environment. The result is not only dissolution of clear-cut occupational roles and identities, but a form of individualisation that depends on norms and values that are embedded in a normatively non-negotiable form of organisation. In this way, the individual's self-organising capacities are turned into a systemic organising principle.

We can now say that the proliferation of ambiguities takes a particular direction in late modernity. While hyper-differentiation increases the level of individual choice, freedom and autonomy that in principle can spark and feed processes of normative negotiation and contestation, marketisation subtly turns that freedom into an organising principle for functional choices, for systemic reproduction and coordination. Thus, individualisation is underpinned by a fundamental ambiguity: the increase in individual autonomy on the one hand, and the growing risk of instrumentalisation through organisations on the other.

2. Three Forms of Individualisation

Individualisation always depends on social structures and organisations. What kind of individualisation develops in a hyper-differentiated society characterised not only by a proliferation of ambiguities, but by an increasing marketisation and corporatisation of the state and society? Hyper-differentiation and the resulting sense of liberation and agony of choice not only brings the boundaries between systemic and normative spheres of society to the fore, but shifts the responsibility to deal with those boundaries on to individuals. Yet in real life this is hardly a clear-cut demarcation. In those terms two analytical dimensions of individualisation can be differentiated: structural individualisation and normative individualisation.

Structural individualisation demonstrates the dependence of individuality on social structures and organisations. This can mean the emergence of both freedom and constraints. Either way, whatever roles and functions structures require, they provide individuals with a source of identification, reference points for identity and means to contribute to and participate in the construction of social reality. To be sure, structural individualisation is generally indifferent to whether its organisational basis is the result of politicisation, marketisation or state-intervention / regulation. All three processes make a whole range of parallel, contradictory, conflictual or complementing roles available to individuals and thus enable them to define their particular individuality.

Structures both enable and constrain individuality, but they also require that individuals play an active role in the creation of their own identity and the structures themselves. In a late modern context, this means that individuals must choose, generate, invent and establish the structures they themselves or others want to live in. This is critical for our understanding of contemporary individualisation, and has not always been the case.

In more traditional societies, roles were ascribed on the basis of rather rigid normative infrastructures. With the rise of modernity, an increasing structural differentiation allowed individuals to make choices according to generalised rules, norms and values. In late modern societies, the individual turns into an 'entrepreneur of the self' who invents, defines and redefines his or her roles – and by doing so not only responds to hyper-differentiated structures, but contributes to their production and reproduction. While the structural underpinnings of late modern societies certainly enable individualisation, hyper-differentiation itself not only requires individualisation, but is its product. Contemporary individualisation is not merely a response to structural requirements, but is essentially the production and reproduction of those structures.

The definition and redefinition of roles can be portrayed as an expansion of individual freedom and as an opportunity for self-organisation, while at the same time this freedom is at risk of turning into instrumentalisation when it reproduces the conditions for systemically required responses. The latter is far from being an individualised negotiation process, but constitutes if not its reversal then at least a fundamental distortion. Thus what makes contemporary individualisation so complex is the blurred boundaries between systemic and normative processes that in turn seem to underpin individuals' thinking, reactions, emotions and feelings. Hence, when we speak of individualisation as the negotiation of these very intersections, it means two things: firstly, the ability to negotiate the norms and values that can feed into public discourses, politicisation and self-organisation; and secondly, the ability to balance, choose and negotiate systemic imperatives, their coordination and reproduction.

While individuals are shaped by structures, they also shape structures. We can call the active shaping of structures through individuals normative individualisation. Normative individualisation is not only about learning a normative infrastructure, it is also about changing the normative bases that fundamentally define us as social beings. Communication, socialisation, individual autonomy, reflexivity, continuity, action and social recognition are aspects through which individuals cannot but make a difference to the normative infrastructure of society. They do so by using the relational space between individual and society to reflect and generate consistency, by acting, by approving and disapproving of others and their actions, by their thoughts and ideas. In this way we weave a web of social interactions where individuals play an active role in the complex and sometimes unconscious formation of their own selves and society.

And yet, as hyper-differentiation breaks down the collective channels for negotiating norms and values (or at least makes them incredibly complex), it is precisely those aspects of individualisation, of making a difference, that are at risk of becoming a means for systemic coordination and reproduction. It is here that the ambiguities between individual autonomy and instrumentalisation, between structural individualisation and normative individualisation become the defining features of contemporary individualisation. It is the obstructed access to the means of negotiating a society's normative infrastructure that is crucial, and that becomes the touchstone for the development of 'organised individualisation'. If anywhere, it is through the formation, negotiation and self-organisation of a society's normative infrastructure that the utopian energies of a sense of liberation can be realised.

Organised individualisation

The decisive point about 'organised individualisation' is not its dependence on organisations. As has become clear, individualisation always depends on social organisation. Equally, we can no longer speak of contemporary individualisation as 'institutionalised individualism', as Beck did drawing on Parsons' work, nor can we consider individualisation as merely a passive response to systemic dependencies. Systems do not precede, but are manifestations of ongoing social interaction – however complex, mediated and dependent these forms of interaction might be. Thus, individualisation is contribution as much as it is reaction. What we can say, however, is that in late modern societies individualisation depends on organisations that individuals have to choose between and which compete for individuals' choices. In network capitalism, individuals are members of work organisations, use service providers and buy goods. By these choices they enter a relationship that draws on aspects of their lifeworlds that systems cannot provide, yet seem to require in order to ensure their own systemic continuity. An interesting co-dependence emerges that is characterised by an underlying power relationship. While individuals' living together is dependent on social organisation, systemic organisation is dependent on social interaction. It is this blurring of the boundaries between systems and lifeworlds that is crucial for the development of 'organised individualisation' today.

What characterises 'organised individualisation' is an almost indistinguishable and thus ambiguous conflation of a sense of liberation and self-realisation and organisational dependence. If the various aspects of individualisation spark and feed public discourses and contestations over norms and values, we can speak of a dialectical relationship between individual and society. This might turn into politicisation producing legitimation, and in the final equation might lead to some form of self-organisation and social integration. At the same time, peoples' qualities, abilities and capacities become mere instruments for the coordination and reproduction of functional processes that are functionally incorporated into self-referential processes in systemic integration. These analytical distinctions cannot easily be grasped in everyday life because of their ambiguity. Yet, on the basis of the empirical material presented, two basic characteristics of 'organised individualisation' can clearly be defined: its function as an organising principle, and its positioning of individuals as active hubs for systemic coordination and reproduction.

Inevitably various aspects of individualisation become absorbed in the negotiation of systemic imperatives and dependencies. Systemic dependencies are coordinated and reproduced through the individual, while the norms and values defining coordination and reproduction are left out of the process. Individualisation becomes an organising principle and aspects of normative individualisation are instrumentalised and become defining features of 'agency'. The individual becomes an instrument, an agent for the handling of systemic imperatives. The coordination of systemic imperatives potentially instrumentalises the various aspects of normative individualisation for functional purposes. Systemic processes imitate the normative negotiation processes in the lifeworld by creating pseudo-lifeworlds, organising functional processes through the individual on the basis of pseudo-negotiations. To be clear, it is not that the complexities of the lifeworld translate simply into systemic media. Rather, by negotiating normative complexities, the individual becomes a lifeworld-based vehicle for organising, processing and reducing systemic complexities.

Moreover, once individualisation has been established as an organising principle, the individual becomes an active hub for the coordination and reproduction of the very systemic processes he or she depends on. While this builds on Beck's understanding of individualisation as a response to systemic dependencies, it goes beyond it because systemic reproduction cannot but be the result of social interaction, of concrete social relationships between individuals. Now the individual is not only an 'entrepreneur of the self', regarding the formation and generation of roles and structures, but the abilities of the self become a means for the realisation of norms and values of particular institutions and organisations. Individualisation is organised in such a way that the systemic dependencies are themselves reproduced and maintained through individualisation, while individuals believe it to be based on their own free choices. What is defining for 'organised individualisation' is that it is dependent on a normative infrastructure that does not match the individual's capacities and abilities to shape and form those very normative underpinnings they reproduce. This is not only the case in the workplace, but is a trend in late modern society in general.

Both individualisation as an organising principle with individuals as active hubs for the coordination and reproduction of systemic dependencies emerged as a consequence of marketisation and corporatisation. It was in particular the 'universalised work ethic' and the threatening of the 'end of work' that came to facilitate the development of 'organised individualisation'. Immersed in a general marketisation, contemporary work society shapes expectations of flexibility and self-responsibility, which are supposed to be fulfilled by individuals. This process of individual adaptation to and coping with systemic pressures generates what we have described as the 'access economy'. Individuals themselves act not only on behalf of organisations, but also try to gain access to knowledge and information. This contributes further to how they themselves turn aspects of normative individualisation into an organising principle for the coordination and reproduction of systemic processes. This becomes even more apparent in the workplace, where individual and organisation visibly face each other. It is not so much that corporations trigger a conflict between the individual and society, but that corporations shift the struggle over individuals' abilities, skills and capacities from an organisational to an individual level. Analytically, it is a shift between individualised normative negotiation and functional coordination. For individuals themselves, this shift is not obvious or straightforward but ambiguous. Corporations 'organise' a struggle over individualisation by creating various more or less instrumentalising pressures in relation to time, task and place, that individuals 'negotiate' drawing on their own qualities and abilities. Individuals' motivations for self-realisation, self-responsibility and even uniqueness are thus exploited as a productive force.

We have sought to identify some of the ambiguities defining the boundaries between systems and lifeworlds on an individual level in the workplace. The capacity to think autonomously, to process information, to make judgements and accept self-responsibility – in short, to act reflectively – is turned into a capacity to act reflexively to systemic processes. Equally, the sense of personal continuity becomes dependent on systemic continuity, thus compelling individuals to foster and reproduce systemic processes to maintain their own personal continuity. At the same time, the struggle for recognition is not based on a normative negotiation of norms. Although individuals might sometimes think so, it is really a struggle against forced systemic adaptation. Individuals have to work out on their own whether or not their actions are triggered by reflection or systemically required reflexes; whether or not their personal sense of coherence and continuity is dependent on and defined by generating systemic continuity; and whether or not social recognition depends on their adaptation to given norms and values or participation in genuine normative negotiation processes.

While individualisation is turned into a work-organisational principle, various management tools facilitate the development of individuals as active hubs for systemic coordination and reproduction. Individuals have to decide where they draw the line between responding to systemic expectations and their own personal interests. It is precisely at this point that individuals would have to differentiate between a sense of liberation or more or less instrumentalisation. However, individuals are hardly in a position to make such differentiations. Individualised negotiation processes can only be successful if they are backed up and informed by some form of collective negotiation of norms and values. And most people draw on public discourses and private discussions to reflect on their daily situation and to form their opinions.

All this, however, involves the question of power. Both individualisation as an organising principle and individuals as active hubs for systemic coordination and reproduction are the result of an imbalance in the distribution of power and access to the means of communication and negotiation. The ability to negotiate norms and values can equally be used as a means of giving and receiving information for instrumental purposes in the worst case manipulation. The individual capacity to learn culture can also mean the internalisation of systemic imperatives, cutting off the ability to go beyond a mere application of learned normative patterns. The quest for life-long learning then turns into an interminable becoming. As competent actors individuals are able to take responsibility, and yet they often have no control over what they assume responsibility for. On the basis of these distinctions and backed up by the interview material, we can see that people management, corporate culture and project management turn individuals into active hubs by instrumentalising trust, communication and individual responsibility. 'Organised individualisation' thus operates on a level that goes beyond the formal power relationship based on work contracts, tapping into the vast resources of individual lifeworlds that, as a consequence of an individualised negotiation process, have been stripped of collective protection mechanisms. The crucial point is that individual qualities are dependent on systemic norms and values that are non-negotiable, which in itself changes the understanding of trust, communication and individual responsibility and might transform them into a one-way street of information and responsibility.

People management tries to get the best out of individuals through a subtle moral 'responsibilisation' designed to realise a given set of goals. Meanwhile, corporate culture highlights the realisation of an incontestable normative infrastructure on the basis of an 'inner-directed' (Riesman et al. 1961) guidance for action in the workplace, thus economising not only economic transactions, but social interaction as well. Project management actually provides an organisational structure enabling individualisation, where roles potentially change on an hourly, daily or weekly basis. In any case, individualisation becomes 'organised' as it becomes dependent on organisations that operate on the basis of norms and values that are beyond public control, are non-negotiable, but draw on individuals' lifeworld capacities for their realisation.

At this point another major late modern characteristic of 'organised individualisation' is revealed. While the demarcations between systems and lifeworlds are individualised, and while the normative negotiation process is sidestepped, processes of systemic integration seem to become overbearing and opportunities for social integration diminish.

3. Deficiencies in Social Integration

What makes social integration such a fragile issue is that it cannot be organised, institutionally prescribed or arranged. While it is not independent of the institutional and organisational landscape of society, it is more reliant on the processual nature of concrete social relationships. Yet this is where the crux of the matter lies. Social interaction is inherently fluid, unpredictable and carries a sense of creativity and spontaneity which makes for never-ending social change. The positive aspect of this is that instrumentalisation from the point of view of diversity and plurality can never be totally encompassing. But social interaction also induces conflict, prejudice, sometimes even violence and thus is also a source of instability, transformation and disintegration. However, it is the heightened sense of flux, of uncertainty, individualisation and fragmentation that challenges the sense of social integration under conditions of hyper-differentiation. In particular, the individualised negotiation of the demarcations between systems and lifeworlds is ambiguous in the sense that it challenges existing forms of, while at the same time constituting new opportunities for, social integration. The proliferation of ambiguities does not result in the disintegration of society, but rather in integrative deficiencies that accelerate the development of organised individualisation.

Social integration is successfully generated if the social order provides individuals with enough rope to be shaped by – and in turn shape – social structures, when the plurality of capable and self-responsible individual voices merge into a process of negotiating the normative infrastructure of society. The crucial point is the access to power to define the 'rules of the game' (or what ordo-liberals refer to as 'political constitution'), and what can also be described as 'membership rules'. Social integration means that individuals are able to contribute to and participate in the formation of norms and values by which they live their lives.

Throughout the discussion we have mainly contrasted social integration with systemic coordination. The difference between the two lies in the fact that social integration is the result of normative self-organisation, while systemic coordination is based on norms and values that are not (or no longer are) negotiable, and are thus perceived as imperatives. It is this difference that defines organisational dependence as a characteristic of 'organised individualisation'. Thus, when the non-negotiable imperative becomes the driving force of individualisation, it generates deficiencies in social integration. This does not facilitate the organisation of normative consent, but is imposed through an unequal distribution of normative negotiating power.

Deficiencies in social integration thus refer to concrete social relationships and memberships that are highly mediated by power or money, where the interpretation and reinterpretation of norms and values seems to be out of reach of individuals. The opportunities for normative contributions and contestations are reduced, or shrunk to systemically organised pseudo-negotiations. We could go as far as saying that deficiencies in social integration amount to systemic coordination without normative control. In that sense, these deficiencies constitute fundamental building blocks of 'organised individualisation', as the norms according to which individuals coordinate systemic interaction are mediated by particular managerial, monetary and profit-driven motivations. Yet this is only half of the picture, as there is also leeway for individuals to negotiate aspects of systemic processes – though rarely the basic norms and values. Thus, it is not that 'organised individualisation' is totally based on deficiencies in social integration, but the ambiguity of instrumental and communicative forces makes it enormously difficult to distinguish between them.

Late modern societies are, to a large extent, defined by network capitalism. Networks, access and knowledge economies require a kind of integration that is based on memberships that can be differentiated along institutional, organisational and individual lines. On an institutional level, civil society, the state and the market all have their own membership rules, regardless of how intertwined they may be. In civil society they can be more or less regarded as voluntary memberships, yet these are not independent of economic, political or social status. The state defines membership rules mainly in terms of citizenship, rights and obligations, most visibly these days not only in immigration and migration, but also in welfare to work policies. In any case, integration is to a large degree an individual task and responsibility. It is based on individual choices or efforts to gain organisational memberships in the various spheres of action that may or may not be tied to some form of normative negotiation process.

What is of particular interest here is that work is still a central means of both social and systemic integration. Despite a proclaimed 'end of work' there can be no doubt that in reference to institutional, organisational and individual questions of integration, there is currently no alternative to work. At the same time, I have pointed out the persisting relevance of a 'universalised work ethic' that normatively defines 'useful' members of society predominantly as individuals in employment. Here again we not only face an ambiguity, but the individualised divide between systemic and normative aspects becomes quite clear. The normative imperative to work is systemically imposed. 'Organised individualisation' thus is not strictly confined to an organisational context, but is relevant to overall work society. While marketisation and corporatisation are supposed to create employment opportunities (and in that sense opportunities for systemic integration), the contestation and debate over what normatively defines a work society is reduced to a minimal democratic election process which concentrates on exactly that, namely, who can provide (apparently) better economic management and subsequently employment opportunities. And yet employment becomes an individual responsibility.

The discussion on the future of work societies could benefit significantly from a greater normative debate and a politicisation of the understanding of work. Instead, current discussions are locked into a systemic, mainly neo-liberal, discourse of deregulation and marketisation. Crucially however, if the normative power to define our understanding of work societies takes civil society, individualisation and politicisation into account, and does not elevate the state and the market as the sole norm defining forces, work can be both systemically and socially integrating. Otherwise state regulation, marketisation and corporatisation become the breeding grounds for 'organised individualisation' not necessarily eliminating, but subtly exploiting the self-organising potentials of individualisation, politicisation and civil society.

The problem lies, however, not just in this reductionist understanding of integration. In reality, not only the market, but society and the state are also becoming increasingly corporatised. Corporations, though, are non-democratic organisations that are in a position to define membership purposive-rationally as 'cultural fit', while the norms and values defining membership are for most individuals incontestable.

The individual responsibility without normative control that defines 'organised individualisation' constitutes an inversion of the sense of liberation individualisation is often associated with. Individuals are supposed to act self-responsibly in order to be a minimal burden on the state, while the state and the market widely define this imperative to secure their own systemic continuity. Furthermore, individuals are expected to gain organisational membership through employment, while the membership rules are non-negotiable set. Members of particular organisations are required to fit into, rather than negotiate, their particular normative culture. Returning to the integrating force of work, this means that contemporary work society might be threatened by an end of work, but it is, equally, threatened by an end of negotiations concerning the normative understanding not only of work, but the role and purpose of the economy as a whole. To be sure, marketisation and corporatisation are not infiltrating civil society and the state; yet in a society characterised by intensifying and globalising market processes, the corporation emerges as the focal point of the tensions between individual and society.

As we no longer live in a society with a unitary, shared normative understanding, the decentralised structure of markets used by corporations also offers the infrastructure for a decentralised organisation of consent, allowing individual and organisational preferences and differences. The first and foremost strength of markets lies in their decentralised form of coordination, which certainly suits a hyper-differentiated infrastructure as it becomes increasingly difficult if not impossible to subsume conflicting collective and individual interests under the roofs of only a few organisations. In this sense, individuals can choose their memberships (while organisations can choose their members) according to their own normative preferences. Secondly, the increasing dependence of individuals in all areas of life on some kind of business, government or non-government organisation, puts most individuals in touch with the market according to which large parts of society and the state operate. Hence, a high level of engagement is almost guaranteed. Thirdly, the workplace is a tangible part of individuals' everyday life; workplaces are not places 'out there', but are of direct individual concern and ask for involvement, responses and engagement. The workplace is a space where individuals matter, where they have an impact and in principle at least can make a difference. From that point of view, corporations have the potential to be concrete places for a decentralised negotiation of the systemic and normative processes of society. Thus we can say that the market and corporations are spaces that bring an individualised negotiation between systemic and normative processes to the fore – but can they be spaces generating normative negotiation and subsequently social integration? The question we have to face here is whether the market and corporations can function as intermediary institutions. To reiterate briefly: intermediary institutions operate as a link between individual and society at a point where the heterogeneity of individual voices are mediated into a form of living together. This cannot be anything but a complex undertaking under conditions of hyper-differentiation. Indeed, it is no longer clear what constitutes an intermediary institution in late modernity. We could say that all kinds of clubs, unions, NGOs or even political parties can fulfil the function of intermediary institutions.

While the structural characteristics of the market and corporations might make them seem like intermediary institutions, they cannot take that role. Before anything else, the market and corporations should not be mistaken as a substitute for a democratically established political order built on the legitimation processes emerging from civil society. This seems to underpin the misperception or inversion of individualisation as a liberating process. Equally importantly, individuals and society can not directly regulate the market or corporate behaviour, but have to take a 'detour through norms' mediated and protected by the state. Deficiencies in social integration thus emerge from weakened links between an individualised normative negotiation process in society and the implementation of those norms and values through the state to regulate the market. More precisely, the normative debates and contestations regarding the roles and function of the market and corporations are sidelined by the state, giving priority to market processes.

As a result, deficiencies in social integration have their origin in an imbalance between purposive-rational justification and legitimation on all three levels of society. On an institutional level, the state and the market give priority to justification (which is often scientific) rather than to public discourse and contestation. On an organisational level, corporations pursue a particular purpose that is, in most cases, not up for negotiation. On an individual level, the ability to negotiate norms and values is turned into the above elaborated organising principle dependent on systemic imperatives on an institutional as well as organisational level. Thus deficiencies in social integration emerge from a distortion of the individualised negotiation process between systemic and normative processes, which is exactly what intermediary institutions ought to prevent.

Many theorists, such as Rifkin and Beck, have suggested that a 'social economy' or 'civil labour' can parallel the market economy. The aim of such suggestions is to broaden the normative understanding of work as an integrating force that in current work societies is totally dependent on the market or corporations, regardless of whether we speak about economic liberalism, Keynesianism, ordo-liberalism, neo-liberalism or basic income models. In particular, neo-liberalism aims to achieve integration through work with a deregulation, flexibilisation and privatisation of the market and corporations. And yet, even if one agrees with the anti-constructivist attitude towards state-regulation and intervention put forward by neo-liberals, one also has to disagree with the 'market-constructivist' attitude. Neither state-regulation nor marketisation alone can produce 'better humans', but currently they do result in 'organised individualisation'. The simple demand for a social economy – if we want to call it that – does not automatically generate social integration. A social economy can only develop successfully if it emerges from politicisation grounded in civil society. Only the latter will be able to spell out the normative understanding of a future work society that is not constructed from above through state-intervention or marketisation, but rather through politicisation anchored in individuals' everyday life experiences and visions of the world they want to live in.

A possible politicisation in the workplace has to run deeper than suggested ideas of worker participation, which is often the basis for pseudo-negotiation. In regard to all three work-organisational developments (that is, people management, corporate culture and project management), employees are not only given a more autonomous role in the execution of tasks – the 'how' – they are also involved in the negotiation and re-negotiation of the underlying values, the 'what'. A possible politicisation in this sense could address questions like how things are produced, or what is produced; corporate culture could be established not only as a managerial tool to achieve self-regulation, but as a negotiable normative infrastructure for employees' self-organisation. This would certainly change the normative infrastructure of overall society, and could lead to a politicisation of corporations in general, as they would have to compete for individuals on the basis of possibilities and opportunities for normative individualisation, as well as organisational skills. On the grounds of a general politicisation of work, economy and corporations, and a more specific politicisation of the workplace, 'organised individualisation' could at least partially lose its dependence on existing structures. Unions could play a crucial role in that respect, if they could develop a negotiation process that went beyond the typical focus on monetary issues (see e.g. Wilson 2004). The important point is that the politicisation of the market, corporations and work would have to be based on a collective organisation of consent, in order to strike a balance of power between individualisation / politicisation and marketisation, and state-regulation or intervention.

The functional and normative fragmentation and pluralisation of late-modern societies and the resulting proliferation of ambiguities challenges existing forms of social integration. Yet in principle, the individualised divide between systems and lifeworlds also provides opportunities for new forms of social integration, if individuals can find and create spaces to successfully make a difference to the existing normative infrastructure. These opportunities, however, have to emerge from a process of negotiation and cannot be organised as a social economy; neither can they emerge from theoretical suggestions. Social integration as a result of individualised negotiating processes can only be successful if it is not limited to an individual responsibility for systemic integration. Integration as an individual responsibility is not problematic as long as it takes the structural and normative dimensions of individualisation into account. Yet if normative negotiation skills are reduced to systemic coordination, it cannot but create deficiencies in social integration facilitating the development of 'organised individualisation'.

At first sight, individualisation is predominantly characterised by a deep-seated sense of freedom and the desire for individual autonomy. In particular, Ulrich Beck has described individualisation as individuals' release from, firstly, the rigid structures of pre-modern societies into more general norms and values of industrial societies; and secondly, from industrially defined class and status into the turmoil of late modernity (1992: 7). Yet the social conditions in late modernity have undergone further changes in particular in the area of the economy and work; changes which have had an enormous impact on overall society, whether we still define it as work society or not. Thus I have argued that contemporary individualisation is different. Its fundamental characteristic is that it is ambiguous and carries both a sense of liberation and compulsion.

However, having established an understanding of individualisation as the negotiation of the boundaries between systems and lifeworlds, I found that individualisation under conditions of contemporary network capitalism is at risk of becoming an organising principle for systemic processes, rather than a normative negotiation process. The ambiguity between a sense of liberation and a possible instrumentalisation finds a continuation in relation to politicisation and marketisation. This becomes particularly obvious in contemporary work society.

The topic of work has allowed us to identify the risk of systemic integration taking priority over social integration.

'Organised individualisation' is an ambiguous characteristic of contemporary society. And while the focus was predominantly on the risk of instrumentalisation, it should be clear from my discussion that the creativity of individuals will always trigger social changes. 'Organised individualisation' is a risk only if we do not think about what we are doing. More directly, the risk of 'organised individualisation' can be minimised if we not only reflect on, but also articulate the ambiguities we encounter, while we do what we do. By no means has it been my intention to portray 'organised individualisation' as an entirely pessimistic situation for the future of late modern society. It provides at least as many opportunities for individuals to make a difference to the world they live in as it contains risks.

Every institutional and organisational order has to strike a balance between material and social reproduction, between systemic and social coordination, between continuity and social change, and between individual autonomy and organisational dependence without putting the negotiation processes between individual and society at risk of instrumentalising individual abilities and capacities, thus diminishing the possibilities for social pathologies and dysfunctions. I have singled out 'organised individualisation' as one possible social pathology in late modern societies. It is the reciprocity of individual autonomy and an emancipated society that ideally finds its expression in a social order that takes the various aspects of individualisation into account, resulting in politicisation, legitimation and social integration. As long as the market and corporations are given priority as the primary forms of organising social interaction, the self is at risk of being caught between freedom and social pathologies.

It is my conviction and indeed, I take great comfort from the fact that the unpredictability of individuals' actions, thoughts and feelings, prevents a total instrumentalisation from occurring. While consensus between the plurality of individuals seems if not impossible at least difficult to achieve, it also means that ambiguity and plurality are the best protection against the risk of instrumentalisation. It is in this plurality and multitude of individual voices and their contributions to a normative negotiation of values and norms that the emancipatory potential of late modern societies lies. Ultimately, however, this means that the meaning and definition of contemporary and future individualisation is not so much a question of theoretical analysis. It is up to individuals in everyday life to creatively build a society in which human beings can develop their abilities and qualities to the utmost. No matter how 'organised' individualisation might be in contemporary society, it is precisely individuals' abilities to act, think, communicate and recognise that can start something new at any moment, in any circumstance and in any society. The ambiguities in the contemporary transformation of network capitalism might just as well be the start of that.

Bibliography

Absetz, E. (2005), 'Work Choices. A simpler, fairer, national workplace relations system for Australia', Canberra: Australian Government.

Adam, B. (2003), 'Reflexive modernization temporalized', *Theory, Culture & Society*, 20(2), pp. 59–79.

Adler, A. (1927), *The Theory and Practice of Individual Psychology*, New York: Harcourt.

Adorno, T.W. (1972), 'Individuum und organisation', in Tiedemann, R. (ed.), *Theodor W. Adorno. Gesammelte Schriften I*, Frankfurt: Suhrkamp, pp. 440–56.

—— (1991), *The Culture Industry. Selected Essays on Mass Culture*, London: Routledge.

—— (1993), *Einleitung in die Soziologie*, Frankfurt: Suhrkamp.

Alexander, J.C. and Colomy, P. (1985), 'Toward neo-functionalism', *Sociological Theory*, 3, pp. 11–23.

Archer, M. (1996), 'Social integration and system integration: Developing the distinction', *Sociology*, 30(4), pp. 679–99.

Arnott, D. (2000), *Corporate Cults. The Insidious Lure of the All-consuming Organization*, New York: Amacom.

Ashmore, R.D. and Jussim, L. (1997), 'Fundamental issues in the study of self and identity – contrasts, contexts, and conflicts', *Self and Identity: Fundamental Issues*, New York: Oxford University Press, pp. 218–30.

Bagnall, D. (1999), 'All work, no jobs', *The Bulletin*, 117(6159), pp. 12–15.

Bandura, A. (1977), 'Self-efficacy: Toward a unifying theory of behavioral change', *Psychological Review*, 84, pp. 191–215.

Barbalet, J.M. (1996), 'Social emotions: confidence, trust and loyalty', *International Journal of Sociology and Social Policy*, 16(9/10), pp. 75–95.

Bauman, Z. (2001), *The Individualized Society*, Cambridge: Polity.

—— (2002), 'Foreword by Zygmunt Bauman: Individually, together', in Beck, U. and Beck-Gernsheim, E. (eds), *Individualization: Institutional Individualism and its Social and Political Consequences*, London: Sage, pp. xiv–xix.

Baumeister, R.F. (1997), 'The self and society. Changes, problems, and opportunities', in Ashmore, R.D. and Jussim, L. (eds), *Self and Identity: Fundamental Issues*, New York: Oxford University Press, pp. 191–217.

—— (1998), 'The self', in Gilbert, D.T., Fiske, S.T. and Linzey, G. (eds), *The Handbook of Social Psychology*, New York: Oxford University Press, pp. 680–740.

Baumeister, R.F. and Tice, D.M. (2001), 'The primacy of the interpersonal self', in Sedikides, C. and Brewer, M.B. (eds), *Individual Self, Relational Self, Collective Self*, Philadelphia, PA: Psychology Press, pp. 25–46.

Beck, U. (1992), *Risk Society: Towards a New Modernity*, London: Sage.

—— (1994a), *The Reinvention of Politics: Rethinking Modernity in the Global Social Order*, Cambridge: Polity Press.

—— (1994b), 'Vom Veralten sozialwissenschaftlicher Begriffe. Grundzüge einer Theorie reflexiver Modernisierung', in Görg, C. (ed.), *Gesellschaft im Übergang*, Darmstadt: Wissenschaftliche Buchgesellschaft, pp. 21–43.

—— (1995), 'Die "Individualisierungsdebatte"', in Schäfers, B. (ed.), *Soziologie in Deutschland. Entwicklung – Institutionalisierung und Berufsfelder; theoretische Kontroversen.*, Opladen: Leske + Budrich, pp. 185–98.

—— (1996), 'Das Zeitalter der Nebenfolgen und die Politisierung der Moderne', in Beck, U., Giddens, A. and Lash, S. (eds), *Reflexive Modernisierung. Eine Kontroverse.*, Frankfurt: Suhrkamp.

—— (2000a), *The Brave New World Of Work*, Cambridge: Polity.

—— (2000b), 'Living your own life in a runaway world: Individualisation, globalisation and politics', in Hutton, W. and Giddens, A. (eds), *On the Edge. Living with Global Capitalism*, London: Jonathan Cape.

—— (2002), 'Beyond status and class?' *Individualization: Institutionalized Individualism and its Social and Political Consequences*, London: Sage, pp. 30–41.

—— (2003), 'The theory of reflexive modernization', *Theory, Culture & Society*, 20(2), pp. 1–33.

Beck, U. and Beck-Gernsheim, E. (1996), 'Individualization and 'precarious freedoms': Perspectives and controversies of a subject-oriented sociology', in Heelas, P., Lash, S. and Morris, P. (eds), *Detraditionalization. Critical reflections on Authority and Identity*, Oxford: Blackwell, pp. 23–48.

—— (2002), 'Authors' preface: Institutionalized individualism', *Individualization: Institutional Individualism and its Social and Political Consequences*, London: Sage.

Beck, U., Bonß, W. and Lau, C. (2001), 'Theorie reflexiver Modernisierung – Fragestellungen, Hypothesen, Forschungsprogramme', in Beck, U. and Bonß, W. (eds), *Die Modernisierung der Moderne*, Frankfurt: Suhrkamp, pp. 11–59.

Bell, D. (1973), *The Coming of Post-industrial Society. A Venture in Social Forecasting*, New York: Basic Books.

Berger, P.L. and Luckmann, T. (1971), *The Social Construction of Reality: A Treatise in the Sociology of Knowledge*, London: Penguin.

—— (1996), *Modernität, Pluralismus und Sinnkrise : Die Orientierung des modernen Menschen*, Gütersloh: Verl. Bertelsmann-Stiftung.

Birch, C. and Paul, D. (2003), *Life and Work. Challenging Economic Man*, Sydney: UNSW Press.

Bollé, P. (2001), 'The Future of Work, Employment and Social Protection (The Annecy Symposium, January 2001)', *International Labour Review*, 140(4), pp. 453–74.

Boltanski, L. and Chiapello, E. (2005), 'The new spirit of capitalism', *International Journal of Politics, Culture and Society*, 18(3–4), pp. 161–88.

Boudreaux, D.J. and Holcombe, R.G. (1989), 'The Coasian and Knightian theories of the firm', *Managerial and Decision Economics*, 10(2), pp. 147–54.

Bourdieu, P. (1977), *Outline of a Theory of Practice*, Cambridge: Cambridge University Press.

—— (1998), *Acts of Resistance. Against the Tyranny of the Market*, New York: The New York Press.

Bowman, S.R. (1996), *The Modern Corporation and American Political Thought. Law, Power, and Ideology*, University Park: The Pennsylvania State University Press.

Bradley, H., Erickson, M., Stephenson, C. and Williams, S. (2000), *Myths at Work*, Cambridge: Polity Press.

Brooks, D. (2000), *Die BoBos: Der Lebensstil der neuen Elite*, München: Econ Ullstein List Verlag.

Brubaker, R. (1984), *The Limits of Rationality. An Essay on the Social and Moral Thought of Max Weber*, Boston, MA: George Allen & Unwin.

Calhoun, C. (1992), 'The infrastructure of modernity. Indirect relationships, information technology, and social integration', in Haferkamp, H. and Smelser, N.J. (eds), *Social Change and Modernity*, Berkeley: University of California Press, pp. 205–36.

Castells, M. (2000), *The Information Age: Economy, Society and Culture. The Rise of the Network Society*, Oxford: Blackwell.

—— (2001), 'Information technology and global capitalism', in Hutton, W. and Giddens, A. (eds), *On the Edge. Living with Global Capitalism*, London: Vintage Random House.

Champy, J. (1994), 'Time to re-engineer the manager', *Financial Times*, 14. January 1994.

Charon, J.M. (1979), *Symbolic Interactionism. An Introduction, an Interpretation, an Integration*, Englewood Cliffs: Prentice-Hall.

Clegg, S.R. (1989), *Frameworks of Power*, London: Sage Publications.

—— (1996), 'Constituting management', in Clegg, S. and Palmer, G. (eds), *Constituting Management. Markets, Meanings, and Identities*, New York: Walter de Gruyter, pp. 1–9.

Clegg, S.R. and Hardy, C. (1996), 'Introduction: organizations, organization and organizing', in Clegg, R.S., Hardy, C. and Nord, R.W. (eds), *Handbook of Organization Studies*, London: Sage, pp. 1–28.

Coase, R.H. (1967), 'The nature of the firm', in Stigler, G.J. and Boulding, K.E. (eds), *Readings in Price Theory*, London: Allen and Unwin, pp. 331–51.

Commons, J.R. (1951), *Institutional Economics: Its Place in Political Economy*, New York: Macmillan.

Côté, J. and Levine, C.G. (2002), *Identity Formation, Agency, and Culture: A Social Psychological Synthesis*, London: Lawrence Erlbaum Associates.

Crouch, M. and McKenzie, H. (2006), 'The logic of small samples in interview-based qualitative research', *Social Science Information*, 45(4), pp. 483–99.

Dahrendorf, R. (2000), 'Zwei Gasthäuser in jeder Strasse. Soziale Bindung ist eine gute Sache. Eine "gute Gesellschaft" aber sollten wir uns nicht wünschen', *Die Zeit*, 5.10.2000.

Deal, T.E. and Kennedy, A.A. (1982), *Corporate Cultures. The Rites and Rituals of Corporate Life*, Amsterdam: Addison-Wesley Publishing Company.

—— (1999), *The New Corporate Cultures. Revitalizing The Workplace After Downsizing, Mergers, And Reengineering*, New York: Perseus Books.

Demsetz, H. (1997), 'The firm in economic theory: A quiet revolution', *The American Economic Review*, 87(2), pp. 426–29.

Dettling, W. (2000), 'Diesseits und jenseits der Erwerbsarbeit', in Kocka, J. and Offe, C. (eds), *Geschichte und Zukunft der Arbeit*, Frankfurt: Campus, pp. 202–14.

Deutschmann, C. (1987), 'The Japanese type of organisation as a challenge to the sociological theory of modernisation', *Thesis Eleven*, 17, pp. 40–58.

Drucker, P.F. (1955), *The Practice of Management*, London: Heinemann.

—— (1995), *Post-capitalist Society*, London: Butterworth-Heinemann.

du Gay, P. (1996), 'Organizing identity: Entrepreneurial governance and public management', in Stuart, H. and du Gay, P. (eds), *Questions of Cultural Identity*, London: Sage, pp. 151–69.

du Gay, P., Salaman, G. and Rees, B. (1996), 'The conduct of management and the management of conduct: Contemporary managerial discourse and the constitution of the 'competent' manager', *Journal of Management Studies*, 33(3), pp. 263–82.

Duffy, F. (1997), *The New Office*, London: Conrad Octopus.

Durkheim, É. (1964), *The Division of Labor in Society*, London: Collier-Macmillan.

Ebert, N. (2001), 'Vom Produktdesign zum sozialen Design. Bürolandschaft und Erfolgsfaktor Mensch.' *Frankfurter Arbeitspapierezur gesellschaftsethischen und sozialwissenschaftlichen Forschung*, 27, pp. 76–95.

—— (2003), *Identität aus dem Nichts*, Norderstedt: BoD.

—— (2010), Decent Society: Utopian Horizon and/or ‚the way is the Goal", in *Thesis Eleven,* Volume 101 (1): 72-80.

—— (2010), Privacy and Work' in Blatterer, H., Johnson, P., Markus, M. (eds) *Modern Privacy, Shifting Boundaries, New Forms*, Palgrave Macmillan, Basingstoke, pp. 133-148.

Emirbayer, M. (1998), 'What is agency?' *The American Journal of Sociology*, 103(4), pp. 962–1023.

Erikson, E.H. (1960), 'The problem of ego-identity', in Stein, M.R., Vidich, A.J. and White, D.M. (eds), *Identity and Anxiety*, New York: The Free Press, pp. 33–87.

Esser, H. (2000), *Soziologie: Spezielle Grundlagen. Band 5: Institutionen*, Frankfurt: Campus Verlag.

Ewen, R.B. (1993), *Theories of Personality*, Hillsdale, NJ: Lawrence Erlbaum.

Flamholtz, E.G. (1989), 'Human resource accounting: An overview', *Behavioral Accounting*, Cincinnati, OH: South-Western Publishing Co., pp. 467–98.

Fletcher, S. (1997), *Competence and Organizational Change. A Handbook*, London: Kogan Page.

Flick, U. (2002), *Qualitative Sozialforschung. Eine Einführung*, Hamburg: Rowohlt.

Fogarty, T.J. and Dirsmith, M.W. (2001), 'Organizational socialization as instrument and symbol: an extended institutional theory perspective', *Human Resource Development Quarterly*, 12(3), pp. 247–66.

Forgas, J.P. and Kipling, D.W. (2002), 'The social self: Introduction and overview', in Forgas, J.P. and Kipling, D.W. (eds), *The Social Self*, New York: Psychology Press, pp. 1–18.

Freud, S. (1974), *The Ego and the Id*, London: The Hogarth Press.

Frisch, M. (1990), *Schweiz als Heimat? Versuche über 50 Jahre*, Frankfurt: Suhrkamp Verlag.

Fromm, E. (1942), *The Fear of Freedom*, London: Routledge & Kegan.

Gaertner, L. and Sedikides, C. (2001), 'A Homecoming to the individual self', in Sedikides, C. and Brewer, M.B. (eds), *Individual Self, Relational Self, Collective Self*, Philadelphia, PA: Psychology Press.

Gantman, E.R. (2005), *Capitalism, Social Privilege and Managerial Ideologies*, Burlington, VT: Ashgate.

Gecas, V. (1982), 'The self-concept', *Annual Review of Sociology*, 8, pp. 1–33.

Gecas, V. and Burke, P.J. (1995), 'Self and identity', in Cook, K.S., Fine, G.A. and House, J.S. (eds), *Sociological Perspectives on Social Psychology*, Boston, MA: Allyn & Bacon, pp. 41–67.

Gehlen, A. (1988), *Man, His Nature and Place in the World*, New York: Columbia University Press.

Geissler, B. (2002), '"Der Flexibilisierte Mensch": Eine These auf dem Prüfstand', in Schnyder, A. and Herfeldt, M. (eds), *Sozialalmanach. Der Flexibilisierte Mensch*, Luzern: Caritas-Verlag, pp. 57–71.

Gerth, H. and Mills, C.W. (1954), *Character and Social Structure*, London: Routledge & Kegan Paul.

Giddens, A. (1979), *Central Problems in Social Theory*, Los Angeles: University of California Press.

—— (1981), *A Contemporary Critique of Historical Materialism*, London: Macmillan.

—— (1984), *The Constitution of Society. Outline of the Theory of Structuration*, Berkeley: University of California Press.

—— (1991), *Modernity and Self-Identity: Self and Society in the Late Modern Age*, Oxford: Polity.

——— (1993), *New Rules of Sociological Method: A Positive Critique of Interpretative Sociologies*, Cambridge: Polity Press.

Gleason, P. (1983), 'Identifying identity: A semantic history', *The Journal of American History*, 69(4), pp. 910–31.

Goffman, E. (1986), *Stigma. Notes on the Management of Spoiled Identity*, New York: Touchstone.

Gordon, C. (1987), 'The soul of the citizen: Max Weber and Michel Foucault on rationality and government', in Lash, S. and Whimster, S. (eds), *Max Weber: Modernity and Rationality*, London: Allen & Unwin, pp. 293–316.

Gorz, A. (1997), 'Die verwendete Zeit wird nicht mehr die Zeit der Verwendung sein', (10/03/2005), pp. online (http://www.oeko-net.de/kommune/kommune12-97/AGORZ.html).

——— (2000), *Arbeit zwischen Misere und Utopie*, Frankfurt: Suhrkamp.

Gramsci, A. (1971), *Selections from the Prison Notebooks of Antonio Gramsci*, London: Lawrence and Wishart.

Gross, P. (1999), *Ich-Jagd*, Frankfurt: Suhrkamp.

Habermas, J. (1971), 'Technology and science as "ideology"', *Toward a Rational Society. Student Protest, Science and Politics*, London: Heinemann Educational Books, pp. 81–122.

——— (1976), 'Moral development and ego identity', *Communication and the Evolution of Society*, Boston, MA: Beacon Press, pp. 69–94.

——— (1979a), 'Historical materialism and the development of normative structures', *Communication and the Evolution of Society*, Boston, MA: Beacon Press, pp. 95–129.

——— (1979b), 'Legitimation problems in the modern state', *Communication and the Evolution of Society*, Boston, MA: Beacon Press, pp. 178–205.

——— (1987), *The Theory of Communicative Action. Vol. 2: Lifeworld and System: A Critique of Functionalist Reason*, Boston, MA: Beacon Press.

——— (1989), 'The new obscurity: The crisis of the welfare state and the exhaustion of utopian energies', *The New Conservatism*, Cambridge, MA: MIT Press, pp. 48–70.

——— (1999), 'The European nation-state and the pressures of globalization', *New Left Review*, 235(May/June 1999), pp. 46–59.

Hall, S. (1992), 'The question of cultural identity', in Hall, S., Held, D. and McGrew, T. (eds), *Modernity and its Futures*, Cambridge: Polity Press in association with the Open University, pp. 273–326.

Hardt, M. and Negri, A. (2000), *Empire*, Cambridge, MA: Harvard University Press.

Harley, R. (2003), 'Putting the 'wow' in tower', *The Weekend Australian Financial Review*, 4./5. October 2003.

Hart, K. (1988), 'Kinship, contract, and trust: The economic organization of migrants in African city slums', in Gambetta, D. (ed.), *Trust: Making and Breaking Cooperative Relations*, Oxford: Basil Blackwell, pp. 176–93.

Hattie, J. (1992), *Self-Concept*, Hove: Lawrence Erlbaum.

Hayek, F.A. v. (1945), 'The use of knowledge in society', *American Economic Review*, 35(4), pp. 519–30.

—— (1946), *The Road to Serfdom*, London: Routledge.

Hermanns, H. (1995), 'Narratives Interview', in Flick, U., Kardoff, E. v., Keupp, L. v. R. and Wolff, S. (eds), *Handbuch Qualitative Sozialforschung*, München: Psychologie Verlags Union, pp. 182–85.

Hewlett&Packard (2002), 'Die neue Welt der Arbeit', *HP Computer News*, 2002(11.03.2002), pp. 1–3.

Honneth, A. (1994), 'The social dynamic of disrespect: On the location of critical theory today', *Constellations*, 1(2), pp. 255–69.

—— (1995a), *The Fragmented World of the Social: Essays in Social and Political Philosophy*, Albany: State University of New York Press.

—— (1995b), 'Work and instrumental action: On the normative basis of Critical Theory', in Mills, C.W. (ed.), *The Fragmented World of the Social. Essays in Social and Political Philosophy*, Albany: State University of New York Press.

—— (1996), *The Struggle For Recognition: The Moral Grammar Of Social Conflicts*, Cambridge, MA: MIT Press.

—— (2004), 'Organized self-realization. Some paradoxes of individualization', *European Journal of Social Theory*, 7(4), pp. 463–78.

—— (2011), *Das Recht der Freiheit*, Frankfurt: Suhrkamp.

Honneth, A. and Hartmann, M. (2006), 'Paradoxes of Capitalism', *Constellations*, 13(1), pp. 41–58.

Hunter, J.D. (2000), *The Death Of Character: Moral Education in an Age Without Good or Evil*, New York: Basic Book.

James, W. (1907), *Psychology*, New York: Henry Holt.

Joas, H. (1987), 'Symbolic interactionism', in Giddens, A. and Turner, J.H. (eds), *Social Theory Today*, Cambridge: Polity Press.

Jones, G.R. (2001), *Organizational Theory, Text and Cases*, New Jersey: Prentice Hall.

Kant, I. (1997 [1781]), *Critique of Pure Reason*, Cambridge: University Press.

Kent, C.A. and Anderson, L.P. (2001), 'Old values for a new economy', *Mid-American Journal of Business*, 16(2), pp. 3–5.

Knight, F.H. (1964[1921]), *Risk, Uncertainty, and Profit*, New York: Augustus M. Kelly.

Kocka, J. (2000), 'Arbeit früher, heute, morgen: Zur Neuartigkeit der Gegenwart', in Kocka, J. and Offe, C. (eds), *Geschichte und Zukunft der Arbeit*, Frankfurt: Campus, pp. 476–92.

Kocka, J. and Offe, C. (2000), 'Einleitung', in Kocka, J. and Offe, C. (eds), *Geschichte und Zukunft der Arbeit*, Frankfurt: Campus, pp. 9–15.

Lafargue, P. (1883), *The Right to be Lazy*, New York: Gordon Press.

Lasky, M.J. (2002), 'The banalization of the concept of culture', *Society*, 39(6), pp. 73–81.

Lemke, T. (2001), "The birth of bio-politics': Michel Foucault's lecture at the College de France on neo-liberal governmentality', *Economy and Society*, 30(2), pp. 190–207.

Liessmann, K.P. (2000), 'Im Schweisse deines Angesichtes. Zum Begriff der Arbeit in den anthropologischen Konzepten der Moderne', in Beck, U. (ed.), *Die Zukunft von Arbeit und Demokratie*, Frankfurt: Suhrkamp, pp. 85–107.

Luckmann, T. (2002), 'Moral communication in modern societies', *Human Studies*, 25, pp. 19–32.

Luhmann, N. (1974), 'Soziologie als Theorie sozialer Systeme', *Soziologische Aufklärung Vol. 1*, Opladen: Westdeutscher Verlag, pp. 113–36.

—— (1995), *Social Systems*, Stanford: Stanford University Press.

—— (1996), *Soziale Systeme. Grundriss einer allgemeinen Theorie*, Frankfurt: Suhrkamp.

Mansbridge, J. (1999), 'Altruistic trust', in Warren, M.E. (ed.), *Democracy and Trust*, Cambridge: Cambridge University Press, pp. 290–309.

Marcuse, H. (1955), *Eros and Civilization. A Philosophical Inquiry into Freud*, Boston, MA: The Beacon Press.

—— (1968), 'Industrialization and capitalism in the work of Max Weber', *Negations. Essays in critical theory*, Ringwood: Penguin Books Australia, pp. 201–26.

Markus, M. (1995), 'Civil society and the politisation of needs', in Gavroglu, K. (ed.), *Science, Politics, and Social Practice: Essays on Marxism and Science, Philosophy of Culture and the Social Sciences: in Honor of Robert S. Cohen*, Dordrecht: Kluwer Academic Publishers, pp. 161–79.

—— (2003), 'Better than 'rational'?' *The Drawing Board: An Australian Review of Public Affairs*, pp. online (http://www.australianreview.net/digest/2003/08/markus.html).

Marx, K. (1970), *The German Ideology*, New York: International Publishers.

Maslow, A.H. (1968), *Toward a Psychology of Being*, New York: Van Nostrand Reinhold.

Mayo, E. (1949), 'Hawthorne and the western electric company', *Organization Theory*, Harmondsworth: Penguin, pp. 60–76.

Mead, G.H. (1956), *The Social Psychology of George Herbert Mead*, Chicago, IL: The University of Chicago Press.

—— (1972), *Mind, Self and Society from the Standpoint of a Social Behaviourist*, Chicago, IL: Chicago University Press.

Meier, C. (2000), 'Das Problem der Arbeit in seinen Zusammenhängen', in Beck, U. (ed.), *Die Zukunft von Arbeit und Demokratie*, Frankfurt: Suhrkamp, pp. 67–84.

Mill, J.S. (1970 [1817]), *Principles of Political Economy*, Harmondsworth: Penguin.

Molina, O. and Rhodes, M. (2002), 'Corporatism: The past, present, and future of a concept', *Annual Review of Political Science*, 5(1), pp. 305–31.

Nassehi, A. (2005), 'Organizations as decision machines: Niklas Luhmann's theory of organized social systems', *Sociological Review*, 53(1), pp. 178–91.

OECD (2005a), *National Accounts of OECD Countries*, Paris: OECD.

—— (2005b), *OECD Science, Technology and Industry Scoreboard*, Paris: OECD.

—— (2006), *OECD in Figures 2006–2007*, Paris: OECD Publications.

Offe, C. (1976), *Industry and Inequality: The Achievement Principle in Work and Social Status*, London: Edward Arnold.

—— (1985a), *Disorganized Capitalism*, Cambridge: Polity Press in association with Basil Blackwell, Oxford.

—— (1985b), 'Social-scientific aspects of the regulation-deregulation debate', *Modernity and the State*, Cambridge: Polity Press, pp. 72–88.

—— (1985c), 'Work: The key sociological category?' in Keane, J. (ed.), *Disorganized Capitalism*, Cambridge: Polity Press in association with Basil Blackwell, Oxford, pp. 129–50.

—— (1995), 'Full employment: Asking the wrong question?' *Dissent* (Winter 1995), pp. 77–81.

—— (1996), *Modernity and the State. East, West*, Cambridge: Polity Press in association with Blackwell Publishers Ltd.

Offe, C., Mückenberger, U. and Ostner, I. (1996), 'A basic income guaranteed by the state: A need of the moment in social policy', *Modernity and the State. East, West*, Cambridge: Polity Press in association with Blackwell Publishers Ltd., pp. 201–21.

Parsons, T. (1960), 'Pattern variables revisited: a response to Robert Dubin', *Sociological Theory and Modern Society*, New York: The Free Press, pp. 192–219.

—— (1963a), 'On the concept of influence', *Sociological Theory and Modern Society*, New York: The Free Press, pp. 355–82.

—— (1963b), 'On the concept of political power', *Sociological Theory and Modern Society*, New York: The Free Press, pp. 297–354.

—— (1964), *The Social System*, London: Routledge & Kegan Paul.

—— (1968), 'The position of identity in the general theory of action', in Gordon, C. and Gergen, J. K. (eds), *The Self in Social Interaction*, New York: Wiley, pp. 11–23.

Parsons, T. and White, W. (1964), 'The link between character and society', *Social Structure and Personality*, New York: Free Press of Glencoe, pp. 183–235.

Peters, T. and Waterman, R. (1982), *In Search for Excellence: Lessons from America's Best-run Companies*, New York: Harper & Row.

Pixley, J. (2002), 'Expectations, emotions and money', in Clegg, S.R. (ed.), *Management and Organization Paradoxes*, Amsterdam: John Benjamins Publishing Company, pp. 199–225.

—— (2004), *Emotions in Finance. Distrust and Uncertainty in Global Markets*, Cambridge: Cambridge University Press.

Pocock, B. (2003), *The Work / Life Collision*, Leichhardt: The Federation Press.

Polanyi, K. (1957), 'The economy as instituted process', in Polanyi, K., Arensberg, C.M. and Pearson, H.W. (eds), *Trade and Market in the Early Empires*, New York: Collier-Macmillan Limited, pp. 243–70.

—— (2001[1944]), *The Great Transformation. The Political and Economic Origins of our Time*, Boston, MA: Beacon Press.

Pusey, M. (1991), *Economic Rationalism in Canberra. A Nation Building State Changes its Mind*, New York: Cambridge University Press.

Ricardo, D. (1821), *On the Principles of Political Economy and Taxation*, London: Murray.

Riesman, D., Glazer, N. and Denny, R. (1961), *The Lonely Crowd: A Study of the Changing American Character*, New Haven, CT: Yale University Press.

Rifkin, J. (1995), *The End of Work*, New York: Tarcher/Penguin.

—— (2000), *The Age of Access*, New York: Tarcher/Putnam.

Sally, R. (2001), 'What is liberalism?' (03. April 2001), pp. online (http://www.lse.ac.uk/clubs/hayek/Ama-gi/Volume1/number2/what_is_liberalism.htm).

Schauenberg, B. (2004), 'Marktversagen und Organisationsversagen', in Schreyögg, G. and von Werder, A. (eds), *Handwörterbuch Unternehmensführung und Organisation*, Stuttgart: Schäffer-Poeschel, pp. 820–28.

Scheier, M. and Carver, C.S. (1981), 'Public and private aspects of the self', in Wheeler, L. (ed.), *Review of Personality and Social Psychology*, Beverly Hills, CA: Sage, pp. 189–216.

Scheler, M. (1961), *Man's Place in Nature*, Boston, MA: Beacon Press.

Schimank, U. (1996), *Theorien gesellschaftlicher Differenzierung*, Opladen: Leske & Budrich.

Schopenhauer, A. (1995 [1819]), *The World as Will and Idea*, London: J.M. Dent.

Schroer, M. (2000), *Das Individuum der Gesellschaft*, Frankfurt: Suhrkamp.

Sennett, R. (1998), *The Corrosion of Character: The Personal Consequences of Work in the New Capitalism*, London: W.W. Norton & Company.

—— (2006), *The Culture of the New Capitalism*, New Haven: Yale University Press.

Sewell, J., William H. (1992), 'A theory of structure: duality, agency, and transformation', *The American Journal of Sociology*, 98(1), pp. 1–29.

Siebold, H. (2001), 'Bezahlt wird sogar das Mittagsschläfchen', *Der Tagesspiegel*, 27.07.2001.

Simmel, G. (1890), *Über sociale Differenzierung*, Leipzig: Dunckcker & Humblot.

—— (1968), *Soziologie. Untersuchungen über die Formen der Vergesellschaftung.*, Berlin: Duncker & Humblot.

—— (1971), 'Freedom and the individual', in Levine, D.N. (ed.), *George Simmel on Individuality and Social Forms*, London: The University of Chicago Press, pp. 217–26.

Simon, R. (1985), *Gramsci's Political Thought*, London: Lawrence and Wishart.

Smith, A. (1974 [1776]), *The Wealth of Nations*, New York: Penguin.

Stiglitz, J.E. (2002), 'Employment, social justice and societal well-being', *International Labour Review*, 141(1–2), pp. 9–29.

Strauss, A.L. (1969), *Mirrors and Masks. The Search for Identity*, London: Martin Robertson.

Taylor, F.W. (1947), *Scientific Management*, New York: Harper & Row.

Tönnies, F. (1955), *Community and Association*, London: Routledge & Kegan.

Trinca, H. and Fox, C. (2004), *Better Than Sex. How a Whole Generation Got Hooked on Work*, Sydney: Random House Australia.

Turner, R.H. (2001), 'The real self: From institution to impulse', in Branaman, A. (ed.), *Self and Society*, Oxford: Blackwell, pp. 242–64.

Ulrich, P. (1989), 'Symbolisches Management. Ethisch-kritische Anmerkungen zur gegenwärtigen Diskussion über Unternehmeskultur', *Beiträge und Berichte der Forschungsstelle für Wirtschaftsethik an der Hochschule St. Gallen für Wirtschafts- und Sozialwissenschaften*, 30, pp. 1–24.

—— (2002), 'Den Markt entzaubern', *Interview in: St. Galler Tagblatt*, 3. Sept. 2002.

Uske, H. (2000), '"Sozialschmarotzer" und "Versager". Missachtung und Anerkennung in Diskursen über Massenarbeitslosigkeit', in Holtgrewe, U., Wagner, G. and Voswinkel, S. (eds), *Anerkennung und Arbeit*, Konstanz: UVK Universitätsverlag Konstanz GmbH, pp. 169–92.

Vanberg, V.J. (2001a), 'The Freiburg school of law and economics. Predecessor of constitutional economics', *The Constitution of Markets*, London: Routledge, pp. 37–51.

—— (2001b), 'Markets and regulation. The contrast between free-market liberalism and constitutional liberalism', *The Constitution of Markets*, London: Routledge, pp. 17–36.

Vielle, P. and Walthery, P. (2003), *Flexibility and Social Protection*, Dublin: European foundation for the improvement of living and working conditions.

Wagner, G. (2004), *Anerkennung und Individualisierung*, Konstanz: UVK.

Wagner, G.G. (2000), 'Erwerbsarbeit sollte Zukunft haben', in Kocka, J. and Offe, C. (eds), *Geschichte und Zukunft der Arbeit*, Frankfurt: Campus, pp. 215–33.

Weber, M. (1961), *General Economic History*, New York: Collier Books.

—— (1974[1930]), *The Protestant Ethic and the Spirit of Capitalism*, London: Unwin University Books.

—— (1978[1946]), 'Science as a vocation', in Gerth, H. and Mills, C.W. (eds), *From Max Weber: Essays in Sociology*, New York: Oxford University Press, pp. 129–56.

Weigert, J.A., Teitge, J.S. and Teitge, D.W. (1986), *Society and Identity. Toward a Sociological Psychology*, Cambridge: Cambridge University Press.

Wheelis, A. (1958), *The Quest for Identity*, New York: W.W. Norton.

Whyte, W.H. (1957), *The Organization Man*, London: Jonathan Cape.

Williamson, O.E. (1981), 'The modern corporation: origins, evolution, attributes', *Journal of Economic Literature*, 19(4), pp. 1537–68.

Willke, G. (2002), *John Maynard Keynes*, Frankfurt: Campus Verlag.

Wilson, S. (2004), *The Struggle Over Work: The 'End of Work' and Employment Alternatives for Post-industrial Societies*, London: Routledge.

Winkler, J.T. (1976), 'Corporatism', *European Journal of Sociology*, 17(1), pp. 100–136.

Index

                    Individualisation at Work